Modeling and Prototyping New Smart Learning Management Systems

Mohammed Ouadoud
National School of Applied Sciences, Abdelmalek Essaâdi University, Morocco

Mohamed Yassin Chkouri
National School of Applied Sciences, Abdelmalek Essaâdi University, Morocco

A volume in the Advances in Educational Technologies and Instructional Design (AETID) Book Series

IGI Global
PUBLISHER of TIMELY KNOWLEDGE

Published in the United States of America by
IGI Global
Information Science Reference (an imprint of IGI Global)
701 E. Chocolate Avenue
Hershey PA, USA 17033
Tel: 717-533-8845
Fax: 717-533-8661
E-mail: cust@igi-global.com
Web site: http://www.igi-global.com

Library of Congress Cataloging-in-Publication Data

Names: Ouadoud, Mohammed, 1990- author. | Chkouri, Mohamed Yassin, 1981- author.
Title: Modeling and prototyping new smart learning management systems / by Mohammed Ouadoud and Mohamed Yassin Chkouri.
Description: Hershey, PA : Information Science Reference, 2021. | Includes bibliographical references and index. | Summary: "This book examines current advances in educational innovation and presents cases that allow for the improvement of personalized and active learning, featuring a wide range of topics dealing with Learning Management Systems "-- Provided by publisher.
Identifiers: LCCN 2020040221 (print) | LCCN 2020040222 (ebook) | ISBN 9781799840213 (hardcover) | ISBN 9781799870906 (paperback) | ISBN 9781799840220 (ebook)
Subjects: LCSH: Instructional systems--Design. | Individualized instruction. | Active learning.
Classification: LCC LB1028.38 .O83 2021 (print) | LCC LB1028.38 (ebook) | DDC 371.3--dc23
LC record available at https://lccn.loc.gov/2020040221
LC ebook record available at https://lccn.loc.gov/2020040222

This book is published in the IGI Global book series Advances in Educational Technologies and Instructional Design (AETID) (ISSN: 2326-8905; eISSN: 2326-8913)

British Cataloguing in Publication Data
A Cataloguing in Publication record for this book is available from the British Library.

All work contributed to this book is new, previously-unpublished material.
The views expressed in this book are those of the authors, but not necessarily of the publisher.

For electronic access to this publication, please contact: eresources@igi-global.com.

Advances in Educational Technologies and Instructional Design (AETID) Book Series

ISSN:2326-8905
EISSN:2326-8913

Editor-in-Chief: Lawrence A. Tomei, Robert Morris University, USA

MISSION

Education has undergone, and continues to undergo, immense changes in the way it is enacted and distributed to both child and adult learners. In modern education, the traditional classroom learning experience has evolved to include technological resources and to provide online classroom opportunities to students of all ages regardless of their geographical locations. From distance education, Massive-Open-Online-Courses (MOOCs), and electronic tablets in the classroom, technology is now an integral part of learning and is also affecting the way educators communicate information to students.

The **Advances in Educational Technologies & Instructional Design (AETID) Book Series** explores new research and theories for facilitating learning and improving educational performance utilizing technological processes and resources. The series examines technologies that can be integrated into K-12 classrooms to improve skills and learning abilities in all subjects including STEM education and language learning. Additionally, it studies the emergence of fully online classrooms for young and adult learners alike, and the communication and accountability challenges that can arise. Trending topics that are covered include adaptive learning, game-based learning, virtual school environments, and social media effects. School administrators, educators, academicians, researchers, and students will find this series to be an excellent resource for the effective design and implementation of learning technologies in their classes.

COVERAGE

- K-12 Educational Technologies
- Educational Telecommunications
- Virtual School Environments
- Collaboration Tools
- Hybrid Learning
- Higher Education Technologies
- Web 2.0 and Education
- Adaptive Learning
- Online Media in Classrooms
- Bring-Your-Own-Device

IGI Global is currently accepting manuscripts for publication within this series. To submit a proposal for a volume in this series, please contact our Acquisition Editors at Acquisitions@igi-global.com or visit: http://www.igi-global.com/publish/.

The Advances in Educational Technologies and Instructional Design (AETID) Book Series (ISSN 2326-8905) is published by IGI Global, 701 E. Chocolate Avenue, Hershey, PA 17033-1240, USA, www.igi-global.com. This series is composed of titles available for purchase individually; each title is edited to be contextually exclusive from any other title within the series. For pricing and ordering information please visit http://www.igi-global.com/book-series/advances-educational-technologies-instructional-design/73678. Postmaster: Send all address changes to above address.

Titles in this Series

For a list of additional titles in this series, please visit:
http://www.igi-global.com/book-series

Leading Schools With Social, Emotional, and Academic Development (SEAD)
Tara Madden-Dent (Sierra Nevada University, USA) and Deborah Oliver (National University, USA & Mindful SEAD, USA)
Information Science Reference • © 2021 • 336pp • H/C (ISBN: 9781799867289) • US $195.00

Simulation and Game-Based Learning in Emergency and Disaster Management
Nicole K. Drumhiller (American Public University System, USA) Terri L. Wilkin (American Public University System, USA) and Karen V. Srba (Saint Francis University, USA)
Information Science Reference • © 2021 • 290pp • H/C (ISBN: 9781799840879) • US $195.00

Applications of Work Integrated Learning Among Gen Z and Y Students
Trevor Gerhardt (University of West London, UK) and Paulette J. Annon (London School of Economics, UK)
Business Science Reference • © 2021 • 345pp • H/C (ISBN: 9781799864400) • US $215.00

Career Ready Education Through Experiential Learning
Karen Rasmussen (University of West Florida, USA) Pamela Northrup (University of West Florida, USA) and Robin Colson (University of West Florida, USA)
Information Science Reference • © 2021 • 305pp • H/C (ISBN: 9781799819288) • US $195.00

Practical Perspectives on Educational Theory and Game Development
Fabio Perez Marzullo (Federal University of Rio de Janeiro, Brazil)
Information Science Reference • © 2021 • 300pp • H/C (ISBN: 9781799850212) • US $185.00

IGI Global
PUBLISHER of TIMELY KNOWLEDGE

701 East Chocolate Avenue, Hershey, PA 17033, USA
Tel: 717-533-8845 x100 • Fax: 717-533-8661
E-Mail: cust@igi-global.com • www.igi-global.com

Table of Contents

Preface

OVERVIEW

We are currently witnessing the launch and development of a large number of new Learning Management Systems (LMSs) innovations, whose main objective is to meet society's requirements and the knowledge economy, which is fully emerging.

Understanding new LMSs innovations are essential for the improvement of the training and learning process. To effectively implement these new LMSs in the classroom, teachers and trainers need access to real-life cases in which these methods were successfully used. We present the modeling and prototyping of a new smart LMS that is easy to create and administer online educational content. This LMS allows the generation and editing of website structures through databases rather than pedagogical models, with a variety of choices that ensure better adaptation to course teaching and learning style. Therefore, it is necessary to find a method of modeling all types of LMS. To model the LMS, we relied on the IMS-LD specification, focusing on four learning theories, namely, traditional pedagogy, behaviorism, cognitivism, and social constructivism. Then, these learning theories that have long inspired the design of computer applications are combined and put into perspective with many emerging educational features to build original modeling of our new smart LMS.

Innovative Trends in Learning Management Systems is a critical scholarly resource that examines current advances in educational innovation and presents cases that allow for the improvement of personalized and active learning. Featuring a wide range of topics such as higher education, teacher education, and learning strategies, this book is ideal for educators, instructional designers, academicians, researchers, and students.

GOAL

This book aims to bring together leading researchers in a New Smart Learning Management System. The objective is to examine diverse issues of social, organizational, economic, cultural, and technological context related to internal and external management of learning and teaching and its technological improvements. We seek different issues, methods, models, constructs, solution applications, or specific architectures and theories related to Learning Management Systems, as well as research and practice.

We propose for the first time, an approach that identifies the essential criteria for the evaluation of LMSs, by analyzing the evaluation dimensions in multimedia documents. Therefore, we propose a comparative study of free LMSs, from the chosen evaluation approach, to measure the degree of adequacy between the technological possibilities they offer and the pedagogical presuppositions of the training. We also exploit the obtained results for the recommendation of the LMSs since the recommendation system, to facilitate the choice of these latter.

According to this comparative study, we find that the problems of most LMSs are, first of all, pedagogical nature problems, and subsequently of a technical nature. Studying these interrelated problems brings new modeling of an LMS, based on the hybridization between four learning theories, namely the traditional pedagogy, behaviorism, cognitivism, and social constructivism. We then try to adapt our modeling of the elaborated LMS to the IMS-LD model. Beyond this, we propose within our modeling a personal office that consists of different activity spaces. We limit ourselves in this book, on modeling and design of the LMS based on the NoSQL, and the UML while respecting the adaptation of our LMS modeling with the IMS-LD model.

The book broadly covered options, issues, strategic improvement, operational management, user access, user-friendliness, capacity development, and other behavioral and organizational administration issues, as well as technological issues around LMS, Adaptive Learning, and solutions.

TARGET AUDIENCE

This book is ideally designed for all academic graduate-level students, researchers and industry practitioners, engineers, research scientists/ academicians, educational administrators, educational professionals, teachers and professors, and researchers involved in practical applications of engineering-pedagogical and didactic aspects, seeking to bring together leading researchers in Learning Management Systems.

ORGANIZATION OF THE BOOK

This book is divided into eight chapters:

- The first chapter determines the state of the art of e-learning platforms for teaching-learning.
- In the second chapter, we present an approach that identifies the essential criteria to be retained for the evaluation of e-learning platforms.
- We then propose in the third chapter, a comparative study of free e-learning platforms, based on the adopted platform evaluation approach.
- In the fourth chapter, we use the results obtained for the recommendation of e-learning platforms based on the LeaderTICE recommendation system.
- The fifth chapter provides a conceptual reference for new modeling of a new smart LMS resulting from an approach, based on the hybridization of the four learning theories mentioned above.
- We thus present in the sixth chapter, from our conceptual model, a meta-model of each activity space of the new smart LMS based on the IMS-LD specification.
- Subsequently, in the seventh chapter, we design an IMS-LD model for a new smart LMS based on UML.
- Finally, in the eighth chapter, we limit ourselves to the design and prototyping of a single activity space for a new smart LMS, that of disciplinary information.

Chapter 1: State-of-the-Art E-Learning Platforms Intended for Teaching and Learning

E-learning experiences have been launched since 2010 in several Moroccan universities as part of an experimental approach. It, therefore, seems to us that a strategy must be put in place to give this choice of teaching its place in training and to provide it with the necessary means to achieve these objectives.

The objective of this chapter is to present an overview, of free and proprietary e-learning platforms, their functional architectures, as well as the types of e-learning devices that can be created from the platforms. e-learning. To deduce the state of the art of the e-learning arrangements of Moroccan universities and compare them with the e-learning arrangements of European and American universities.

This chapter consists of three main sections:

- In the first section, we define e-learning, and we present the typologies of e-learning systems, e-learning platforms as well as standardization in the field of e-learning.
- In the second section, we determine the free and proprietary e-learning platforms
- We compare in the third chapter of the university teaching and learning systems

Chapter 2: Studying and Analyzing the Evaluation Dimensions of Learning Management Systems

We are currently witnessing the launch and development of many distance training devices at Moroccan universities, the major objective of which is to meet the demands of society and the knowledge economy which is rapidly emerging. All of these devices use LMSs, the choice of which is problematic for the carriers and designers of the devices, for different reasons (costs, utility, usability, etc.), that any random choice leads to a loss of money, effort, and time. Aware of the impact of these technological tools on learning. Therefore, this chapter proposes a methodical, systemic approach that identifies the essential criteria to be retained for the evaluation of LMS, to meet the needs of users (teachers and learners) based on an analysis of dimensions of evaluation in multimedia documents, until our study settled on the dimensions of utility and usability. Then, we followed a detailed analysis on each of them separately, to deduce the necessary LMS assessment approach.

This section mainly consists of three sub-sections:

- In the first section, we will categorize the utility characteristics discussed, according to various studies. After the analysis, we retained six utility characteristics. Thereafter, we attempted to subject the tools of currently recognized LMSs to filter the criteria that met the pedagogical principles of training. Then we checked their utility and their operability through interactive technologies that met the retained characteristics.

- In the second section, we categorize the most important usability criteria, according to various studies. After the analysis, we selected eight usability criteria to be part of our evaluation gait.
- Finally, in the third chapter, we present the measures and criteria adapted for the evaluation of LMSs according to a scalable approach and synthesis of the two analyzed dimensions.

Chapter 3: Comparative and Evaluative Study of Free Learning Management Systems

LMSs are constantly evolving, they have transformed the daily lives of teachers and students. A study of free LMS is therefore necessary. In this chapter, we propose a comparative study of free LMS, from a methodical and systemic approach, which identifies the dimensions, specifications and essential criteria to be retained for the evaluation of LMS. Thus, within the framework of this chapter, we try to evaluate the most recognized LMS, to measure the degree of adequacy between the technological possibilities which they offer and the educational presuppositions of the training. Finally, we use the results obtained, to facilitate the choice of the e-learning platform most suited to the objectives, specifications, and criteria are chosen by any institution. This chapter is motivated by our desire to clarify and support users in their choice of the platform most suited to their needs so that they can benefit from the maximum potential offered by technologies in education.

This chapter mainly consists of five sections:

- In the first section, we presenting a general introduction to our chapter.
- The second section presents the definition and benefits of LMSs.
- The third section presents the selected LMSs and the approach used for the evaluation. Then, it specifies the chosen rating method and describes each rating score.
- In the fourth section, we put the selected LMSs in comparison.
- finally, in the fifth section, we are putting the obtained results in contribution.

Chapter 4: A New Smart Recommendation System of Learning Management Systems

This chapter presents the functional and technical architecture of a recommendation system of free learning management systems that we have implemented to facilitate the choice of the most suitable LMS to meet the objectives, specifications, and criteria chosen by the institution. Thus, any random choice entails a loss of money, effort, and time loss, for porters and device designers, and this is for various reasons (cost, utility, usability, etc.). Notably, this system takes into account more than 20 LMSs. The choice of these LMSs is based on a methodical and systemic approach that identifies the adequate criteria to the objectives and specifications chosen by the institution, depending on the objects and pedagogical tools related to the recommended teaching and learning device, to retain the most suitable LMS.

This chapter is motivated by our will to clarify and support users in their choice of the most suitable LMS to meet their needs and to benefit a maximum from the potential offered by technologies in pedagogy

For our study, in section 3, we present the functional architecture of the recommendation system of used LMSs. This section mainly consists of three subsections:

- The system will facilitate the selection of the LMS and will allow choosing the one that suits best your training ecosystem.
- The system gives you the possibility to choose the characteristics and pedagogical tools adapted to your specifications.
- The system does the analysis and treatment of the choices obtained, to recommend the most suitable LMS to institutional goals.

Chapter 5: Educational Modeling of New Smart Learning Management System

The problems of most LMSs are first of all of a pedagogical nature and then of a technical one. Studying these interrelated problems provides a useful conceptual reference that enables us to design a new model for a more relevant solution. In this chapter, a new conceptual model of an LMS is presented. The model, which stems from a methodological and systemic approach, is based on the hybridization of four learning theories, namely the traditional pedagogy, behaviorism, cognitivism, and social constructivism. We will present at first each of these learning theories by discussing both their advantages and limits. Then, together with the main principles of these learning theories and the technical functionalities of the proposed LMS that result from the hybridization of these principles are outlined. We finally discuss the implications of the new conceptual model for how to design and develop a new LMS that fits the needs of their final users, in particular learners.

This chapter consists mainly of four sections:

- In the first section, we present the main theoretical currents.
- The second section presents the LMS and underlying learning theories.
- The third section presents educational modeling of an LMS
- of which we present the conceptual model, the modular approach, the customizable personal office, and the generic activities and tools spaces.
- Finally, in the fourth section, we discuss the various related works by comparing them with our educational modeling.

Chapter 6: Designing an IMS-LD Meta-Model of a New Smart Learning Management System

The context of this work is that of designing an IMS-LD meta-model of an LMS. Our approach is to first think about the conditions for creating an LMS between learners and designing the IT environment that supports this system. In this chapter, we try to adapt the IMS-LD model with a meta-model for LMS based on the hybridization between learning theories. This adaptation will go through three stages. Firstly, the development of the meta-model of LMS. Secondly, the study of the correspondence between the developed meta-model and IMS-LD model. Finally, their transformation to IMS-LD meta-model.

To concretize our modeling work, we present in the first section, the LMS consists of different activity spaces for activities of teaching and learning. In the second section, we determine the different theories of learning used for the modeling of this space, namely the traditional pedagogy and the social constructivism. We also present the IMS-LD e-learning specification and related work. Next, in the third section, we present the ATL transformation language to perform the transformation between the developed meta-model and the IMS-LD model. We also determine in this section, the reasons why we did not use the ATL language for the transformation of models. Finally, we present in the last section, the modeling Driven Architecture (MDA). Thus, we try to adapt the proposed meta-model of the LMS to the equivalent IMS-LD model.

Chapter 7: Modeling a New Smart Learning Management System Based on the EML

The context of this work is that of designing an IMS-LD model for a new smart LMS. Our work is specifically in the field or seeking to promote, using information technology from a distance. Our approach is to first think about the conditions for creating a real new smart LMS between learners and designing the IT environment that supports this LMS. In this chapter, we try to adapt the IMS-LD model with a new smart LMS based on traditional pedagogy, behaviorism, cognitivism, and social constructivism. This adaptation will go through three stages. Firstly, the development of an LMS model. Secondly, the study of the correspondence between the developed model and the IMS-LD model. Finally, their transformation to the IMS-LD model.

To make our modeling work concrete, we present in the first section the LMS consists of different activity spaces for activities of teaching and learning. We also present in the second section, the IMS-LD e-learning specification. Then in the last section, we present the design of our new smart LMS, of which we create the LMS use case diagrams. Thus, we try to adapt the LMS class diagram models to the IMS-LD model.

Chapter 8: Prototyping a New Smart Learning Management System Based on the NoSQL

The context of this work is that of prototyping a disciplinary information space for a new LMS. Our work is specifically in the field or seeking to promote, using information technology from a distance, a collective knowledge construction. Our approach is to first think about the conditions for creating a real LMS between learners and designing the IT environment that supports this LMS. We chose to base on the hybridization between four learning theories as a basis for teaching this LMS, namely the traditional pedagogy, behaviorism, cognitivism, and social constructivism. These pedagogies have already proven themselves, mostly in learning situations in the classroom.

The LMS consists of different activity spaces for teaching and learning activities. We limit ourselves in this work to the prototyping of disciplinary information space for a new smart LMS based on IMS-LD, the NoSQL MongoDB database, and the Symfony framework.

CONCLUSION AND E-LEARNING IMPACT

In this book, we have proposed the original conceptual modeling of a new smart LMS based on the hybridization of four theories of learning, namely: traditional pedagogy, behaviorism, cognitivism, and social constructivism. Our primary motivation was to offer a more learner-centered LMS while opening up dynamically to the teacher. Indeed, the proposed modeling is equipped with a bouquet of customizable web services according to the needs and behaviors of end-users. In this way, freedom of choice is left about teaching and learning concerning the creation, adaptation, and personalization of the different components of the LMS.

Beyond that, we are in the process of modeling and designing a new smart learning management system model compatible with IMS-LD and NoSQL, to develop a prototype of the information space. disciplinary via the Symfony Framework. This design is based on active learning centered on the learner. To achieve a goal, we must reach the stage of validating the model, which is one of the tasks to be accomplished in our future work. Also, we are developing the rest of our smart LMS via the Symfony Framework which will guide us better to complete this phase. The development of the proposed LMS is still ongoing. We are planning to implement its prototype as part of university training with a group of teachers and learners. Thus, we will be able to verify the validity of our modeling work with the target audience and therefore make relevant decisions for better use and wide dissemination of the LMS in the future, to promote distance training.

Acknowledgment

The production of this brief was made possible thanks to the help of several people to whom I would like to express my gratitude.

In memory of my dear father Driss. He was for me an example of the perfect father, an example of honesty and seriousness. There aren't enough words to describe how much he means to me and the influence he still has on me. May ALLAH have his soul and welcome him to his Paradise, and surrounding him with his holy mercy.

In memory of my dearest grandmother Fatima. She has always advised and guided me in the path of work, and righteousness. May ALLAH have his soul and welcome him to his paradise, and surrounding him with his holy mercy.

To my dearest mother Drissia. She worked for my success, with her love, her support, all the sacrifices made, and this precious advice, for all her assistance. No dedication can be eloquent enough to express what it deserves for all that it has given me since my birth. May this Book be the reward for all the effort and the answer to these so formulated prayers.

To my dearest wife Khadija. There are no words that can describe the wonderful soul that she is. She has always encouraged and consoled me in my difficult times. Without his help, advice, and encouragement, this book would not have come into being. May ALLAH bring us together for a long, common, and peaceful journey, and may this book bear witness to my sincere and faithful gratitude and love.

Acknowledgment

All of my thanks and thoughts are with my mother Drissia and my wife Khadija. They have never ceased to encourage and support me, especially during the final stages of writing this manuscript.

Many thanks to all of my family for the help and moral support throughout this period of research.

To all those who participated directly or indirectly in the realization of this research work.

THANK YOU

Introduction

Since the mid-2000s, the academic world has experienced an expansion in the use of e-learning as in other spaces for the dissemination of knowledge. While access to knowledge was previously conditioned by physical presence in the classroom, technologies have now made it possible to go beyond this condition of presence and to open up to other learning methods. E-learning presents many and interesting possibilities for teaching. The development of the use of e-learning in academic and professional education is at the heart of many projects of educational actors. The evolution of teachers' training needs to meet pedagogical requirements, the forward management of skills, the need to maintain their level of competence throughout their working life and the development of practices for recognizing prior learning are modifying substantially the methods of teaching. E-learning seems to provide answers to these expectations. While access to information or knowledge was generally possible through face-to-face (classical learning), e-learning was able to break this hegemony of being present in a classroom with a trainer. E-learning provides solutions within the framework of continuing education without claiming to be exhaustive. Among these solutions, it is considered that distance training seems to be the alternative for the current situation of initial and continuing training.

In the age of e-learning, universities, among others, seem to be increasingly concerned about the quality of the courses they offer their students for successful integration into the labor market. Also, distance education helps students and teachers to research, explore, and deepen knowledge. Thus, it helps to communicate and interact without taking into account the constraints of space or time. It also helps to win the bet on the quality of the lessons and helps to solve the problem of overcrowding in the classroom. Notably, Moroccan and international universities suffer from overcrowding among the ranks of students in lecture halls, and this is due to the high rate of schooling in recent years. As a result, national and international discussions are looking for a new so-called intelligent pedagogical engineering platform orienting the learner towards autonomy in his learning, capable of disseminating innovative training in a teaching-learning context. where a large place is given to distance and hybrid training, nomadic learning, the use of web tools, and social networks. These reflections would thus lead to the establishment of support strategies for the learner, on the one hand, the scripting of contextualized educational content and the establishment of an appropriate technical and human device on the other.

We are currently witnessing the launch and development of many distance training devices in Moroccan and international universities. All these devices use e-learning platforms, which are constantly evolving, the choice of which proves to be problematic for the carriers and designers of the devices, knowing that any random choice entails a loss of money, effort, and of time. We, therefore, propose a comparative study of e-learning platforms. We evaluate the most recognized e-learning platforms, to measure the degree of adequacy between the technological possibilities they offer and the educational presuppositions of the training.

In the light of our comparative study, we see that most e-learning platforms, in particular LMSs, were initially developed around ten years ago following a classic training model. A teacher who has pieces of knowledge and forwards, following different training modalities. They are mostly tools to teacher's service to create and manage courses, rather than to learner's service and the learning process. Therefore, we decided to work on a new conceptual model that combines learning theories to promote teaching-learning processes. The present study attempts to shed light on the above questions by first exposing the four learning theories considered to be the most important and most relevant for our modeling, namely traditional pedagogy, behaviorism, cognitivism, and social constructivism. Then, these theories, which have long inspired the design of e-learning applications, are combined and put into perspective with several emerging educational functions to serve as the birth of an original model of a new LMS. The use of any tool in the field of education and training must be justified based on its educational value and its response to the needs of learners. However, it should be noted that although they are seen as an effective solution to overcome space-time restrictions, platforms can act as a barrier to the learning process as pedagogical principles are neglected in their design. Therefore, a rigor challenges us in the comparative study, and the modeling to be adopted at this stage and prompts us to ask ourselves the following questions:

- Which norms and standards meet the requirements for the evaluation of these platforms?
- What approach in terms of Multimedia Pedagogical Engineering should we apply to evaluate these platforms?
- To what degree of specificity of training, can LMS e-learning platforms respond to as innovative technical systems?
- What are the choices, in terms of multimedia engineering, on which we must base ourselves for the modeling of an LMS platform of this type, which better meets the norms and standards recognized in distance training devices?
- To what degree of the specification can the recommended learning theories promote distance education?

Its various questions are investigated as part of our approach, to assess its contribution for experimental purposes. For our study, a reading of the literature specialized in the analysis of LMS shows two orientations, the first is dedicated to the technical analysis of these (computer language, script, metadata), and the second looked at the educational scope of these systems and the development of learners' skills. Our approach is then oriented towards a reconciliation of these two orientations, considering that the technological and the educational are not mutually exclusive, however, to cross their elements for a purpose where the technology is at the service of the pedagogy. We suggest making the right choice of LMS from a comparative evaluative, technical and educational study of these LMS based on our approach to have the choices, in terms of multimedia engineering, on which we must base ourselves for the modeling of an LMS platform. Our major objective was to test and verify whether our proposed model is worthy and useful for the design, development, and distribution of e-learning platforms, in particular LMSs.

Our new platform modeling will therefore offer a better balance between what the teacher does and what the learner does by allowing more distributed control in the use of the platform. It will give the learner room to learn and make him an actor in his learning. For example, a personal desktop and various activity spaces have been made available to all users of the proposed LMS to allow them to personalize them using a variety of web services.

We offer an easy-to-create and administer LMS platform meta-model for online educational content. Therefore, it is necessary to find a method to model all types of LMS. To model the LMS, we have based ourselves on the IMS-LD specification which uses pedagogical concepts, allowing us to model learning units. And this, by focusing on the four learning theories mentioned previously considered the most important and relevant for our modeling. This reveals that this modeling presented to readers and seeks ways to take advantage of technology for learning by considering users as human actors and not human factors.

Chapter 1
State-of-the-Art E-Learning Platforms Intended for Teaching and Learning

ABSTRACT

Distance learning experiments have been launched since 2010 in several Moroccan universities as part of an experimental approach. It, therefore, seems that a strategy must be put in place to give this choice of education its place in training and grant it the means necessary to achieve these objectives. The objective of this chapter has presented an overview, on free and proprietary e-learning platforms, on their functional architectures, as well as the types of e-learning devices that can create from platforms e-learning, and to deduce the state of the art of the e-learning provisions of Moroccan universities and to compare them with the e-learning provisions of European and American universities.

INTRODUCTION

E-learning is a fast and efficient way of providing and sharing knowledge with learners in different parts of the world.

According to (Liu, 2010; Karim and Goodwin, 2013), it is defined as the following: "E-learning uses the Internet or other digital content for learning and education activities, that takes full advantage of modern educational

DOI: 10.4018/978-1-7998-4021-3.ch001

technology to provide a new mechanism for communication and learning environment rich in resources to achieve a new way of learning."

Since the mid-2000s, the Moroccan academic world has experienced an expansion in the use of e-learning as in other spaces for the dissemination of knowledge in general. Besides, to enrich dissemination support (sounds, images, animations, through a website or a PowerPoint presentation), e-learning offers many interesting teaching possibilities. The development of the use of e-learning in academic and professional education is at the heart of many projects of educational actors. The evolution of teacher training needs, to meet educational requirements, the provisional management of skills, the need to maintain one's level of competence throughout one's active life, and the development of practices for recognizing experience acquired modify substantially the modalities of teaching. E-learning seems to provide answers to these expectations. If access to information or knowledge was generally possible through face-to-face (classical learning), e-learning could break this hegemony of being in a class with a trainer. E-learning provides solutions in the context of continuing education without claiming to be exhaustive. Among these solutions, distance training is considered an alternative for the current situation of initial and continuing training.

The culture of e-learning in the practice of students and teachers is already installed. However, e-learning cannot be used for their new status and to replace old pedagogical tools, but rather to be planned as a more global approach to training manager reconstitution. It is this technology offered by distance learning e-learning platforms, which gives meaning to proximity management. It thus makes it possible to replace face-to-face training, to bring the learner closer to his teacher while ensuring a better understanding of the training and support for the possible mobility of educational actors.

In the 20th century, there was an international movement in favor of e-learning integration in higher education. This movement has been operationalized due to the variety of the educational offer by universities, which most have opted to diversify knowledge dissemination means (sounds, images, animations ... etc.) to meet the needs of their target public. If access to knowledge was previously conditioned by the physical presence in the classroom, technology enables its learners to exceed this condition of presence and be opened towards other learning modalities today. We can say that e-learning provides solutions in the context of distance learning without claiming to represent the solution to all educational dysfunctions. Among these solutions, distance learning seems to be the challenge ahead to face the new training requirements in the digital era.

In the case of our study, the e-learning solutions that interest us are free e-learning platforms, because their costs, their states of development, their directions, and used technologies rendered them very close to the axis of this research.

If e-learning has many advantages in training, it cannot be said that its use sometimes poses certain problems.

Among these problems, we can point out the reluctance of teachers towards this new approach to academic and professional training. The change in habits indeed requires time to settle in. Bringing people to adapt to the journeys of change requires taking up this problem of integrating e-learning into training by university teachers.

Distance learning experiments have been launched since 2010 in several Moroccan universities as part of an experimental approach. It, therefore, seems to us that a strategy must be put in place to give this choice of education its place in training and grant it the means necessary to achieve these objectives.

E-LEARNING

For several years, information and communication technologies (ICT) have been not only a new tool, a new medium, but also a means of opening up resources from around the world. ICT can be considered the result of the convergence of three technologies: IT, telecommunications, and audiovisual, these three fields are associated with the connected computer. The Internet has made this convergence a reality today.

We are thus faced with a new mode of communication which, by the quantity of information which it makes available and the variety of its sources, poses problems with considerable educational stakes in parallel to the certain advantages which it provides at all levels.

We hear about distance learning, online training, e-learning, distance education, ... It's a whole multitude of terms with similar apparent meaning, but which refers to different aspects of new educational technology to the fashion, and that should be distinguished.

1. Definitions

The most possible and most current distance learning is currently based on the Internet. For this, the term E-learning is increasingly used to include any open and distance learning using information and communication technologies. We adopt this term as moreover in the rest of this book.

- E-learning: This means "electronic education"; it is a discipline where teaching theory and computer network technologies are combined to allow learners to complete their courses via a computer network (Internet or Intranet) (O'Neil, 2001).
- Distance learning: A more general concept in the sense that the means used to communicate between learners and trainers are not specified. Traditional correspondence training, communication by telephone, fax, etc. can be part of distance learning. We will note the linguistic nuance between the terms "teaching" and "training", the first evokes a longer duration and the compulsory sanction by a diploma while the second can mean a simple improvement of knowledge as is the case for training staff of companies. We also speak of ODL for open and distance learning; the opening is made to a large audience. The most used opening tool today remains the Web.
- Tele-education or tele-training: The use of telecommunication means it is more important in this case (telephone, fax, Internet…
- E-learning platform: is software that supports the conduct of distance learning. This type of software brings together the tools necessary for the three main users - teacher, student, administrator - of a system, which aims at the remote consultation of educational contents, the individualization of learning, and tele-tutoring (OVAREP, 2000). These systems aim to put online comprehensive lessons where the student can prepare his contrives, his license, his baccalaureate ... via these platforms.

2. Typologies of e-Learning Systems

Moving from the implementation of "face-to-face" training to the development of e-learning requires cultural, organizational, and educational changes. The relationships between trainees, content, and trainers are disrupted, making this development delicate.

In fact, according to the needs of each learning situation (target audience, type of training, area of training, etc.), we should end up with multiple systems articulating in varying proportions remote working time, time of self-study work, and face-to-face working times to adapt to the educational process and approach. Several categorizations have been proposed for e-learning systems ranging from the most global to the most detailed. The most general classification offers two categories (O'Neil, 2001):

- Synchronous systems define a "virtual classroom" where communication between distance learning players is in real-time using sound, video, or chat
- Asynchronous systems where the student is not necessarily online with the teacher, he can work in offline mode and communicate at scheduled times or on-demand. The necessary and most used mode of communication in this kind of system is electronic mail.
- Training with tutored and synchronized self-learning: This type of training combines remote work at a given time and face-to-face work. The system combines self-learning at a distance (a tool and its concepts for example) with a common "reformulation" and an appropriation in the classroom. Self-learning is based on different activities based on documents of different natures (reading, guided handling, exercises) described in a standardized guide sheet for the whole training, all available for download from the training site. This self-learning takes place over a day identified in the timetable of the trainees containing compulsory contacts with the trainers by sending documents, replies to questionnaires or productions. Trainers and tutors, present remotely, can be reached during this period at any time by various means (telephone, messaging, etc.) to resolve any difficulties.
- Training with tutored and desynchronized self-learning: In this type of training is found all the principles of the previous type. The difference lies in the desynchronization of the distance. In this case, the work to be done remotely takes place within a given period with a deadline. Contact with trainers and tutors still exists, but the answers to the questions are not immediate.
- Self-training: This system is based on tools integrating the entire learning process, from initiation to assessment without resorting to face-to-face. It is necessarily desynchronized and the use of the tutor is limited since the tool should in principle guide the learner as well as possible.
- Cooperative production: The distancing of trainees, if it individualizes their training, isolates them at the same time. However, group work remains a learning system, which must continue within the framework of these new methods. The setting up, for example, of cooperative productions by precise specifications, generates a dialogue and a

confrontation between the different members of a group thus restoring the interactivity between them. The trainers follow the progress of the work by observing the development of production and reacting to it. All of the players are therefore involved in the work. This modality probably requires the greatest inventiveness on the part of the trainers.

- Alternating training tutored the use of remote communication tools to help develop learning by action, at the place of action, and by the specificity of the work-study program. Organized around work to be carried out in establishments, based on theoretical contributions in face-to-face or online and the use of an electronic logbook. Each trainee has a referent trainer-tutor who follows the progress of the work through this logbook and the delivery of the requested productions. The tutor can be asked by the trainee any questions he has about his work.
- Autonomous work: The concept of autonomy naturally exists in the different types of situations listed above. However, it is possible to identify forms of work that do not require the presence of trainees at the training site. For example, the reading, document, and information gathering phases, clearly identified in the training systems and the schedule are not subject to face-to-face. They thus allow trainees to broaden their research possibilities by using personal, local, academic resources, whether documentary, material, or human.

3. E-learning Platforms

The development of an e-learning platform poses the constraints relating to the development of websites but also presents certain specificities coming from its use for learning. The main considerations are:

- On the technical level: They relate mainly to computer and communication hardware and software such as the hardware and operating system of platform users and at the server level, multimedia tools, Internet connection (type, speed, etc.), download and messaging tools…
- On the pedagogical level: They consist of taking into account the distance of the teacher and possibly the pedagogical place on the one hand and the individuality of the training on the other hand, and define the pedagogical contents and the standard courses so that the platform

has interest and motivation. It is also within this framework that we define the modules, lessons, and envisaged courses.

- On the administrative level: They relate to the management of learners' schooling (registration, transcript of marks, etc.), the management of trainers (recruitment, remuneration, etc.), assignment of learners to groups, assignment of trainers to groups, etc.
- Modeling Considerations: This is the engineering of e-learning systems. At this level, models are chosen for the acquisition and representation of knowledge as well as the design of interfaces to facilitate interoperability with other systems related to the platform, the reusability of modules, adapting to changes in the platform environment…

The structure of an e-learning platform essentially comprises three actors: the learner, the teacher, and the administrator of the platform. The role of a teacher can be subdivided into teacher-designer, teacher-trainer (or teacher-tutor), teacher-corrector, etc. We also find the administrator of educational materials and administrator of schooling as a subdivision for the role of administrator. Each role is assigned specific modules for its management. The main features of a platform are:

- Creation of courses, tests, and standard courses,
- Management of educational documents (indexing, classification, updates, etc.),
- Management of a cooperative workspace between learners and/or teachers,
- Monitoring of the learner's learning and evaluation,
- Management of the learner's education,
- Provision of work tools to the learner (specific editors, download tools, T.P simulation tools, etc.).
- Making available to the various actors' communications tools and the procedures for their management (forums, messaging, chat, videoconferencing, etc.).

There are a large number of distance learning platforms on the international market, around more than 600 including around forty under free licenses. Among the platforms under a free license (or GPL license), we can cite Claroline, Ganesha, and Moodle, etc.

There are also proprietary licensed platforms such as e-doceo, myTeacher, Blackboard…

4. Standardization in the e-Learning Field

Standardization work in the field of educational technologies is mainly linked to the work of the following organizations: IEEE, IMS, and ARIADNE, ADL, AICC, and W3C. Two features are subject to standardization:

- Importing and integrating external educational resources into a platform,
- The reuse of courses and materials from one platform to another.

We will note the difference with general standardization work on Internet technologies (carried out by W3C) because this work will have an essential impact on the standardization of educational technologies; this is the case for standards and protocols such as:

- XML, a general standard for structuring and exchanging documents on the Web,
- WebDav, collaborative creation protocol for Web pages,
- SMIL, the standard for structuring multimedia documents,
- CSS, standard defining style sheets for HTML documents.

Likewise, the .Net strategy launched by Microsoft in July 2000, which consists of using a set of a protocol called SOAP (Simple Object Access Protocol) which defines how applications can communicate on a network, will influence the standardization processes of educational technologies.

Standardization in the field of educational technologies has been coordinated since 1998 by the IEEE LTSC. This Committee for the development of standards in the field of educational technologies has established an action program aimed at promoting standards, good practices, and practical guides facilitating the development, maintenance, and interoperability of computer applications relating to education and training.

The LTSC has set up a structure, which includes 20 working groups interested in different themes such as:

- architecture and vocabulary,

- Questions of interest to learners (learner model, task model, identification of learners, etc.),
- Questions relating to the content (interoperability languages, internal course organization model, etc.),
- Signage and documentation of educational objects (materials, courses, etc.),
- Management platforms and systems.

Among the educational technology standardization projects, we can cite:

4.1 Instructional Management Systems

IMS, which is supported by the Educause group (of American origin) and which brings together a large number of companies in the IT sector, the multimedia training sector, the training organizations, and educational institutions, companies in general, and administrations (more than 160). IMS was launched in 1994 and aims to develop standards in the following areas:

- Description of educational materials (cataloged as metadata) to make possible publication and research on the Web (and on any information system),
- Interoperability of these materials,
- Interoperability of platforms with materials and general information systems of educational establishments for exchanging information,
- Recording of information on students (diplomas, skills, etc.),
- Exchange data between administration systems.

IMS has led to the LOM standard. Figure 1 shows the main specifications proposed by this standard.

There are adaptations of the LOM such as LOMFR proposed in 2006 by the CN36 group of AFNOR. LOMFR slightly modifies the LOM specification by notably adding four elements to the general category:

- Resource reference date (date of a particular event on the resource: modification, publication, etc.),
- Type of documentary (text, dynamic resource, etc.),
- Induced activity (briefly describes the activity that will use the resource: creating, leading, self-training, etc.),

- Validation of acquired knowledge (allows you to express the quantity of teaching or credit unit obtained after having reached educational objectives).

Figure 1. The hierarchical structure of the LOM (Jarraud and De La Passardière, 2004)

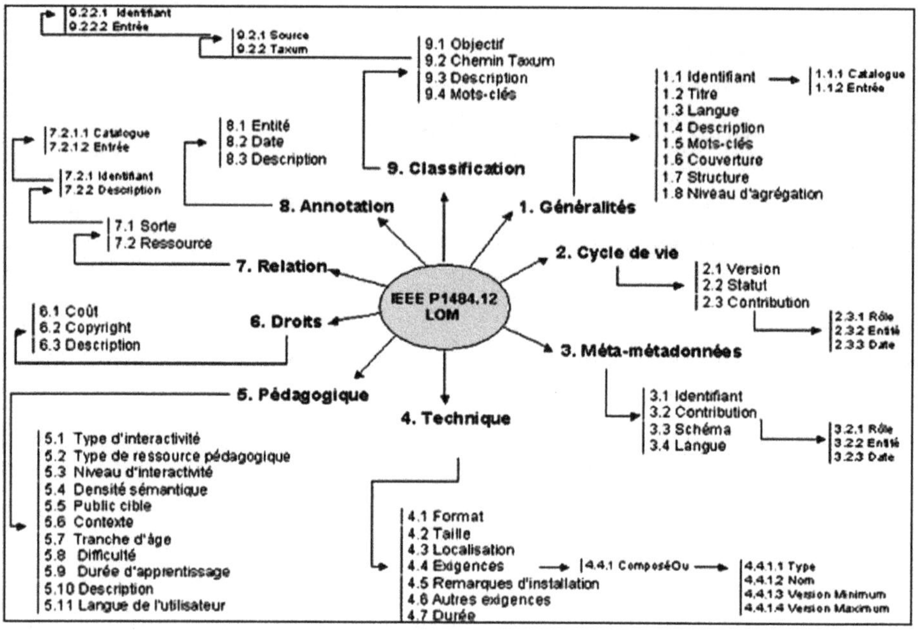

LOMFR induces the concept of validation of acquired knowledge to inform the result of the use of the resource, but we do not know the criteria of the evaluation method to obtain this result.

4.2 Shareable Course Object Reference Model

SCORM is also a standard developed at the initiative of the United States Department of Defense. It is part of the spectrum of IMS work. SCORM tries to solve three problems:

- Transferring a course, including student information, from one platform to another.
- The creation of "granular" materials used in different courses,

- Computerized research (in databases, on the Internet) of training materials and documents.

The means envisaged are the standardization of the description of the materials and the standardization of the exchange functionalities on the networks of these materials. In October 2000, the following were defined within the framework of SCORM:

- Specifications to represent the structure of a course,
- Specifications relating to the launch of applications supporting these courses,
- "Meta-data", document description items.

The techniques used are those of XML standardization (insertion of labels in documents).

Today, various platforms such as Moodle, Claroline, etc. run SCORM-type resources in the form of packages. Content is packaged to make educational resources available to the learner, LMS, and content creators. It is a standard means (per IMS specifications) for structuring and exchanging educational content between different systems and tools, i.e. it allows the transfer of educational content between the LMSs, the development tools, and thc content bases.

The Content Package is represented by a compressed file in ZIP format, consisting of two main components (see Figure 2):

- A file in XML format describing the structure of the content and the association of the content with the resources. This file is called imsmanifest.xml and is located at the root of thc packagc.
- The physical files constituting the Content Package.

4.3 Instructional Management Systems – Learning Design

We can also cite the IMS-LD specification, resulting from the work of the Open University of the Netherlands on educational modeling languages called EML, which is a metalanguage for describing pedagogical models or scenarios (accompanied by resources and services required to achieve one or more learning objectives).

Figure 2. Conceptual diagram of a package [37]

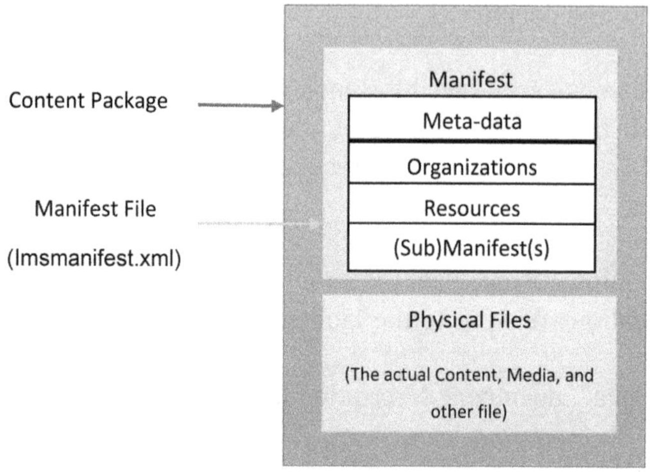

4.4 Instructional Management Systems – Question and Test Interoperability

The QTI specification of IMS allows us to represent the data structure of a question (item) and a test (assessment), as well as the corresponding results particularly, attracted our attention given the interest of this thesis for evaluation. However, as shown in Figure 3 which shows the main elements of version v2.1, this specification is based on tests and therefore questionnaires and does not deal with open questions.

4.5 Synthesis

Standardization in the field of educational technologies and the Internet has an obvious effect on the engineering of learning systems. Indeed, the possibility of interoperability and the existence of a metadata bank will lighten the development of this kind of system and will facilitate their updating to adapt them to new parameters. Only, these standards must cover all the functionalities of learning and a uniform level of granularity that can meet the expectations of each designer. Their use by using adequate software tools will accelerate the production of courses with possible questionnaires. However, if we want to work on the knowledge of a teaching field with more dynamic and more "intelligent" processes as is the case of the evaluation of the learner progression in the learning of a field when there are open questions (without predefined answers) or the appropriate generation of content, we quickly notice the limitations of these standards. This is mainly because the standards cannot model the semantics of a domain, which would allow automatic processing of the represented components, which are in the majority of the cases educational resources.

Figure 3. Different roles of IMS QTI components (Née Dahmani, 2010)

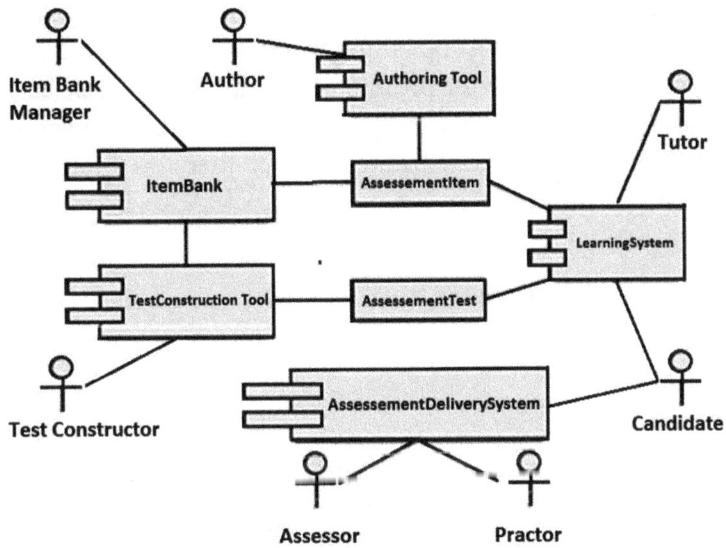

FREE AND PROPRIETARY E-LEARNING PLATFORMS

Proprietary e-learning platforms are developed for the commercial activity of selling a distance-learning product (e.g. Captera, Training Industry, eLearning Industry, Coursera ...

Free e-learning platforms are offered in open code and are based on the philosophy of "free software" defined by the "Free software Foundation" which considers free software available in the form of source code, freely reusable and modifiable (see figure 4). However, free software does not mean free because professionalism and the quality of services require the expertise and costs associated with this quality.

Proprietary e-learning platforms have certain differences from free e-learning platforms. The first important difference concerns the educational approach.

1. Social Constructivism Pedagogical Paradigm

Traditional teaching is often criticized for being too centered on the teacher, therefore for being unidirectional since the student has only a passive role, which consists of capturing information and memorizing it while the teacher is considered the expert who transmits knowledge.

In contrast, social constructivism, which is a sociological theory of knowledge developed by Berger and Luckhman (Benyounes, 2009), places the student and not the teacher, at the center of the learning process. And stipulates that knowledge must be built collectively between the teacher, the student, the group of courses, the professionals and specialists in learning, the social environment such as the family and the community (hence the name of social constructivism). The learning links are therefore bidirectional and multidirectional as illustrated in Figure 5.

Figure 4. Principle of Open Source

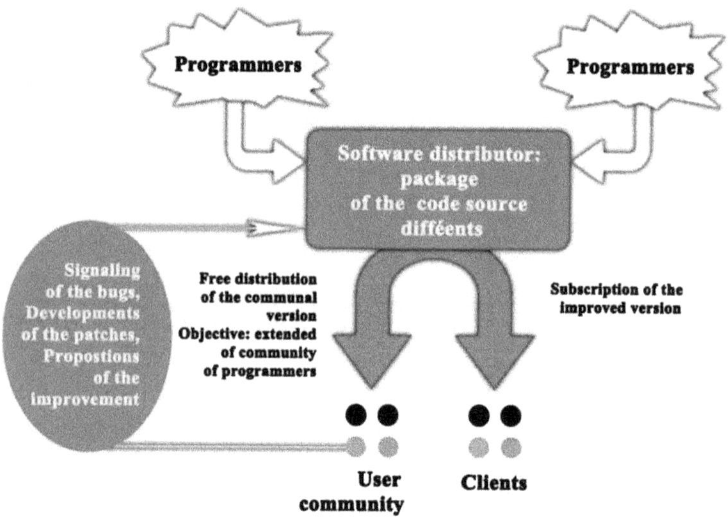

As a result, even if the knowledge is personal, it is carried out in a social framework, which brings benefits in the sense that the information comes not only from what one thinks but also from social interactions with many other social workers (see Figure 6).

The imbalance is a disturbing element, which requires an effort of understanding to pass to a higher level of knowledge.

Figure 5. Learning in society: socio-constructivism (Guité, 2011; Benyounes, 2009)

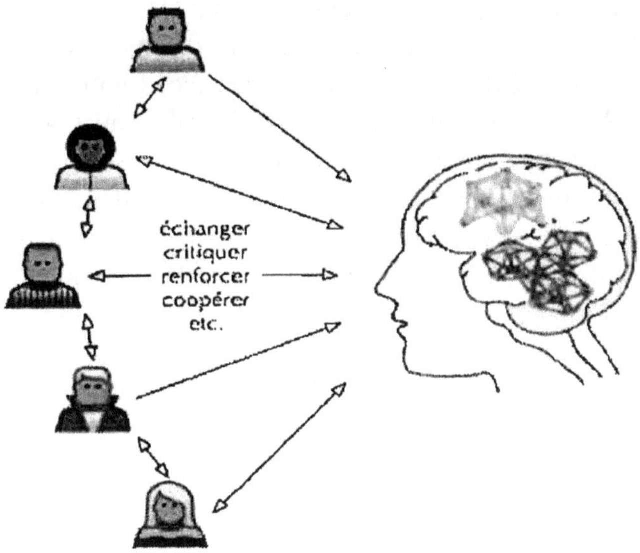

Figure 6. The Social constructivist model (Benyounes, 2009)

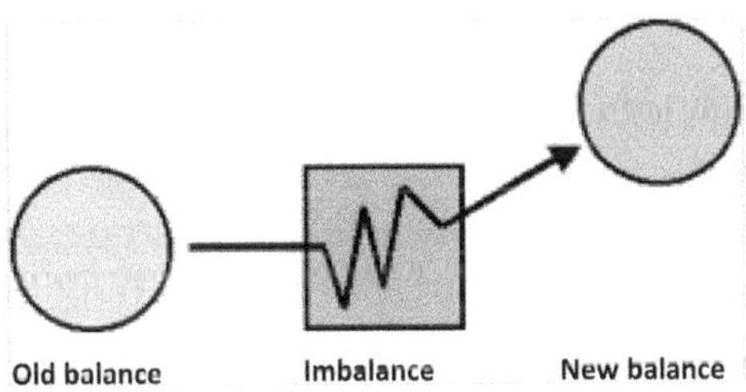

In this new paradigm, educational contents are no longer at the center of the learning process, what matters is the richness of social interactions that allow knowledge sharing as illustrated in figure 6.

This modern learning philosophy is, therefore, more than a form of distance learning because it not only motivates students. This latter, who now plays an active role by transmitting their knowledge, but also allows the teacher to have personalized contacts adapted to the needs of each student and to animate the discussions and the activities to achieve the common objectives of the class. Technologically, Open Source learning platforms allow this kind of pedagogical approach, as evidenced by the approach of Martin Dougamias, designer of Moodle, which is based on this social constructivist pedagogy, which places the user, and not the platform, at the learning center.

The PLUME university team, which has set up a platform in France inspired by this learning philosophy, even asserts about traditional platforms that more than 70% of systems fail due to poor needs analysis, but also due to the wear and tear that users experience when faced with the virtuality of the platform. All these seven exchanges on the Web must be supported by exchanges between humans and not between humans and platforms, because of weariness, discouragement then failure (Dossou and al., 2007).

The emphasis on social interactions explains why Moodle now benefits from a large international community of members, an annual conference of users who are no longer just professional developers but also ordinary users, documentation online developed in wiki media and translated into 85 languages around the world, and finally interactive multimedia services to better understand the pedagogy of the platform.

2. IT Environment

Among the technological and functional advantages of open source platforms, which differentiate them from proprietary platforms, we can cite the following aspects:

2.1 Standardization, Normalization, and Interoperability

An important aspect of functionality is that of interoperability, which is very limited in proprietary environments when it is a fundamental requirement for developers of free and open-source software. Compliance with standards guarantees good interoperability with other software. Since the sources are open, there is no point in using incompatible protocols or non-standard file formats. The standardization of data also makes it possible to reuse it by other software in a reliable manner and at a lower cost.

As a result, standardization not only ensures an improvement in the educational efficiency of software products but also a better economic efficiency of investments in online training. In his study on the standardization of online training, Simard (Simard, 2002) presents the main attributes of this standardization, which have been grouped in Table 1. These attributes are considered by the author as advantages because they are not found, or only partially, in environments that do not conform, or hardly conform, to norms (jury recognition) or standards (de facto recognition only).

Table 1. Benefits of standardizing e-learning

Criteria	Description
Accessibility	Enable research, identification, access, and delivery of online training content and components in a distributed manner.
interoperability	Allow the use of content and components developed by an organization on a given platform by other organizations on other platforms;
Reusability	Allow the reuse of contents and components for different purposes, in different applications, in different products, in different contexts, and different modes of access.
Durability	Allow the contents and components to face technological changes without the need for reengineering or redevelopment.
Maintainability	The ability to support the constant evolution of pedagogical content at a low cost.
Adaptability	Allow tailor-made modulation of contents and components

(Simard, 2002)

We will not discuss in the brief how-to standardize e-learning because it is a vast and very complex subject that does not fit into the objectives of our research which were defined when the brief was introduced.

If we go from generic standards relating to all aspects of software quality (eg ISO 9126 (ISO/IEC 9126-1, 2001; ISO/IEC 9126-2, 2003; ISO/IEC 9126-3, 2003; ISO/IEC 9126-4, 2004) to specific standards relating to a particular aspect such as interoperability with its standards like SCORM and IMS specific to e-learning. We can cite a study carried out for Sun Micro-System and in which the authors' Collier and Robson (Collier and Robby, 2002) describe well the advantages of interoperability standards for all stakeholders.

For the software system purchaser, the main advantage is the non-dependence on the manufacturers of these systems. For the latter and their designers, the work and therefore the cost of designing interfaces is reduced because it is no longer necessary to develop interfaces specific to each software product, as in the proprietary approach. As a result, the manufacturer achieves significant economies of scale when demand increases. Finally, for the user, interoperability standards allow them to access and share the contents of a wide variety of educational resources.

2.2 Efficiency, Reliability, and Reusability

The availability of source codes allows users not only to consult them but also to modify them. Consequently, experienced developers can resolve errors located in code quickly. This ensures free software better efficiency compared to proprietary software whose design flaws are not quickly modified because their publishers often have the habit of not fixing these flaws until the release of a new version of their software. Besides, this efficiency is also accompanied by good reliability because, as the popular jargon says about free software: "With enough eyes to watch, bugs can no longer hide" (Benyounes, 2009).

Free software development is a process to which a large community of developers and publishers, spread across the world, contributes. This development process is effective because it allows, therefore, considering several technical solutions, the best of which are selected by a natural selection process. The development process is not only effective but it is also profitable because the reuse of the code is an important source of saving time and therefore money.

For all these advantages, free software is often considered free or is bought at a relatively modest price compared to the high purchase costs of proprietary software such as Captera, Training Industry, eLearning Industry, Coursera… However, free software publishers generally offer service contracts associated with their products to give professional guarantees to their customers who have the freedom to subscribe or not according to the needs and the IT resource management policy of each of them. Free software is therefore not free software. However, the relatively low acquisition costs, thanks to the availability of source code for a very large number of users, and less dependence on suppliers are added to reduce operating costs thanks to the adoption of interoperability standards and the sharing of reusable educational objects.

3. Functional Architecture

Functional architecture refers to the general structure of "the degree to which a product or system provides functions that meet the expressed and implicit needs when used under specified conditions" (ISO/IEC 25010, 2011). This structure follows a set of strategic decisions taken during the design of all or part of the IT system, through the exercise of a technical and industrial discipline in the IT sector, also called architecture, and for which the manager is an IT architect.

We will first present the basic architecture of the platform and then that of its two main components.

3.1 Basic Architecture

Open Source platforms are based on open and distance learning, which combines modern communication supports for the professor (telephony, videoconferencing, electronic mail, discussion forum, chat ...).

Figure 7. The external architecture of online training (Benyounes, 2009)

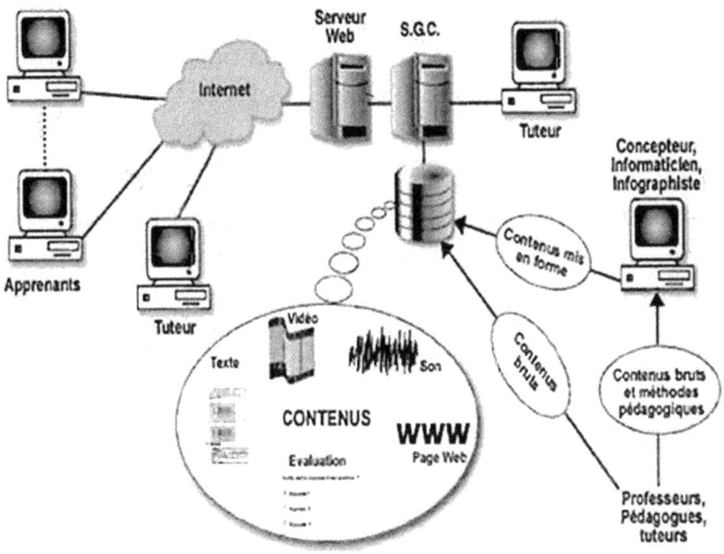

Figure 7 summarizes all the elements of a distance-training system:

- The architecture center represents the learning platform, which offers a library of courses and various educational resources on the web
- Communication tools are adapted to learning activities, for example:
- In synchronous mode (real-time), teachers and students can communicate by chat, application sharing, or videoconference;
- In asynchronous mode, tools such as messaging, blogs, or forums are used for deferred exchanges.
- The second category of tools concerns management and administration tools such as:
- Registration and monitoring of students.
- Managing their files (notes)
- Their educational path

- Course design (content)
- Course management
- Survey tools
- Etc.

3.2 The Architecture of the Components

The platforms revolve around two complementary systems (see Figure 8):

- An LMS is often referred to as a "distance learning platform".
- Learning Content Management System or LCMS

3.2.1 Learning Content Management System

LCMS is a software system focused only on learning content, as the name suggests. More specifically, its main features are as follows (see Figure 9):

- Content creation: this is the primary function of LCMS. The courses constructed with reusable educational objects are then validated for publication.
- Storage of content in a central database. Content distribution: LCMS finally ensures the dissemination of educational content to students either on the Internet or on a private local network.

Figure 8. The architecture of a platform (Colace and al., 2003; Benyounes, 2009)

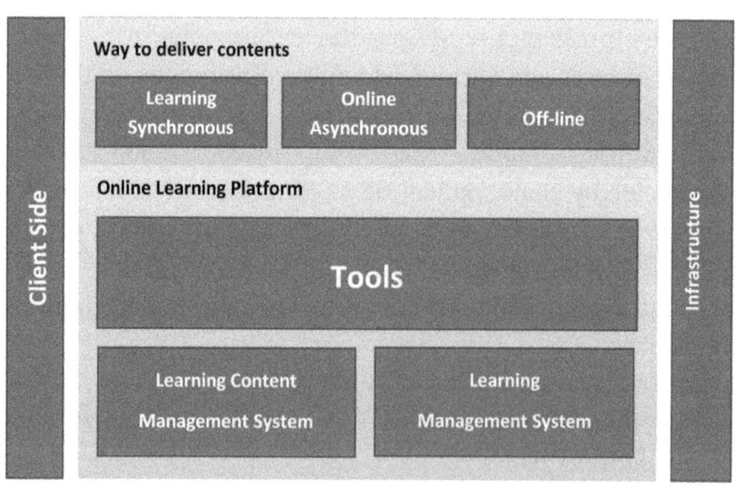

Figure 9. LCMS functional architecture

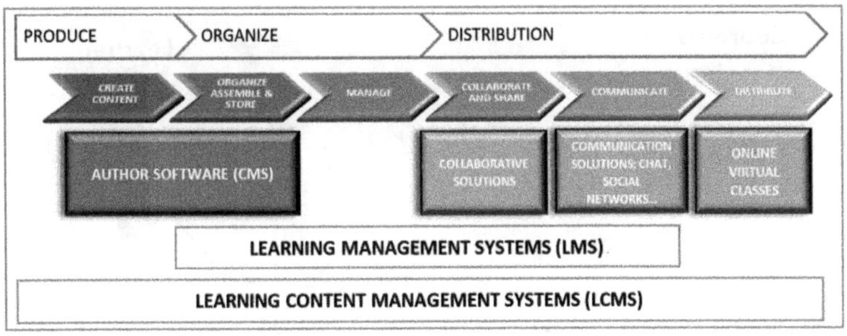

3.2.2 Learning Management System

The LMS is software-comprising services intended to help teachers in the management of their lessons. It offers services that allow content management, in particular for creation, import, and export. The set of tools represents the set of services that manage teaching processes and interactions between users such as access control service, synchronous and asynchronous communication tools, and a service for managing user groups.

More specifically, its services relate to many features such as:

- Management of educational content (creation, import, export).
- The individual path through the training modules.
- The availability of sharing tools.
- Distribution of communication tools.
- Registration of students and management of their files (monitoring and results).
- Distribution of online courses and other educational resources.

Figure 10 illustrates the general principle of the operation of an LMS by presenting the main functionalities associated with the main contributors, namely:

- The designers create educational content.
- Teachers who manage educational content.
- Students taking the training.
- The administrator configures the platform.

Figure 10. LMS architecture

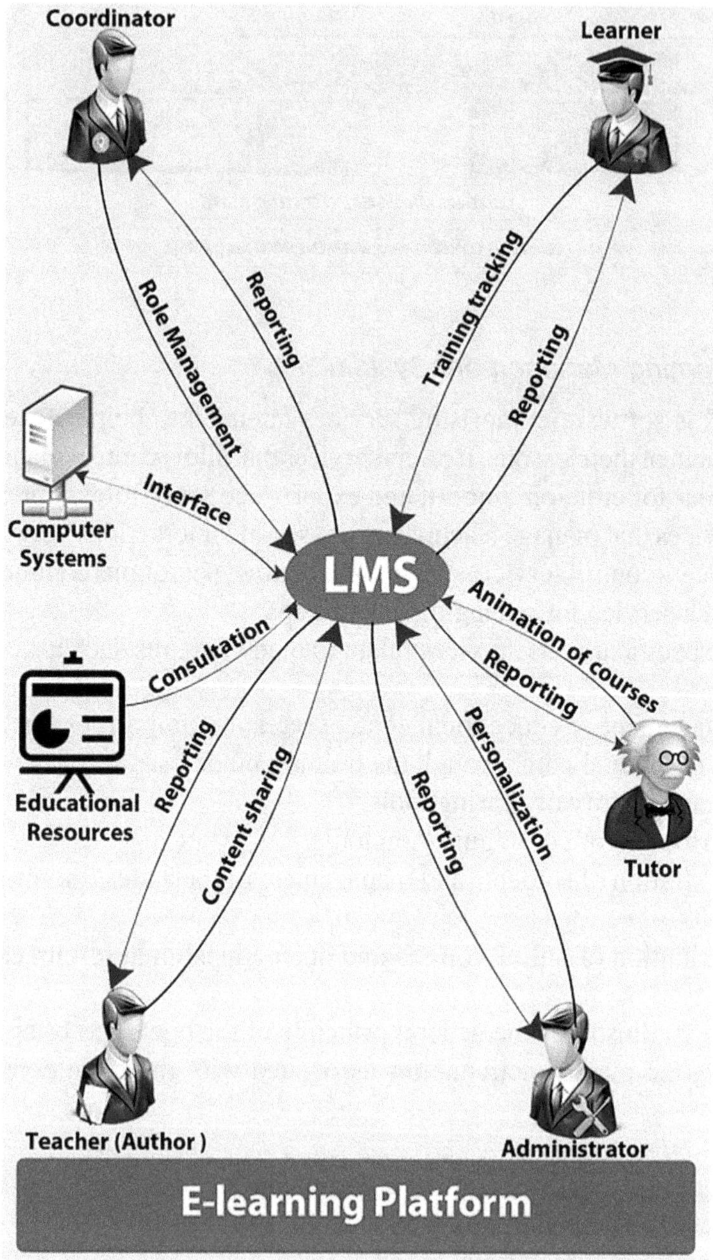

4. Teaching-learning Systems

It is a coherent whole made up of resources (material and human), strategies, methods, and actors interacting in a given context to achieve a goal "(Lebrun, 2005). He specifies that: "The learning system aims to allow someone to learn something with the technological tool.

We propose to integrate the role of the teacher in the learning system. Research in CEHL studies the means of assisting the learner and to those who favor this learning (teacher, trainer, tutor, peers, etc.).

In national and international research in EIAH, there are already many types of personalized systems from LMSs or LCMSs such as Moodle, Claroline, ATutor, and Sakai… where the courses are online and open. These systems are developed within the framework of DE, face-to-face training, and open training. They are called Virtual Campuses. Online University. Virtual Universities… namely:

- MOOC (Massive Open Online Course),
- PLE (Personal Learning Environment),
- VLE (Virtual Learning Environment),
- C3MS (Community, Content, & Collaboration Management Systems).

4.1 Massive Open Online Course

Massive Open Online Course. MOOCs are open online courses that bring together a large number of students. They have not failed to interest many economic and political actors who see in them a successor to e-learning or distance learning systems to train a large number of people.

Table 2. Comparison between cMOOCs and xMOOCs

Comparison of MOOCs	cMOOCs	xMOOCs
Learning outcomes	Develop digital, social, and intellectual skills associated with the web. "Choose an answer"	Acquire knowledge. "Find an answer"
Thematic	Open and forward-looking, knowledge is to be built through experience, the debate of ideas, analysis, model identification ...	Elementary or at least thematic where knowledge is formalized, stable, delimited introductory course
Pedagogical model	Connectivist approach, building your learning by sharing and discussing with others	Traditional approach: well-structured course, the material provided, work and tests, reassuring
Target audience	Learners with digital skills prerequisites	Larger audience, learners with fewer digital skills

The MOOC movement was created to provide access to high-quality education in remote corners of the United States and the world. (Sonwalkar, 2013) MOOCs are at such an early stage of development that there is not yet an agreed or preferred way to describe their approach (Porter, 2015). The latter is a model of educational provision, which is, to varying degrees:

- Massive. The course can accommodate, in principle, an unlimited number of participants, sometimes tens of thousands.
- Open. The course is open to all Internet users, regardless of origin, level of study, without institutional affiliation necessary, generally free of charge.
- Online. Comments, evaluations, conferences, Tutoring, and follow-up are carried out remotely without the obligation of presenting,
- Course. There are training programs structured around a set of learning objectives in a defined field of study. An expert or a group of experts in a particular field creates the outline of the course and facilitates a series of interactive readings and discussion forums on a given theme.

Two types of MOOCs are now commonly discussed. The first is based on the connectivism theory of learning, which promotes informal learning networks, those students co-construct the course with the teaching team. The latter is known as cMOOC. The second builds on a cohesive and organized set of resources, known as xMOOC is more traditional, content-based, and much more like traditional educational models. Depending on the content, xMOOC is more likely to have one or more speakers, usually by broadcasting conferences via YouTube-style videos, with tasks and discussions online via proprietary software. This organization allows the university to integrate the MOOC into existing programs. Deadlines for completing tasks and a form of continuous online assessment allow course administrators to assign brands and credits. Online participants who are not interested in obtaining credits may or may not participate as they wish.

4.2 Personal Learning Environment

PLE is a system, a set of tools, or an ecosystem, which helps learners to build and organize their learning. Personal learning is learning in which the learner controls his learning process, his environment, the resources he has access to, and the people with whom he interacts.

Personal learning environments as an idea that first integrates "pressures and movements" such as lifelong learning, informal learning, learning styles, new approaches to assessment, cognitive tools. Also, the PLEs are inspired by the success of new "sticky" technologies in ubiquitous computing and social software (Attwell, 2007).

There is no consensus on the definition of a personal learning environment. Broadly speaking, Graham presents it as "a new approach to the use of technologies to learn" (Roland, 2013). According to Nicolas Roland, a researcher in education science, it is "an ecosystem of people and tools that the individual mobilizes, and organizes within the framework of knowledge-building activities" (Attwell, 2007). This means a centralized learning environment, unlike the LMSs. Some authors (Terry Anderson, Ron Lubensky, and Mark van Harmelen) highlight the digital aspect of the system (software, applications, web service) while others (Clive Shepherd ...) add physical resources (family, friends, books, magazine, newspaper, television ... In the different definitions, the same objective of a PLE appears: to build and manage your learning, to take charge. The trainer Marc Dennery summarizes the PLE as the set of tools and methods available to the learner allowing him to achieve his learning objectives" (Dennery, 2013).

4.3 Virtual Learning Environment

A Virtual Learning Environment in educational technology is a web-based platform for the digital aspects of study courses, usually in educational institutions. VLEs generally allow participants to be organized into cohorts, groups, and roles, resources, activities, and interactions in a course structure provide the different stages of the evaluation report on participation; and have a certain level of integration with other institutional systems (Britain and Liber, 1999; Weller, 2007).

For those who edit them, VLEs can have a de facto role as a design architecture and design (Masterman, 2013). Almost all higher education institutions in the English-speaking world have adopted VLEs.

Here are the main components required for a virtual learning environment or an online education program to take place:

- Content management - creation, storage, access, and use of learning resources.
- Mapping and planning of the study program – course planning, evaluation, and personalization of the learning experience.

- Learner engagement and administration – managing access to learner information and resources and monitoring progress and success.
- Communication and collaboration - emails, reviews, chat, wikis, blogs.

4.4 Community, Content, and Collaboration Management Systems

C3MS, that is to say, a software based on the Web, which makes it possible to manage a community, the collaboration between the members and the contents. C3MS can refer to an existing portal that includes several generally simple modules or to a portal (i.e. the toolbox) necessary to install and configure the portal.

Simple Internet technologies (web pages, forums, email, FTP, etc.) have been successful in education because they have responded to the basic needs for information exchange, communication, and collaboration necessary for constructivist scenarios.

In addition to being simple, yet powerful, the Internet allows the user (teachers) to have control over it. While simple web technology allows for creative scenarios, it has four drawbacks:

- Maintaining static websites (including student pages) takes time,
- Simple discussion systems, like forums or mailing lists, don't do very good knowledge management,
- More sophisticated scenarios are poorly supported,
- Moreover, there is no glue to put all these elements together.

Community websites face very similar problems and seem to have found at least a partial answer. Over the past two years, an impressive number of what the authors represent C3MS have cropped up in existence.

Inspired by personal weblogs (also called blogs, increasingly popular journaling systems), Slashdot-like weblog/information systems, simple content management systems, and various popular groupware applications, they offer a modular system for setting up interactive community websites.

Besides, most of these systems provide documented extension mechanisms allowing third parties to contribute modules with additional functionality.

C3MS systems are a form of web portals. A portal brings together a variety of useful information, and communication resources into a single web page (Looney and Lyman, 2000). A portal is, therefore, a collection of objects (information bricks) and services (operation on these bricks) that can be accessed from the portal page (Web).

COMPARISON OF UNIVERSITY TEACHING-LEARNING SYSTEMS

To justify such a study, a set of factors mentioned below seems to be determinants:

- Media news implementing the meteoric enthusiasm of young people for social media;
- Data on the generalization of ICT in Higher Education (E-Sup) program;
- Needs of students and teachers to integrate ICT into learning and university practices;
- Following the CNPN project, the start of the 2014-2015 academic year must bring with it, among other things, an innovative distance-training system.

Our question today is to know where we stand with this training innovation perspective. To support our research around this subject, two tracks seem to us for the moment essential to investigate:

- What about the technologies and arrangements, put in place to make this distance-learning system?
- What choice of multimedia educational engineering adopted for such a system?

Following these two lines of investigation immediately leads us to question the status of this study in national universities is international. We are trying to assess the level of university dispositions as part of this study.

We can consider that the evaluation generally consists of comparing the object evaluated with a reference model to deduce conclusions from it (Huart and al., 2008). Of course, the "reference model" can be virtual and envisaged as a combination of recommendations adapted to the field of the object to be evaluated. What can be assessed in a distance-learning context? The assessment must be based on formal and explicit criteria. What are the dimensions of evaluation to favor? Many evaluation criteria can be used for the evaluation of digital documents and in the context of learning; we can add some that are more specific. There are usually three main evaluation dimensions of interactive systems (Senach, 1993), namely utility, usability, and aesthetics.

Tricot (Tricot and al., 2003) adds acceptability to these three dimensions (positive or negative feeling about the product, "intention" of use depending on many parameters: motivation, affects, culture, values). From the work of Senach and Tricot, as well as that of ISO 25010 (ISO/IEC 25010, 2011) and the various discussions which comfort them (Ouadoud and al., 2016), we are interested in utility and usability.

Table 3 identifies e-learning platforms implemented in growth establishments, which we have assessed their utility and usability. In Table 4, we followed a detailed evaluation grid, of e-learning systems at the national level versus e-learning systems at the international level, referring to the two evaluation dimensions chosen, namely: utility and usability.

1. Moodle-Based e-Learning System

The Moodle platform has topped the list of platforms used as an e-learning system in universities, notably the Moroccan (Cadi Ayyad, Ibn Zohr, Ibn Tofail…) and French (Paris I, Paris VIII…) universities. Moodle has a very good degree of utility and usability. The platform can accommodate thousands of learners, teachers, and tutors (+10000 accounts, +30 course materials completely scripted and divided into educational activities, Fully remote management of IT module lessons). It is one of the most widely used free platforms in the world, with its large French-speaking and international community, its clear, well-structured, useful documentation, its numerous discussion forums focused on all the issues generated by the complexity of training in the distance. The Moodle platform is based on the creation of communities of learners around content and educational activities. Moodle favors human exchanges, builds communities of practice, and promotes mutual aid and support between learners as well as between teachers and tutors.

Table 3. Identification of e-learning platforms of promising establishments

Promising ESTABLISHMENT	Identification						
	Moroccan Universities			French Universities		American Universities	
	Cadi Ayyad	Ibn Tofail	Ibn Zohr	Paris I	Paris VIII	Harvard	Duke
Platform used	Moodle	Moodle	Moodle	Moodle	Moodle	edX	Coursera
Platform type	LMS / LCMS / VLE	LMS / LCMS / VLE	LMS / LCMS / VLE	LMS / LCMS / VLE	LMS / LCMS / VLE	MOOC	MOOC
The educational model of the platform	social constructivism	social constructivism	social constructivism	social constructivism	social constructivism	Classic: Lessons, exercises, and test of acquired knowledge	Classic: Lessons, exercises, and test of acquired knowledge
Platform license	Open source (GPL)	Open source (GPL)	Open source (GPL)	Open source (GPL)	Open source (GPL)	Open source	Commercial
Technology used	PHP (5.4.4+)	PHP (5.4.4+)	PHP (5.4.4+)	PHP (5.4.4+)	PHP (5.4.4+)	-	-
Language used	French, English, and Arabic	French, English, and Spanish	French, English, Arabic, and Spanish	French, and English	French, English, Arabic, and Spanish	English	English
Platform website	http://moodle.org	http://moodle.org	http://moodle.org	http://moodle.org	http://moodle.org	www.edx.org	https://www.coursera.org
Institution website	http://learn.uca.ma/	http://ead.uit.ac.ma/	http://www.cvm.ac.ma/	https://cours.univ-paris1.fr/	https://moodle.univ-paris8.fr	https://online-learning.harvard.edu/	https://www.coursera.org/duke

Table 4. Evaluation grid for teaching and learning devices at national and international level

Promising Establishment Evaluation Criteria	Moroccan Universities			French Universities		American Universities	
	Cadi Ayyad	Ibn Tofail	Ibn Zohr	Paris I	Paris VIII	Harvard	Duke
The establishment already offers DL	☑	☒	☑	☑	☑	☑	☑
The establishment has a regularly updated website	☑	☑	☒	☑	☑	☑	☑
The system presents a strategy of the establishment in terms of ICTE and/or DL or a section dedicated to this (these) theme (s)	☒	☒	☑	☑	☒	☑	☑
The Utility of the Device							
Target audience specify and justify	☑	☑	☒	☑	☑	☒	☑
The rationale for switching to distance learning	☒	☒	☑	☒	☒	☒	☒
Learning based on an existing face-to-face diploma	☑	☑	☒	☑	☑	☒	☒
Availability of courses in electronic format	☒	☒	☑	☒	☒	☑	☑
Explicit educational choices (tutoring in particular)	☒	☒	☒	☑	☑	☑	☑
Functional capacity of the device	☑	☑	☒	☑	☑	☑	☑
The Usability of the Device							
Ease of learning	☒	☑	☒	☒	☒	☑	☑
Ease of use	☑	☑	☑	☑	☑	☑	☑
Quality of documentation	☒	☒	☒	☑	☑	☑	☑
Quality of course descriptions	☒	☑	☑	☑	☑	☑	☑

In table 4, we see that:

- The Cadi Ayyad University of Marrakech. As shown, the University's e-learning platform is based on Moodle's LMS support. The CAU of Marrakech is in line with the distance learning system and seems to be ahead of other Moroccan universities in such a system. However, the university uses only a few features of the Moodle platform. For that, it is necessary to set up the system, which will be integrated as well as possible into the learning ecosystem of the university, the system must:
    - Present a university strategy in terms of ICTE or distance learning,
    - Give the justification for the transition to distance learning,
    - Have courses available in electronic format,

  - Have the educational choices explained, tutoring in particular,
  - Keep the ease of learning,
  - Ensure the quality of documentation,
  - Ensure the quality of the course descriptions.

However, we cannot deeply judge or evaluate this training at this time since access is limited to registered students of the UCA. An attempt is made to access and evaluate this distance-learning platform.

- The Ibn Zohr University of Kenitra. The IZU subscribes to the Moodle platform and uses its services, but it seems that university teachers use it to diversify course materials. However, the university uses only a few features of the Moodle platform. For that, it is necessary to set up a system that will be integrated as well as possible into the learning ecosystem of the university, the system must:
  - Be updated daily,
  - Have a target audience specified and justified,
  - Have training based on an existing face-to-face diploma,
  - Have the educational choices explained, tutoring in particular,
  - Have functional capacity,
  - Keep the ease of learning,
  - Ensure the quality of documentation.

As mentioned in the system, a restriction of visits to online courses does not leave us for the moment to make technical and pedagogical analyses on this platform.

- The Ibn Tofail University of Agadir. The ITU likewise uses Moodle's services and seems to generalize this experience in almost all disciplines of the dies taught. However, the university uses only a few features of the Moodle platform. For that, it is necessary to set up a system that will be integrated as well as possible into the learning ecosystem of the university, the system must:
  - Present a university strategy in terms of ICTE or distance learning,
  - Give the justification for the transition to distance learning,
  - Have courses available in electronic format,
  - Have the educational choices explained, tutoring in particular,
  - Ensure the quality of documentation.

Access on an anonymous basis is not authorized and registration seems impossible, which does not leave the possibility for the moment to study and deeply evaluate the technical and educational elements in this system.

- Paris I University of Paris likewise uses the services of Moodle and seems to generalize this experience almost on all the disciplines of the dies taught. However, the university uses almost the majority of the functionality of the Moodle platform. For that, it is necessary to set up a system that will be integrated as well as possible into the learning ecosystem of the university, the system must:
    - Give the justification for the transition to distance learning,
    - Have courses available in electronic format,
    - Keep the ease of learning.

However, we cannot deeply judge or evaluate this training at this time since access is limited to students enrolled at the University of Paris I. An attempt is made to access and evaluate this distance-learning platform.

- Paris VIII University of Saint-Denis also uses the services of Moodle and seems to generalize this experience almost on all the disciplines of the dies taught. However, the university uses almost the majority of the functionality of the Moodle platform. For that, it is necessary to set up a system that will be integrated as well as possible into the learning ecosystem of the university, the system must:
    - Present a university strategy in terms of ICTE or distance learning,
    - Give the justification for the transition to distance learning,
    - Have courses available in electronic format,
    - Keep the ease of learning.

Anonymous access is not allowed and registration seems impossible, which does not leave the possibility for the moment to study and deeply evaluate the technical and educational elements in this platform.

2. edX-Based e-Learning System

We see that the edX platform used as an e-learning system at the American University of Harvard also has a very good degree of utility and usability. edX can accommodate thousands of learners, teachers, and tutors (it had more than 10 million users following: + 1569 online courses, + 89 programs, and + 11 languages). It is one of the most used open-source platforms in the world, it is clear, well-structured, useful documentation, its many discussion forums, and videoconferences focused on all the issues generated by the complexity of distance learning. The edX platform is a MOOC (online learning platform). It hosts and provides free online university-level courses around the world. It also researches online learning and how users use it.

In table 4, we see that:

- The Harvard University of Cambridge uses the services of edX and seems to generalize this experience across all disciplines of the subjects taught. However, the university uses the majority of the functionality of the edX platform. But there are still a few functionalities to set up the system that will best integrate with the university's learning ecosystem, the system must:
    - Have a target audience specified and justified,
    - Give the justification for the transition to distance learning,
    - Have training based on an existing face-to-face diploma,

Access to the courses is authorized and registration seems essential, which leaves the possibility to study and deeply assess the technical and educational elements in this system.

3. Coursera-Based e-Learning System

Coursera platform used as an e-learning system at the American University of Duke also has a very good degree of utility and usability. Coursera can accommodate thousands of learners, teachers, and tutors (it had over 24 million registered users and over 2,000 courses); Coursera is a MOOC offering online training open to all. Coursera is dedicated to making the best learning in the world available free of charge to anyone looking for it.

- The Duke University of Durham uses the services of Coursera and seems to generalize this experience across all disciplines of the dies taught. However, the university uses the majority of the functionality of the Coursera platform. But there are still a few functionalities to set up the system that will best integrate with the university's learning ecosystem, the system must:
    - Give the justification for the transition to distance learning,
    - Has training based on an existing face-to-face diploma?

Access to the courses is authorized and registration seems essential, which leaves the possibility to study and deeply assess the technical and educational elements in this system.

4. Synthesis

We can argue that the beginning of the e-learning era in Morocco is launched under the impetus of certain Moroccan universities (Ibn Zohr, Cadi Ayad, Ibn Tofail ...), but remains to be seen its development and momentum while respecting the favorable conditions for teaching and learning Moroccan students.

The use of this assessment grid of the state of play at the national level against the international level, allows us to make a comparative study between Moroccan, European, and American studies.

We can deduct from this grid that French, and English experiences in e-Learning and launched under the impulse of most French and English universities (Paris I, Paris VIII, Harvard, Duke ...), but remains to be seen in its development to do critical work. Moreover, especially in teaching and learning at universities.

CONCLUSION

When teaching in Morocco started in the e-learning era, dropout and failure rates were very high. Research on this learning has shown that learners need a personalized system and in particular personalized follow-up. Similarly, the first observations of university systems indicate that around 10% of learners go until the end of the course. This type of situation covers situations that we can problematize in research. In this number of students who drop out. So providing a personalized and customizable system could help them maintain their motivation and learning.

To provide such a system, we suggest exploring three phases: assessing the need for personalization, personalization, and validating its impact. The first phase is to identify the reasons why students drop out on the one hand. On the other hand, it consists of identifying the conditions, which make it possible to maintain/relaunch their motivation until the end of the course or to predict the quality of learning. The second phase is to provide personalized and customizable environments. To validate their impact in the third phase.

In this vein, a comparative and evaluative study of e-learning platforms is presented in chapter 3 to validate what has been developed in the context of this chapter. Indeed, it will be based on the results from the study and analysis of the evaluation dimensions of e-learning platforms that we conducted in chapter 2 to build a quality evaluation approach to e-learning platforms to justify our choice.

REFERENCES

Attwell, G. (2007).. Personal Learning Environments - the future of e-learning? *e-learning Papers, 2*(1). https://issuu.com/elo-wiki/docs/informallearning

Benyounes, B. (2009). *Évaluation de la fonctionnalité et l'utilisabilité de la plateforme d'apprentissage Moodle: une approche du génie logiciel*. Mémoire présenté comme exigence partielle de la maîtrise en informatique - université du Québec à Montréal.

Britain, S., & Liber, O. (1999). *A Framework for Pedagogical Evaluation of Virtual Learning Environments*. JISC Technology Applications Programme.

Charpille, J. L., & Couniliufm, E. (2002). *Mettre à distance la formation.* Publication de l'Académie de Nancy-Metz de décembre 2001.

Colace, F., De Santo, M., & Vento, M. (2003). Evaluating Online learning platforms: a Case Study. *Proceedings of the 36th Hawaii International Conference on System Sciences (HICSS'03)*. http://csdI2.computer.org/comp/proceedings/hicss/2003/1874/05/187450154c.pdf

Collier G., Robby, R., (2002). *SUN Microsystems, e-learning interoperability standards*. by Eduworks Corporation.

Dennery, M. (2013). *Bâtir son environnement d'apprentissage personnel : la première des formations.* Le blog de C-Campus.

Dossou A., Koffi, D., Durand, A., Leproust, M., & Vanderstichel. (2007). *Étude comparative de plateformes de formation à distance.* Projet de fin d'étude, Master Ingénierie Pédagogique MultiMedia, CUEEP de Lille.

Gerhardt-Powals, J. (1996). Cognitive engineering principles for enhancing human-computer performance. *International Journal of Human-Computer Interaction, 8*(2), 189-221. doi:10.1080/10447319609526147

Guité, F. (2011). *Constructivisme, socioconstructivisme et connectivisme*. http://www.francoisguite.com/2007/10/constructivisme-socioconstructivisme-et-connectivisme/

Huart, J., Kolski, C., & Bastien, C. (2008). L'évaluation de documents multimédias. Etat de l'art. In Leleu-Merviel (dir.), Objectiver l'humain? Volume 1, Qualification, quantification, Paris, Hermès Sciences Publications. *Revue des Interactions Humaines Médiatisées*, *9*(2), 52.

ISO/IEC 25010:2011. Systems and software engineering -- Systems and software Quality Requirements and Evaluation (SQuaRE) -- System and software quality models

ISO/IEC 9126-1: 2001. Software Engineering -Software product quality -Part 1: Quality Model

ISO/IEC 9126-2: 2003. Software Engineering -Software product quality -Part 2: External Metrics

ISO/IEC 9126-3: 2003. Software Engineering -Software product quality -Part 3: Internal Metrics

ISO/IEC 9126-4: 2004. Software Engineering -Software product quality -Part 4: Quality in use Metrics

Jarraud, P., & De La Passardière, B. (2004). *Un profil d'application du LOM pour Campus Sciences* (Vol. 11). Revue STICEF.

Karim, F., & Goodwin, R. (2013, October-December). Using Cloud Computing in e-learning Systems. *International Journal of Advanced Research in Computer Science & Technology*, *1*(1), 66–67.

Liu, C.-H. (2010). The comparison of learning effectiveness between traditional face-to-face learning and e-learning among goal-oriented users. In *Digital Content, Multimedia Technology and its Applications (IDC), 2010 6th International Conference on*. IEEE.

Looney, M., & Lyman, P. (2000, July/August). Portals in Higher Education: What are they and what is their potential. *EDUCAUSE Review*, *35*(4), 28–36.

Masterman, L. (2013). The challenge of teachers' design practice. Routledge.

Née Dahmani, F. B. (2010). Modélisation basée ontologies pour l'apprentissage interactif - Application à l'évaluation des connaissances de l'apprenant (PhD dissertation). Computer Science Department, Mouloud Mammeri University of Tizi-Ouzou, Algeria.

O'Neil, M. (2001, May). What is E-learning. *Home Magazine*.

Ouadoud, M., Chkouri, M.Y., Nejjari, A., & El Kadiri, K.E. (2016). Studying and Analyzing the Evaluation Dimensions of E-learning Platforms Relying on a Software Engineering Approach. *International Journal of Emerging Technologies in Learning, 11*(1), 11-20. doi:10.3991/ijet.v11i01.4924

OVAREP. (2000). *Étude comparative technique et pédagogique des plateformes pour la formation ouverte et à distance*. Academic Press.

Porter, S. (2015). *To MOOC or Not to MOOC: How Can Online Learning Help to Build the Future of Higher Education?* Academic Press.

Roland, N. (2013). *EPA : système ou écosystème*. Hypomnematon.

Senach, B. (1993). L'évaluation ergonomique des interfaces homme-machine: une revue de la littérature. In L'ergonomie dans la conception des projets informatiques. Toulouse: Octares éditions.

Simard, C. (2002). *"Normalisation de la formation en ligne, Enjeux, tendances et perspectives", document d'orientation stratégique, préparé pour l'Agence universitaire de la francophonie(AUF)*. Bureau Amérique du Nord.

Sonwalkar, N. (2013). The First Adaptive MOOC: A Case Study on Pedagogy Framework and Scalable Cloud Architecture—Part I. In MOOCs Forum (Vol. 1, pp. 22-29). Mary Ann Liebert, Inc.

Tricot, A., Plégat-Soutjis, F., Camps, J. F., Amiel, A., Lutz, G., & Morcillo, A. (2003). Utilité, utilisabilité, acceptabilité: interpréter les relations entre trois dimensions de l'évaluation des EIAH. In C. Desmoulins, P. Marquet, & D. Bouhineau (Eds.), Environnements informatiques pour l'apprentissage humain, ATIEF / INRP éditions (pp. 391–402). Academic Press.

Weller, M. (2007). *Virtual Learning Environments: Using, Choosing and Developing your VLE*. Routledge. doi:10.4324/9780203964347

ADDITIONAL READING

Ouadoud, M., Chafiq, T., Rida, N., & Chkouri, M. Y. (2019). Generate a Meta-Model Content for Collaboration Space of Learning Management System Compatible with IMS-LD. *International Journal of Interactive Mobile Technologies, 13*(01), 37–52. doi:10.3991/ijim.v13i01.9440

Ouadoud, M., & Chkouri, M. Y. (2019). Generate a Meta-Model Content for Communication Space of Learning Management System Compatible with IMS-LD. In M. Ezziyyani (Ed.), *Advanced Intelligent Systems for Sustainable Development (AI2SD'2018), Advances in Intelligent Systems and Computing* (pp. 24–39). Springer International Publishing. doi:10.1007/978-3-030-11928-7_3

Ouadoud, M., & Chkouri, M. Y. (2019). Designing an IMS-LD Model for Communication Space of Learning Management System. In M. Ezziyyani (Ed.), *Advanced Intelligent Systems for Sustainable Development (AI2SD'2018), Advances in Intelligent Systems and Computing* (pp. 40–54). Springer International Publishing. doi:10.1007/978-3-030-11928-7_4

KEY TERMS AND DEFINITIONS

ADL: Advanced distributed learning.
AICC: Aviation Industry CBT Committee.
C3MS: Community, content, and collaboration management systems.
CAU: Cadi Ayyad University.
CEHL: Computer environments for human learning.
DE: Distance education.
DL: Distance learning.
DoD: Department of Defense.
EML: Educational modeling languages.
GPL: General public license.
ICT: Information and communication technologies.
ICTE: Information and communication technologies for education.
IEEE: Institute of Electrical and Electronics Engineers.
IMS: Instructional management systems.
ITU: Ibn Tofail University.
IZU: Ibn Zohr University.

LCMS: Learning content management system.

LMS: Learning management system.

LOM: Learning object metadata.

LTSC: Learning Technology Standards Committee.

MOOC: Massive open online course.

ODL: Open and distance learning.

PLE: Personal learning environment.

PLUME: Promoting useful, controlled, and economic software.

SCORM: The SCORM® (sharable content object reference model) was created to address these interoperability, reusability, and durability challenges. As a reference model, it was intentionally designed to leverage standard web technologies as well as existing learning technology specifications that already existed. SCORM® is comprised of a collection of interrelated technical specifications and guidelines designed to meet the DoD's high-level requirements for creating interoperable, plug-n-play, browser-based e-learning content. It consists of three different technical specifications "books" that collectively address challenges associated with interoperability, portability, reusability, and the instructional sequencing of self-paced e-learning content (Available at https://www.adlnet.gov/adl-research/scorm).

Social Constructivism: Is centered on the learner. The learner learns through its representations. The construction of knowledge although personal is carried out in a social setting. The context and come from both what we think and what others bring as interactions.

VLE: Virtual learning environment.

W3C: World Wide Web Consortium.

Chapter 2
Studying and Analyzing the Evaluation Dimensions of Learning Management Systems

ABSTRACT

We are currently witnessing the launch and development of a large number of distance training devices in Moroccan universities, whose main objective is to meet society's requirements and the knowledge economy, which is fully emerging. All of the devices are based on the use of LMSs, which can be problematic for designers for different reasons (costs, utility, usability, etc.). Being conscious of the impact of these technological tools on learning, the authors propose a methodical approach that identifies the essential criteria for evaluation of LMSs to fit the needs of teachers and learners from analysis of the evaluation dimensions in multimedia documents, particularly through the dimensions of utility and usability.

INTRODUCTION

One of the essential features of the knowledge economy is the acceleration of interactive software life cycles, which are part of LMSs. The choice of these LMSs, which constitute the cornerstone of initial and continuing training systems, is not obvious to most users. However, why is this so difficult?

DOI: 10.4018/978-1-7998-4021-3.ch002

As part of our study, we will show that choosing between the various tools available on the market forced us to identify the challenges and the specific needs. It was crucial to ensure these tools would provide rich services motivated by the online sharing of structured information and interactivity among different users. To this, we added the tracking services of the learning paths of different users, notably learners.

It was obvious that the use of any tool in the field of education and training had to be justified according to its pedagogical interest and its response to the needs of the learners, but if the LMS is supposed to address the spatial and temporal constraints between tutors and learners, it must not hinder the learning process.

Consequently, any random choice that entails a loss of money, effort, and time challenges us and invites us to ask the following questioning:

On the one hand, how can we choose an LMS that meets the norms and standards as they are acknowledged in distance education systems?

On the other hand, LMSs are objects of evaluation, so to what degree of training specificity can they respond? What are the choices in terms of multimedia engineering on which we must analyze these LMSs? What norms and standards do the requirements meet in the evaluation of these LMSs?

These issues and others are the subjects of the investigations as part of our approach to judging its intake for experimentation purposes.

For our study, the reading of the specialized literature in the LMSs analysis shows two orientations. The first is dedicated to the technical analysis (computer language, script, metadata), and the second covers the pedagogical extent of these LMSs and the development of the learners' skills.

Our approach is oriented toward a reconciliation of these two orientations. The technological and pedagogical are not mutually exclusive; however, crossing their elements in a goal or technology is at the pedagogical center.

To concretize our approach, in the "theoretical frame" section, we initially took the evaluation dimensions of interactive systems conducted by Senach (Senach, 1993), Tricot (Tricot and al., 2003), and ISO 25010 (ISO/IEC 25010, 2011). Then we categorized these works and the various discussions (Bastien and Scapin, 2001; Huart and al., 2008). After analysis, we retained the dimensions of utility and usability.

Then, in the "analysis of assessment dimensions" section, we followed a specific methodology for analyzing the evaluation dimensions obtained according to the three steps indicated:

- Comparison of studied outcomes,
- Personal position relative to the outcomes,
- Analysis and results (choose criteria and tools suitable for the evaluation of the LMSs).

This section mainly consists of three sub-sections:

1. Utility analysis: In this sub-section, we will categorize the utility characteristics discussed, according to various studies (Senach, 1993; Tricot and al., 2003; ISO/IEC 25010, 2011; ISO/IEC 9126-1, 2001). After the analysis, we retained six utility characteristics. Thereafter, we attempted to subject the tools of currently recognized LMSs to filter the criteria that met the pedagogical principles of training, based on various studies (Lablidi and al., 2009; Aska and al., 2000), to check the quality and the presence of the tools available to the various players in distance training. Then we checked their utility and their operability through interactive technologies that met the retained characteristics (ISO/IEC 25010, 2011).
2. Usability analysis: In this sub-section, we categorize the most important usability criteria, according to various studies (Norman, 1988; Nielsen, 1995; Gerhardt-Powals, 1996; ISO 9241-11, 1998; Bastien and Scapin, 1993; ISO/IEC 9126-1, 2001; Baker and al., 2002; Tricot and al., 2003; ISO 10075-3, 2004; Shneiderman and Plaisant, 2005; Stone, 2005; Johnson, 2008; ISO 9241-171, 2008; ISO 9241-210, 2010; ISO/IEC 25010, 2011; Tognazzini, 2014). After the analysis, we selected eight usability criteria to be part of our evaluation gait.
3. Evaluation approach of LMSs: In this sub-section, we present the measures and criteria adapted for the evaluation of LMSs according to a scalable approach and synthesis of the two analyzed dimensions.

LEARNING MANAGEMENT SYSTEMS

1. Definition

As we defined OVAREP (Lablidi and al., 2009), the LMS is a computing system that groups several tools and ensures the educational conduits. Across dedicated LMSs to the ODL, all conduits are preserved and expanded for the learner, tutor, administrator, etc. within the LMS.

Thereby, the tools offered by these LMSs enable tutors and learners to communicate individually or collectively and discuss themes and shared documents.

The learner is invited to consult on the course, to realize the homework, to follow its development, and to receive self-generated feedback or feedback given by the tutor. In this environment, the learner exchanges his knowledge, his remarks, and contributions (production or document) with other learners to self-evaluate and transmit his work to a teacher, whether it is individually or collectively.

A training coordinator is responsible for the learners' inscription management, of the time, and the rhythms of the formation and activity of the teaching team.

The teacher (course designer) is responsible for the preparation of courses and tutors. The tutor is supposed to bring the necessary support to the learners at both cognitive and methodological levels. The tutor's role differs according to the pedagogical presuppositions inherent to the LMSs.

He can be an animator in a collaborative educational system, facilitator in a constructivist educational system, organizer of learning situations conducive to dialogue to cause and resolve conflicts in a social-constructionist educational system; presenter of information via a structured, hierarchical, and deductive in a cognitivist educational system; or an expert on a transmissive educational system.

The administrator plays a technical role and cannot be confused with the role of the coordinator who has as a function in the following tasks:

- Installs and maintains the system,
- Manages access and rights,
- Creates links with external information systems (school, catalog, teaching resources, etc.).

2. LMS Features

An LMS exists to bring answers to the following problems:

- Expand the training offered through the ODL and allow those who find training constraints to have opportunities to overcome them,
- Access to the best management of time jobs by reducing the supply in face-to-face training,
- Develop exchange, inter-actors of training,

- Innovate the teaching practices by using new technologies for communication and training,
- Introduce other modalities of training such as management of collaborative projects,
- Foster the role of tutoring that allows reducing the sensation of isolation, often the cause of stalling and abandonment.

An LMS fits well in several pedagogical models. We defined our expectations in matters of content and teaching modalities for all the actors: learners, integrators, tutors, coordinators, and administrators.

Learners are invited to

- Attend pedagogical activities that take various forms, both specific and general (problems, simulations, QCM, tests self-correcting),
- Include interactive teaching resources in various formats (text, image, audio, video, PDF, Flash),
- Realize situations for assessments,
- Access collaborative working from shared documents.

The learning path is divided into two entities:

- Entity 1 consists of creating modules that are broken into several units that contain various resources (documents, activities, quiz) and learning path-oriented supports (individual or a group),
- Entity 2 consists of achieving a set of activities (about the objective of the module) as part of project-based teaching, courses-oriented activities.

Teachers (course designers) are responsible for the preparation of training courses about

- Creation of the teaching resources interface with the training management systems (AICC, SCORM, etc.),
- Sharing educational resources (course modules, evaluations, etc.),
- Planning of pedagogical resources.

Tutors are responsible for

- Taking charge of learners by an individual tracking system, animation and/or moderation of forums,
- Initializing the conversation within the chat, which is responsible,
- Follow-up the learners in the videoconference,
- Monitoring activities and proposed projects,
- Planning the interventions,
- Monitoring the groups' management.

Administrators and coordinators are responsible for customizing the LMS about

- Establishing the groups,
- Monitoring the activities of teachers,
- Managing the courses,
- Customizing the LMS,
- Managing the roles.

3. Constraints of LMS

The reason for this section is that it is important to look at the constraints of LMS because it makes it possible to be objective when choosing the method of dissemination of training or different e-learning training tools. Among the major constraints of LMS, include:

- Lack of informal learning. Often Learning Management Systems are so focused on the course; they do not envisage learning opportunities outside the LMS platform. Between the Internet, which allows developing the opportunities for social learning, by sharing experiences, reflections, instantly and free.
- Learners are easily unmotivated. It is difficult to assess the lack of deep motivation in learning curves other than to interpret them as irregular course monitoring. This indicator cannot be with him, only a factor that will explain the unmotivated of the learner. The dropout rate of e-learning courses is higher than that of traditional courses. Individuals must be motivated because e-learning requires more autonomy than traditional courses.
- Lack of social interaction. Learners often feel very isolated because it lacks social interaction. With blended learning and virtual classes, social networks, occupy an integral part of the LMS. Web 2.0, an

e-learning type called e-learning 2.0, has made that relied on the use of social tools such as blogs, wikis, podcasts, as well as existing social networks. Informal learning finds a place through meetings (conversations, group meetings, etc.) and social interactions.

- The infrastructure is too expensive. The investment in a paid LMS platform is expensive.
- Loss of money, effort, and time. LMSs are constantly evolving, the choice of which is problematic for wearers and designers of systems, and this for various reasons (cost, utility, usability ...), that any random choice leads to a loss of money, effort, and time.
- Speed. With difficult access and inflexible structure, current LMSs are based on the SQL language for data storage. However, NoSQL succeeds in the SQL database in the speed department, because simply NoSQL takes less time to access data than SQL.

Consequently, LMSs are always part of a uniform and techno-centric logic and architecture that reduced the learning conception to a particular pedagogical theory independently of others. The problems of most LMS are first of all problems of a pedagogical nature and subsequently of a technical nature.

THEORETICAL FRAME

LMSs, like any software, must be subjected to a set of criteria that make the process of evaluation possible. These criteria are order, pedagogical, technical, and ergonomic functions, etc. As part of this section, we will introduce and synthesize our theoretical foundation, taking into account the approaches of Senach and Tricot (Senach, 1993; Tricot and al., 2003) as well as the ISO 25010 standard (ISO/IEC 25010, 2011) and the various discussions they confront (Bastien and Scapin, 2001; Huart and al., 2008).

1. Approach of Senach

In light of Senach's work, including (Senach, 1993), we distinguished three main evaluation dimensions of interactive systems: utility, usability, and aesthetics.

Similarly, Figure 1 presents the evaluation criteria of the three main evaluation dimensions adapted by Senach.

Figure 1. Dimensions of evaluation, adapted by Senach (Senach, 1993)

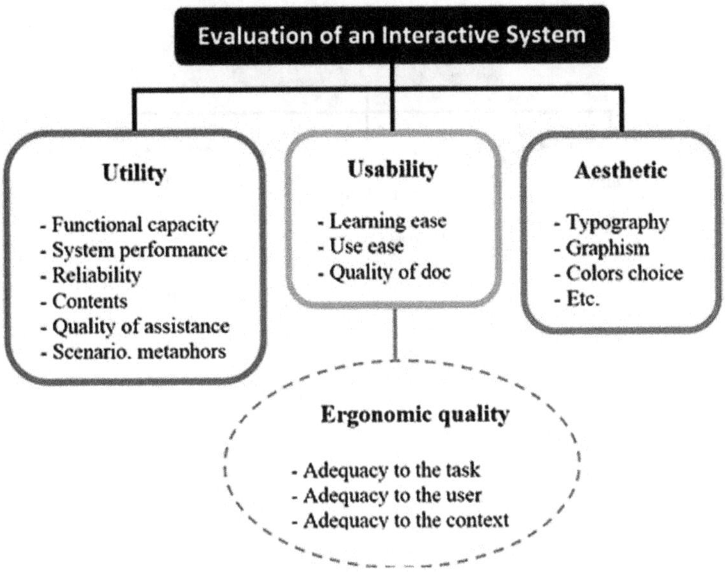

2. Approach of Tricot

Tricot added the dimension of acceptability to these three dimensions (utility, usability, and aesthetics) (Senach, 1993): in other words, feeling positive or negative concerning the product, "intention" of use depending on many parameters: motivation, affects, culture, values (Tricot and al., 2003). Figure 2 presents criteria that are possible for the evaluation of utility, usability, and acceptability (Tricot and al., 2003).

In what follows, the ISO 25010 standard completes what has been developed by different studies and presents a model of the quality of interactive systems of the eight characteristics.

3. The Approach of ISO 25010 Standard

In the quality model of interactive systems, the most famous characteristics are those of the ISO / IEC 9126-1: 2001 (ISO/IEC 9126-1, 2001). These characteristics were originally developed in 2001 and revised in 2011 by the ISO / IEC 25010: 2011 (ISO/IEC 25010, 2011), which incorporates the same software quality characteristics with some modifications.

Figure 2. Presentation of measures and criteria for evaluation by inspection of an HSI (Tricot, 2003)

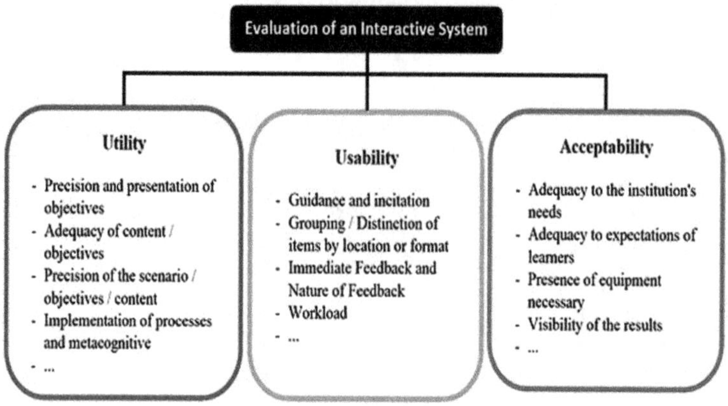

The quality model of interactive systems of ISO 25010 standard consists of eight characteristics: functional suitability, performance efficiency, compatibility, usability, reliability, security, maintainability, and portability. Each characteristic is composed of a set of related sub-characteristics.

Table I presents a quality model interactive system of the eight main evaluation characteristics of the ISO 25010 standard.

4. Synthesis

Regarding these three dimensions, according to the work of Senach (Senach, 1993) and other researchers, such as Bastien and Scapin, found that the aesthetic dimension is sometimes regarded as a component of satisfaction on the part of the user, as are the preferences of the user (Bastien and Scapin, 2001). Besides, the aesthetic dimension is suspicious of great subjectivity and is likely to be abandoned.

On the other hand, and according to Tricot's approach (Senach, 1993), the most important seem to be utility and usability. Also, Huart found that the notions of utility and usability are often discussed in the literature (Huart and al., 2008). Consequently, based on the work of Senach and Tricot, as well as that of ISO 25010 and the various discussions, which comfort them, we are therefore interested in the utility and usability dimension.

Table 1. Quality model interactive systems of ISO 25010

Characteristic	Sub Characteristic
Functional suitability	Functional completeness
	Functional correctness
	Functional appropriateness
Performance efficiency	Time behavior
	Resource utilization
	Capacity
Compatibility	Co-existence
	Interoperability
Usability	Appropriateness recognizability
	Learnability
	Operability
	User error protection
	User interface aesthetics
	Accessibility
Reliability	Maturity
	Availability
	Fault tolerance
	Recoverability
Security	Confidentiality
	Integrity
	Non-repudiation
	Accountability
	Authenticity
Maintainability	Modularity
	Reusability
	Analysability
	Modifiability
	Testability
Portability	Adaptability
	Installability
	Replaceability

(ISO/IEC 25010, 2011)

Table 2. Comparison of characteristics users in the design interface of the utility

Utility Criteria Categories	Functional Capacity	Maintainability	Compatibility / Interoperability	Compatibility / Co-existence	System Performance	Security	Assistance Quality	Portability	Contents	Scenario
Senach (1990)	x				x		x		x	x
ISO 9126-1 (2001)	x	x	x			x		x		
Tricot (2003)									x	x
ISO 25010 (2011)	x	x	x	x	x	x		x		

STUDY AND ANALYSIS OF EVALUATION DIMENSIONS OF LMSS

In the project, we followed a detailed evaluation strategy of the LMS's evaluation criteria while referring to two retained evaluation dimensions.

1. Study and Analysis of the Utility

In the development of interactive software, the most popular utility criteria were presented in the "theoretical frame" section. Thus, in Table 2, we selected the basic criteria that constituted the cornerstone of the utility dimension, and we have them placed in comparison to users' characteristics established by different studies, depending on the possible declensions of the cited criteria.

We distinguished (see Table 2) that functional ability is often recommended in most studies. For this, we retained this characteristic because it is often the subject of interactive systems evaluation.

In 1990, Senach treated the functional capacity. Then, in 2001, ISO 9126-1 standard completed what Senach started and nicknamed this characteristic "functionality," which consists of sub-related characteristics in particular: compatibility/interoperability and security.

Besides, in 2011, the ISO 25010 standard reviewed what had been originally developed by ISO 9126-1 and incorporated the same software quality characteristics with some changes. Among these changes, we found that this standard gave more importance to compatibility and security, which originally were the sub-characteristics of the functionality characteristic of ISO 9126-1 standard, nicknamed "functional suitability."

Thereby, we also retained compatibility and security.

Moreover, we added the characteristic of portability because it is practically discussed (see Table 2), and it gives more importance to the adaptability of the LMSs for mobile systems because it facilitates distance learning.

We, therefore, selected four criteria of utility, namely:

- Functional suitability,
- Compatibility,
- Security,
- Portability.

Subsequently, we used these retained criteria, in comparison to users' characteristics established by different studies, based on Table 3. After analysis, we found that the four criteria of usefulness address the characteristics of ISO 25010 because they are often recommended in most studies.

Usually, the ISO 25010 consists of eight related characteristics; however, in this dimension, we treated just six characteristics of this standard: functional suitability, performance efficiency, compatibility, security, maintainability, and portability. These characteristics, in our view, are best suited to assessing the usefulness of the LMSs.

Thus, the two other characteristics of ISO 25010: usability and reliability will be treated in the usability dimension.

In what follows, we used the currently recognized functionality tools of LMSs to filter the criteria that meet the six characteristics of utility.

1.1 Analysis of Utility Tools

Based on Lablidi's table (Lablidi and al., 2009) and OVAREP's study (OVAREP, 2000) as well as Aska's table and Anne Bouthry's study (Aska and al., 2000), after analysis, we tried to adapt these criteria to the specific needs of our approach. Thus, a set of functionalities were identified for each actor of the LMS to perform his task. Among these IT functionalities, we are providing actors tools of communication, monitoring, sharing, security, interoperability, and organization, etc.

Table 3 associates the criteria to the given tools at disposition for each actor. Five actors were distinguished:

Table 3. Selected criteria and tools for choosing an LMS

Actors	Criteria	Tools
Learner	Synchronous communication	Chat, virtual classroom (videoconferencing / webinar)
	Asynchronous communication	Forum, messaging, mailing
	Document Sharing	Deposit space of the document, virtual library, database, forum, Wiki, Dropbox, Shared folders
	Historical of documents	Social networks, forum
	Organization	Calendar, Post-it, dashboard
	Evaluation	Tests, dashboard, portfolio, quiz
	Collaboration	Wiki, classroom (videoconferencing / webinar), portfolio, forum
	Plagiarism Detection	Plagiarism detection tools
	Certification	Followed certificate of training
Teacher, tutor	Registration of learners	Calendar, dashboard
	Groups management	Registration to one or more groups, calendar, dashboard
	Tracking of learners	Tracking, number of times that the learner has logged in, the connections dates, executed activities (courses, discussions, forums, tests, etc.), % success, progress monitoring
	Management of tests	The generator of QUIZ and test, self-evaluation tests, managing notes: average calculation, displaying notes, report on the test results
Administrator, coordinators	Assignment of courses to learners and tutors	Data processing by group and tutors
	Dissemination of results	Import and export formats supported by different file types
	Management of user roles	Multi-profile management (learners, teacher, tutor, integrator/author)
	Course transfer from one LMS to another	Example: Transfer of a course on Moodle LMS to Claroline LMS
	Customizing the LMS	Managing roles, groups, modules, access rights, etc.
Teacher, course designer	Multimedia content	Audio, video, flash, etc.
	Resource Management	Filing space of documents
	IMS interoperability standards	SCORM, IMS QTI, AICC, IMS XML
	Support of multiple authors	The right to create, manage its course and give the right of access to another teacher
	Import and export	Import and export of the tests

continues on following page

- Learners,
- Teachers (course creators), responsible for the preparation of tutors and training courses,

Table 3. Continued

Actors	Criteria	Tools
All actors	Presence of other actors	Awareness
	Identification	Visit card, profile, badge, and dashboard.
	Security	Possibility to use SSL, security by login/password, Assigning username and password, security barrier, backup system.
	Compatibility with common browsers	Compatibility with common browsers such as Firefox, Chrome, Opera, etc.
	File diffusion means	RSS
	Used technology	PHP, JAVA, ASP, PITON, etc.
	Used Database	SQL, NoSQL
	Interaction with other operating systems	Unix, Linux, Mac OS X, Microsoft Windows, FreeBSD, etc.
	Interaction with other databases	PostgreSQL, SQLite, MS SQL, MySQL, Oracle DB, MariaDB, Percona, etc.
	Possibility of using plugins	Such as PDF, Excel, PowerPoint, Word, etc.
	Portability	Adaptation to mobile terminals
	Adapting to different training devices	Creating MOOC or SPOC

- Tutor, responsible for monitoring learners,
- Coordinator, responsible for the LMS integration into the overall operations of the tutors' establishment,
- And administrator, responsible for customizing the LMS.

For each actor, we analyzed the breadth of functionalities to which he has access, integration of these functionalities, ease of use, and requirements about competence.

Conscious that LMSs are not generic to evaluate adequacy between technological tools and pedagogical intakes for the different actors, we evaluated the ease of editing courses, the process of monitoring and coaching, and the interactive aspects among users of the LMS.

We know that the mission of an LMS is made available to users through pedagogical activities. Thus, the functionalities offered would first help the different actors fulfill their respective tasks and enable cooperation and communication among the users.

Our analytical work advocated determining the functionalities by using a checklist (see Table 3) and then checking their utilities and categorical location, according to a method of analysis by characteristic.

We usually distinguished six characteristics previously retained:

- Functional suitability,
- Performance efficiency,
- Compatibility,
- Security,
- Maintainability,
- Portability.

For each of the characteristics and its sub-characteristics, we analyzed the functionality with which it has access and the integration of these characteristics to available tools for each characteristic based on the criteria and selected tools in Table 3.

In the following, the six essential characteristics were retained to conduct distance training with functional tools to meet the previously outlined criteria (see Table 3).

1.2 Functional Suitability Analysis

Functional suitability means "the degree to which a product or system provides functions that meet stated and implied needs when used under specified conditions" (ISO/IEC 25010, 2011).

Table 4 projects the essential functionalities for functional suitability and the sub-characteristics meeting the previously outlined criteria. Three sub-characteristics related to functional suitability were distinguished and defined per ISO 25010:

- Functional completeness: "the degree to which the set of functions covers all the specified tasks and user objectives"
- Functional correctness: "the degree to which a product or system provides the correct results with the needed degree of precision"
- Functional appropriateness: "the degree to which the functions facilitate the accomplishment of specified tasks and objectives"

Table 4. Functional suitability tools adapted for choosing an LMS

Functional Suitability	Yes	No
Functional Completeness		
Forum		
Synchronous causerie (chat)		
Virtual Classroom (videoconferencing / webinar)		
Sharing documents		
Calendar		
Awareness (list of connected people)		
Tests management		
Collaboration (Wiki)		
Learners' management (registration, schedule...)		
Learners' management in working groups		
Users' roles management		
Customizable LMS		
Advancement Scale or progression percentage in the course		
Resource Management (course)		
Support of multiple authors		
Functional Correctness		
Management of working time of learners and teachers		
Results and notes		
Notes display		
Tracking statistics of course		
Control Connections (tracking of learners)		
Report on the test results		
Glossary		
Report on the frequency or the use of a course		
Functional Appropriateness		
Certification (certificate of training follow–up)		
Foyer (family group)		
Registration chat		
Messaging		
Plagiarism detection tools		
RSS / podcast: means of distributing files (audio, video or other)		

1.3 Analysis of Performance Efficiency

Performance efficiency means "the performance relative to the number of resources used under stated conditions" (ISO/IEC 25010, 2011).

In Table 5, we project the essential functionalities for performance efficiency and the sub-characteristics meeting previously outlined criteria. Two sub-characteristics related to performance efficiency were distinguished and defined per ISO 25010:

Table 5. Performance efficiency tools adapted for choosing an LMS

Performance Efficiency	Yes	No
Resource Utilization		
Is that LMS functionalities tools meet the distance requirements Learning		
Capacity		
Is that the LMS meets all the distance requirements learning		
Assistance quality		

- Resource utilization: "the degree to which the amounts and types of resources used by a product or system, when performing its functions, meet requirements"
- Capacity: "the degree to which the maximum limits of a product or system parameter meet requirements"

1.4 Compatibility Analysis

Compatibility signifies "the degree to which a product, system or component can exchange information with other products, systems or components, and/or perform its required functions, while sharing the same hardware or software environment" (ISO/IEC 25010, 2011).

Table 6 presents the essential functionalities for compatibility and the sub-characteristics meeting the previously outlined criteria. Two sub-characteristics related to compatibility were distinguished and defined:

- Co-existence: "the degree to which a product can perform its required functions efficiently while sharing a common environment and resources with other products, without detrimental impact on any other product"

- Interoperability: "the degree to which two or more systems, products or components can exchange information and use the information that has been exchanged"

Table 6. Compatibility tools adapted for choosing an LMS

Compatibility	Yes	No
Co-existence		
Course transfer from one LMS to another of the same type		
SCORM (allows creating grains of course, reusable and interoperable).		
IMS QTI (set of specifications allowing interoperability to test systems)		
AICC (sets the interoperability between the LMS and content)		
IMS XML		
Interoperability		
Information and application sharing		
Import and export of resources		
Possibility of using plugins (Word, Excel, etc.)		
The technology used (PHP, J2EE, ASP…)		

1.5 Security Analysis

Security means "the degree to which a product or system protects information and data so persons or other products or systems have the degree of data access appropriate to their types and levels of authorization" (ISO/IEC 25010, 2011).

Table 7 shows the essential functionalities for security and their sub-characteristics meeting the previously outlined criteria. Five sub-characteristics related to security were distinguished and defined per ISO 25010:

- Confidentiality: "the degree to which a product or system ensures that data are accessible only to those authorized to have access"
- Integrity: "the degree to which a system, product or component prevents unauthorized access to, or modification of, computer programs or data"
- Non-repudiation: "the degree to which actions or events can be proven to have taken place so that the events or actions cannot be repudiated later"
- Accountability: "the degree to which the actions of an entity can be traced uniquely to the entity"

- Authenticity: "the degree to which the identity of a subject or resource can be proved to be the one claimed."

Table 7. Security tools adapted for choosing an LMS

Security	Yes	No
Confidentiality		
Secured by login/password		
Assigning access rights		
Integrity		
Ability to use SSL		
Non-repudiation		
Tracking system		
Backup system		
Accountability		
Barrier of security		
Authenticity		
Assigning username and password		
Identity card (visit card / profile)		

1.6 Maintainability Analysis

Maintainability means "the degree of effectiveness and efficiency with which a product or system can be modified by the intended maintainers" (ISO/IEC 25010, 2011).

In Table 8, the essential functionalities for maintainability and their sub-characteristics meeting the previously outlined criteria. Five sub-characteristics related to maintainability were distinguished and defined per ISO 25010:

- Modularity: "the degree to which a system or computer program is composed of discrete components such that a change to one component has minimal impact on other components"
- Reusability: "the degree to which an asset can be used in more than one system, or in building other assets"
- Modifiability: "the degree to which a product or system can be effectively and efficiently modified without introducing defects or degrading existing product quality"

- Testability: "the degree of effectiveness and efficiency with which test criteria can be established for a system, product or component and tests can be performed to determine whether those criteria have been met"

Table 8. Maintainability tools adapted for choosing an LMS

Maintainability	Yes	No
Modularity		
Is that the LMS contains discrete plugins		
Reusability		
Interaction with other operating systems (multi-operating systems option)		
Interaction with other databases (multi-database option)		
Modifiability		
Modifiability of the system without errors		
Testability		
Maintenance and updating		

1.7 Portability Analysis

Portability signifies "the degree of effectiveness and efficiency with which a system, product or component can be transferred from one hardware, software or other operational or usage environment to another" (ISO/IEC 25010, 2011).

Table 9 shows the essential functionalities for portability and their sub-characteristics meeting the previously outlined criteria. Three sub-characteristics related to portability were distinguished and defined per ISO 25010:

- Adaptability: "the degree to which a product or system can effectively and efficiently be adapted for different or evolving hardware, software or other operational or usage environments"
- Installability: "degree of effectiveness and efficiency with which a product or system can be successfully installed and/or uninstalled in a specified environment"
- Replaceability: "the degree to which a product can replace another specified software product for the same purpose in the same environment."

Table 9. Portability tools adapted for choosing an LMS

Portability	Yes	No
Adaptability		
Adaptation to mobiles terminals		
Compatibility with common browsers		
Adapting to different training devices (creating MOOC or SPOC)		
Installability		
Instability of without errors LMS		
Replaceability		
Replaceability with the new LMS version		

2. Study and Analysis of the Usability

2.1 Study of the Usability Principles of Nielsen

In software development and interface design, the best-known usability criteria are ones by Nielsen (Nielsen, 1995). The "Nielsen ten usability criteria" were originally developed in 1990 and revised in 1994 after a factor analysis of 249 usability problems. Nielsen's ten principles are composed of a general list and offer broad categories. Namely:

- Conform to the real world
- Consistency and Standards
- Help and Documentation
- User Control and Freedom
- Visibility of the system status
- Flexibility and Efficiency
- Error prevention
- Recognition and No Reminder
- Help users recognize, diagnose, and correct errors
- Aesthetics and minimalist design

2.2 Study the Usability Criteria of Bastien and Scapin

Other usability criteria like Bastien's eight principles (Bastien and Scapin, 1993), which were also, originally developed in 1993, namely:

- Guidance (Advice, guide the user in his interaction with the system)
    - Incentive: Elementary criteria (status bar, measure, space, format, index, title, help ... any element facilitating navigation.
    - Grouping/distinction: Visual organization of information to illustrate a class relationship of type membership/distinction by:
        - The localization
        - The format
    - Immediate feedback: System feedback
        - The quality
        - The rapidity
    - Readability (Basic criterion): lexical characteristics of the presentation of information on the screen (luminance, contrast, characters, size, spacing, line length, etc.)
- Workload (Reduced perceptual or memory load)
    - Brevity:
        - Concision: individual elements of input or output.
        - Minimum actions = input sequences (sequences of actions to reach a goal).
    - Information density: Perceptual or memory charge for sets of elements and not individual items
- Explicit control
    - Explicit actions: System transparency
    - User control (Reversibility): the possibility to retrace your steps, to cancel your actions.
- Adaptability
    - Flexibility: Alternatives (procedures, options, commands) for the same objective.
    - Taking into account the experience of the user: Beginner, intermediate, advanced.
- Error management
    - Protection against errors: Detect and prevent errors during input vs validation.
    - Quality of error messages: Relevance, accuracy, ease of reading the nature and reasons for the errors and solutions.
    - Correction of errors: Means available to the user to facilitate the correction of errors.
- Consistency / Coherence
    - Internal coherence: General coherence of the different elements of the system between them.

  - Metaphor: consistency of the system's referents.
  - Mapping: consistency of all the signifiers.
  - Evidence (affordance): pragmatic physical evidence of the elements.
- Meaning of codes and denominations
  - Strong semantic relationship: Relation between object or information displayed and referent.
- Compatibility (Basic criterion)
  - External consistency: similarity between various elements, environments, and applications.

2.3 Study of the Usability Rules of Donald Norman

Norman's seven rules, (Norman, 1988) were originally developed in 1988, namely:

- Error Mode: suggest the need for better feedback.
  - Description of errors: suggest the need for better system configuration.
  - Lack of consistency: leads to errors.
  - Capture errors: imply the need to avoid overlapping command sequences.
- Activation problems: suggest the importance of memory reminders.
- People will make mistakes so that the system is insensitive.
- Feedback: The state of the system should be available to the user, ideally in a format that is unambiguous and makes a set of options readily available to avoid mode errors.
- The similarity of intervention sequences: The different action classes should have very different command sequences (or menu models) to avoid typing and description errors.
- Actions must be reversible: As much as possible and where both irreversible and relatively high consequences, they must be difficult to do, thereby preventing involuntary performance.
- System consistency: The system should be consistent in its structure and order design to minimize memory problems in retrieving operations.

2.4 Study of the Usability Rules of Shneiderman and Plaisant

Shneiderman's eight golden rules (Shneiderman and Plaisant, 2005), that they too were originally developed in 2005 and which largely overlapping the ones with the others, namely:

- Ensuring consistency
- Meeting the needs of universal ease of use
- Offer informative feedback
- The design of the flow task, to obtain closure
- Error prevention
- Easy stock reversal license
- The User is the master who controls
- Reduce the memory load in the short term

2.5 Study of the Usability Rules of Deborah Stone

Stone's eight rules (Stone, 2005), were originally developed in 2005 and largely overlap with each other, namely:

- **Visibility:** The first step of this objective must be clear.
- **Affordance:** Control suggests how to use it.
- **Comments:** Should be clear what happened where is happening.
- **Simplicity:** As simple as possible and task-oriented.
- **Structure:** Content organized judiciously.
- **Consistency:** similarity of predictability.
- **Tolerance:** avoid errors and contribute to the recovery.
- **Accessibility**: Usable by all intended users, despite the handicap, of the access system, or environmental conditions.

2.6 Study the Usability Principles of Jeff Johnson

Johnson's eight principles (Johnson, 2008), which they too were originally developed in 2008, namely:

- Focus on users and their tasks, not on technology
    - Understanding the users
    - Understand the tasks
    - Take into account the context in which the software will operate

- Consider the primary function, the presentation later
    - Develop a conceptual model
- Complies with the user's view of the task
    - Strive for naturalness.
    - Use user vocabulary and not your own.
    - Keep the internal program within the program.
    - Find the exact point on the power/complexity compromise.
- Design for the current case
    - Ensures it is easy to accomplish common results.
    - Two types of common: the number of users compared to the number of times
    - The basic case design, cases do not sweat the edge
- Do not complicate the task of users
    - Do not give users additional problems
    - Do not make users reason by elimination
- Facilitate learning
    - Think outside, not inside
    - Consistency
    - Provide a low-risk environment
- Provide information, not just data
    - Design displays carefully; get professional help
    - The screen belongs to the user
    - Preserve display inertia
- Responsiveness design
    - Acknowledgment of user actions instantly
    - Let users know when the software is busy and when it is not
    - Free users to do other things while waiting
    - Movement Animate smoothly and clearly
    - Allow users to thwart one of the long operations they don't want
    - Allow users to estimate how long operations will take
    - Attempt to let users define their own work pace.

2.7 Study of the Usability Rules of Tricot

Tricot's ten rules (Tricot and al., 2003) largely overlapping the ones with the others, namely:

- Guidance and incentive
- Grouping / Distinction of items by location or format

- Immediate feedback and feedback nature
- Workload
- Explicit control
- Adaptability
- Error management
- Quality of messages
- Homogeneity and consistency
- The signing of codes and denominations

2.8 Study the Usability Standards Adopted by ISO

As well as the standards adopted by the International Committee ISO, namely:

- **ISO 9241-11 standard's eleven principles (ISO 9241-11, 1998)**
  - **Usability** Extent to which a product can be used by specified users to achieve specified goals with effectiveness, efficiency, and satisfaction in a specified context of use.
  - **Effectiveness** Accuracy and completeness with which users achieve specified goals.
  - **Efficiency** Resources are expended to the accuracy and completeness with which users achieve goals.
  - **Satisfaction** Freedom from discomfort, and positive attitudes towards the use of the product.
  - **Context of use** Users, tasks, equipment (hardware, software, and materials), and the physical and social environments in which a product is used.
  - **Work system**, consisting of users, equipment, tasks, and a physical and social environment, for achieving particular goals.
  - **User** Person who interacts with the product.
  - **Goal** Intended outcome.
  - Task Activities required for achieving a goal.
  - **Product** Part of the equipment (hardware, software, and materials) for which usability is to be specified or evaluated.
  - Measure (noun) Value resulting from measurement and the process used to obtain that value.
- **ISO 10075-3 standard's eight characteristics (ISO 10075-3, 2004)**
  - **Objectivity.** The degree to which results obtained with an instrument are independent of the person responsible for the instrument, analysis, and interpretation of the data

- **Fidelity.** The degree to which a method or instrument is capable of measuring what it should measure
    - Homogeneity: degree according to which all the parts or all the elements of a measurement procedure measure the same characteristics.
    - Internal consistency: the degree to which different parts or parallel shapes of a measuring instrument lead to identical results, for example by splitting a scale into two or more parts, or by using at least two parallel shapes of an instrument.
    - Stability: the degree to which the (generally delayed) reproduction of a measurement procedure leads to identical results
    - Inter-judge fidelity: the degree to which two or more assessors achieve the same results when they measure the same characteristics
- **Validity.** The degree to which a method or instrument is capable of measuring what it is supposed to measure.
- **Sensitivity.** The degree to which a method or instrument is capable of distinguishing the different degrees of variation of the object of measurement, for example, the different degrees of on-call or mental tiredness.
- **Diagnosticity.** The degree to which a method or instrument is capable of distinguishing the different types of sources of mental workload, for example, perceptual solicitations, etc., or their effects, for example making the difference between fatigue, monotony, saturation, or drowsiness.
- **Generalizability.** The degree to which an observed score (unit of measure) can be generalized to apply to a defined domain of situations (conditions of constraint) and/or to a population of workers.
    - Relative generalizability. The degree to which a hierarchical ranking of workload conditions/population, for example from lowest to highest, can be reproduced (as is the case in decisions regarding relative positions).
    - Absolute generalizability. The degree to which an absolute level of mental stress/strain associated with specific working conditions/people, regardless of the stress/strain associated with other conditions/people, can be reproduced (as is the case in decisions concerning absolute values).

    - **Usability.** The degree to which a product can be used by identified users, to achieve defined goals with efficiency, effectiveness, and satisfaction, in a context of specified use.
    - **Critical reference standard values** for the evaluation of measured ratings and/or pass / fail decisions
- **ISO 9241-171 standard's thirty-eight criteria (ISO 9241-171, 2008)**
    - Accelerator keys
    - Accessibility
    - Accessibility feature
    - Activation
    - Assistive technology
    - Chorded key-press
    - Closed system
    - Color scheme
    - Contrast
    - Cursor
    - Effectiveness
    - Efficiency
    - Explicit designator
    - Focus cursor
    - Icon
    - Implicit designator
    - Individualization
    - Input focus
    - Keyboard emulator
    - Keyboard equivalent
    - Keyboard focus
    - Keyboard focus cursor
    - Label
    - Latch
    - Lock
    - Modifier key
    - Name
    - Natural language
    - Platform software
    - Pointer
    - Pointer focus
    - Pointing system
    - Satisfaction

    - Screen reader
    - Text cursor
    - Usability
    - User interface
    - user-interface element
- **ISO 9241-210 standard's eighteen rules (ISO 9241-210, 2010)**
    - **Accessibility,** the usability of a product, service, environment, or installation by people presenting the widest possible range of capabilities.
    - **Context of use Users,** tasks, equipment (hardware, software, and documents), and physical and social environments for using a product.
    - **Precision efficiency:** the degree of completion according to which the user achieves specified objectives.
    - **Efficiency:** the ratio of resources spent to the accuracy and degree of completion by which the user achieves specified objectives.
    - **Ergonomics study of human factors,** the scientific discipline which aims at understanding the interactions between man and the other components of a system, and the implementation in the conception of theories, principles, methods, and relevant data to improve human well-being and the overall system efficiency.
    - **Goal to be achieved.**
    - **Human-centered design:** systems design and development approach aimed at improving the usability of interactive systems by focusing on the use of the system concerned, and by applying existing knowledge and techniques in terms of human factors/ ergonomics and usability.
    - **Interactive system:** the combination of hardware, software, and/ or services that receive data from users and provides them with the resulting information.
    - **Prototype "interactive system":** representation of all or part of an interactive system which, although more or less limited, can be used for analysis, design, and evaluation.
    - **Satisfaction:** the absence of discomfort, and positive attitudes in the use of the product.
    - **Stakeholder:** individual or organization having a right, a share, a claim, or an interest in a system or having in its possession characteristics meeting its needs and expectations.
    - **Task:** activities required to achieve a goal.

 - **Usability:** the degree to which a system, product, or service can be used, by specified users, to achieve defined goals with efficiency, effectiveness, and satisfaction, in a context of specified use.
 - **User:** the person who interacts with the product.
 - **User experience:** perceptions and reactions of a person resulting from the effective and/or anticipated use of a product, system, or service.
 - **User interface:** all the components of an interactive system (software or hardware) that provide information and commands to the user to accomplish specific tasks with the interactive system.
 - **Validation:** confirmation by tangible evidence that the requirements for a specific use or intended application have been met.
 - **Verification:** confirmation by tangible evidence that the specified requirements have been met.

- **ISO 9126-1 standard's principles (ISO/IEC 9126-1, 2001), which were developed in 2001 and revised in 2011 by ISO 25010 (ISO/IEC 25010, 2011)**
 - **Appropriate recognizability.** The degree to which users can recognize whether a product or system is suitable for their needs.
 - **Ability to learn.** The degree to which a user or system can use a product or system to achieve the specified objectives of learning to use the product or system effectively, efficiently, without risk, and satisfied in a specific context of use.
 - **Operability.** The degree to which a product or system has attributes that facilitate operation and control.
 - **Protection against user errors.** The degree to which a system protects users from errors.
 - **The aesthetics of the user interface.** The degree to which a user interface allows a pleasant and satisfying interaction for the user.
 - **Accessibility.** The degree to which a product or system can be used by people with the widest range of characteristics and abilities to achieve a specified goal in a specific usage context.

2.9 Study the Usability Principles of Tognazzini

Tognazzini's nineteen first principles of user interface design that were originally developed in 2003 and revised in 2014 (Tognazzini, 2014) largely overlap with each other, namely:

- Aesthetics
- Anticipation
- Autonomy
- Color
- Consistency
- Defaults
- Discoverability
- The efficiency of the User
- Explorable Interfaces
- Fitts's Law
- Human-Interface Objects
- Latency Reduction
- Learnability
- Metaphors
- Protect Users' Work
- Readability
- Simplicity
- State: Track it
- Visible Interfaces

2.10 Study Other Less Recognized Usability Criteria

The usability rules redefine and reorder the same principles, as is also the case with other less known usability criteria such as:

- **Gerhardt-Powals's ten rules (Gerhardt-Powals, 1996):**
    - Automate unwanted workload.
    - Reduce uncertainty.
    - Data fuses.
    - Provide new information with effective means to interpret the use of the familiar setting, making it easier to accommodate
    - Use names that are conceptually related to the function

- Significantly consistent Group data to reduce research time
- Reduce tasks that rely on data
- Include in screens only the information needed by the user at a given time
- Ensure multiple coding of data, if applicable
- Repetitions of judicious practice (to resolve the possible conflict between heuristics 6 and 8)

- **Backer's eight rules (Baker, 2002):**
  - Provide the means of verbal, intentional, and appropriate communication.
  - Provide the means of gestural, intentional, and appropriate communication.
  - Provision of telecommunications dependency of the individual's embodiment.
  - Provision of telecommunications dependence on common objects (ie crossing artifact).
  - Provide protection.
  - Management shifts cooperation between tightly coupled and loosely coupled
  - Support people in coordinating their actions.
  - Facilitate the search for collaborators and establish contact
- **Brown's nine directives (Brown, 1999):**
  - Display formats. Request for prose text;
  - Language. Asks target audience familiar language;
  - Color. The colors have a code each and having a particular meaning;
  - Graphics. Pay attention to the icons, they must have a clear meaning;
  - Dialogue. Consistency at the level of orders to the user;
  - Data entry. Pay attention to the format specifications, they must be precise;
  - Control and display systems. Pay attention to the keys and the speed of the mouse cursor;
  - Error messages and online help. Useful error messages, relevant online help content;
  - Implementation of the interface.
- **Aaron's principles (Aaron, 1992).**

2.11 Analysis of Usability Criteria

In Table 10, we selected the basic criteria that constitute the cornerstones of the usability dimension and placed them in comparison with user characteristics established by different studies, depending on possible declensions of the cited criteria, to deduce the most important usability criteria for evaluation of LMSs.

We selected (see Figure 3) the most affordable usability criteria identified by the different studies. The seven usability criteria recommended in most studies are

- Status visibility
- Errors control
- Consistency/Coherence
- Efficiency/Flexibility
- Simplicity
- Guidance/Feedback
- Effectiveness/Reliability

Figure 3. Analysis of usability criteria

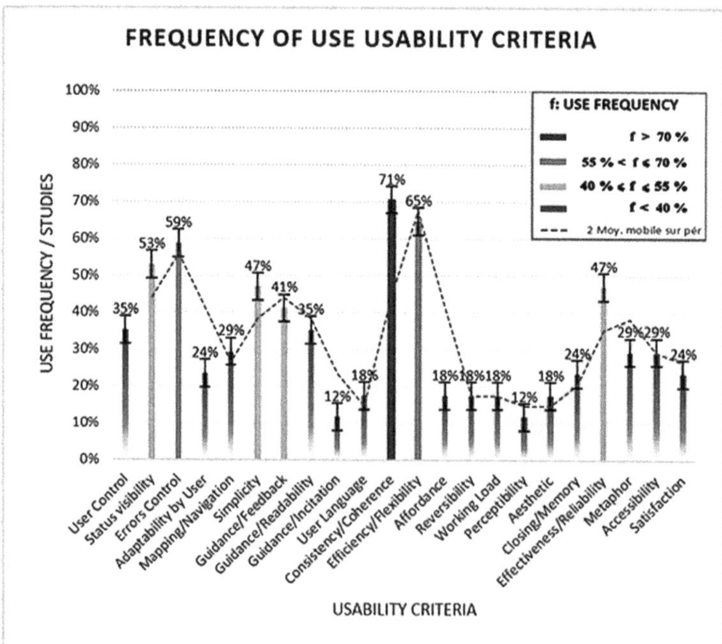

Table 10. Comparison of characteristics users in the design interface of usability

Usability Criteria Categories	User Control	Status visibility	Errors Control	Adaptability by User	Mapping / Navigation	Simplicity	Guidance / Feedback	Guidance / Readability	Guidance / Incitation	User Language	Consistency / Coherence	Efficiency / Flexibility	Affordance	Reversibility	Working Load	Perceptibility	Aesthetic	Closing / Memory	Effectiveness / Reliability	Metaphor	Accessibility	Satisfaction
Norman (1988)		x	x		x	x	x				x			x				x				
Nielson (1995)	x	x	x				x			x	x	x		x			x	x		x		
Gerhardt-Powals (1996)		x						x			x	x			x				x			
ISO 9241-11 (1998)												x							x			x
Bastien et Scapin (2001)	x		x	x	x		x	x	x		x	x	x		x					x		
ISO 9126-1 (2001)		x		x		x													x		x	
Baker et al. (2002)	x	x	x			x	x	x														
Tognazzini (2003)		x	x		x	x		x			x	x				x				x		
Tricot et Al. (2003)	x		x	x	x		x		x		x	x	x		x					x		
ISO 10075-3 (2004)											x	x							x			
Schnederman (2005)	x		x				x				x			x				x	x			x
Stone (2005)		x				x	x				x		x								x	
Johnson (2008)	x		x			x				x	x											
ISO 9241-171 (2008)										x		x						x	x		x	x
ISO 9241-210 (2010)												x							x		x	x
ISO 25010 (2011)		x	x	x		x		x			x	x					x		x		x	
Tognazzini (2014)		x	x		x	x		x			x	x				x	x			x		

Subsequently, we put these selected criteria, in comparison with users' characteristics established by different studies, see Table 10. After analysis, we found that the usability requirements of ISO 25010 standard correspond correctly with most selected criteria, except the criterion "Feedback." However, "Feedback" has great importance in evaluating LMSs. For this, we retained the usability criteria of ISO 25010 by adding "Feedback" as part of our evaluation process. In Table 11, we present the selected usability criteria.

Table 11. Usability criteria retained

Usability Criteria	Yes	No
Appropriateness recognizability		
Learnability		
Operability		
User error protection		
User interface aesthetics		
Accessibility		
Reliability		
Guidance / Feedback		

3. Evaluation Approach of LMSs

To be used effectively, all LMSs need utility and usability components to be well exploited and used in the best conditions. These preconditions are known and presented in different forms. The element of requirements covers a set of specifications, such as functional suitability tools (Table 4), performance efficiency tools (Table 5), compatibility tools (Table 6), security tools (Table 7), maintainability tools (Table 8), and portability tools (Table 9) as well as the usability criteria (Table 11).

We present the evaluation approach to determine the quality of the LMSs (Table 12) in an overview of the dimensions of utility and usability and the adapted criteria for evaluating the LMSs.

Similarly, we present Figure 4, a quality model of our main evaluation criteria of LMSs, which were inspired from two dimensions: utility and usability.

Table 12. Evaluation Approach of the LMSs quality

Assessment and Analysis Grid of the Quality of LMSs
Identification of the LMS
o LMS's name:
o LMS designer:
o LMS type:
o LMS genre:
o LMS's pedagogical model:
o LMS license:
o Description:
o Version & Edition:
o Used technology:
o Language:
o Website:
Utility Specifications
Functional suitability tools (Table 4)
Performance efficiency tools (Table 5)
Compatibility tools (Table 6)
Security tools (Table 7)
Maintainability tools (Table 8)
Portability tools (Table 9)
Usability Specifications
Usability criteria (Table 11)

Figure 4. The quality model selected for choosing an LMS

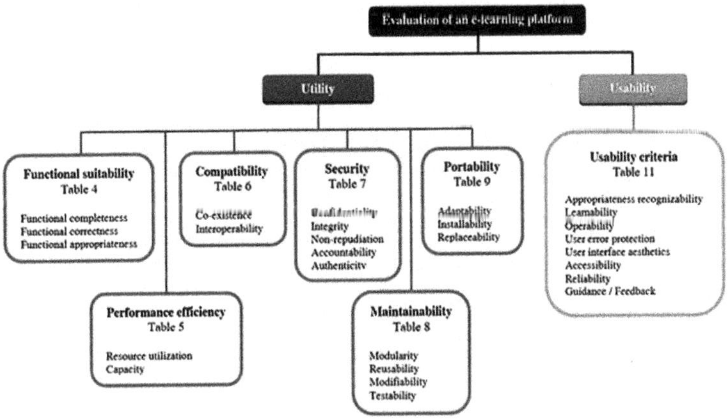

CONCLUSION

Evaluation of LMSs was the subject of an experiment. The actions of the learners and the interactions among them and with their tutors constituted a means for appreciating the achievement of the training goals.

This approach set up tags for the exploration of LMSs. It organized and prepared our comparative study to assess LMSs and allowed us to live the experience of distance training via a suitable LMS on which we built our judgment of the relevance of the teaching and technological choices and meeting most of our expectations.

REFERENCES

Aaron, M. (1992). *Graphic Design for Electronic Documents and User Interfaces*. ACM.

Baker, K., Greenberg, S., & Gutwin, C. (2002). Empirical development of a heuristic evaluation methodology for shared workspace groupware. In *Proceedings of the 2002 ACM conference on computer supported cooperative work (CSCW'02)*. New York, NY: ACM. 10.1145/587078.587093

Bastien, J.M.C., & Scapin, D. (1993). *Ergonomic Criteria for the Evaluation of Human-Computer interfaces*. Institut National de recherche en informatique et en automatique.

Bastien, J. M. C., & Scapin, D. L. (2001). Evaluation des systèmes d'information et critères ergonomiques. In *Environnements évolués et évaluation de l'IHM, Interaction homme-machine pour les SI 2* (pp. 53–80). Hermès Sciences Publications.

Gerhardt-Powals, J. (1996). Cognitive engineering principles for enhancing human-computer performance. *International Journal of Human-Computer Interaction*, *8*(2), 189–221. doi:10.1080/10447319609526147

Huart, J., Kolski, C., & Bastien, C. (2008). L'évaluation de documents multimédias. Etat de l'art. In Leleu-Merviel (dir.), Objectiver l'humain? Volume 1, Qualification, quantification, Paris, Hermès Sciences Publications. *Revue des Interactions Humaines Médiatisées*, *9*(2), 52.

ISO 10075-3:2004. Ergonomic principles related to mental workload -- Part 3: Principles and requirements concerning methods for measuring and assessing mental workload

ISO 9241-11:1998. Ergonomic requirements for office work with visual display terminals (VDTs) -- Part 11: Guidance on usability

ISO 9241-171:2008. Ergonomics of human-system interaction -- Part 171: Guidance on software accessibility

ISO 9241-210:2010. Ergonomics of human-system interaction -- Part 210: Human-centred design for interactive systems

ISO/IEC 25010:2011. Systems and software engineering -- Systems and software Quality Requirements and Evaluation (SQuaRE) -- System and software quality models

ISO/IEC 9126-1:2001. Software Engineering -Software product quality -Part 1: Quality Model

Johnson, J. (2008). *GUI bloopers 2.0 common user interface design don'ts and dos*. Morgan Kaufmann.

Lablidi, A., Abourrich, A., & Talbi, M. (2009). *Démarche préconisée pour évaluer une plate-forme*. Association EPI. Available: www.epi.asso.fr/revue/articles/a0912b.htm

Marlin, C. (1999). *Human-Computer Interface Design Guidelines*. Wiltshire: Intellect Books.

Nielsen, J. (1995). *10 Heuristics for User Interface Design*. Available: https://www.nngroup.com/articles/ten-usability-heuristics/

Norman, D. A. (1988). *The psychology of everyday things*. Basic Book.

Senach, B. (1993). L'évaluation ergonomique des interfaces homme-machine: une revue de la littérature. In L'ergonomie dans la conception des projets informatiques. Toulouse: Octares éditions.

Shneiderman, B., & Plaisant, C. (2005). *Designing the user interface: strategies for effective human-computer interaction*. Boston: Pearson/Addison Wesley.

Stone, D. L. (2005). *User interface design and evaluation*. San Francisco, CA: Elsevier/Morgan Kaufmann.

The OVAREP (Observatoire des ressources multimédias), 2000 « Étude comparative technique et pédagogique des plateformes pour la formation ouverte et à distance »

Tognazzini, B. (2014). *First Principles of Interaction Design (Revised & Expanded).* Available: https://asktog.com/atc/principles-of-interaction-design/

Tricot, A., Plégat-Soutjis, F., Camps, J. F., Amiel, A., Lutz, G., & Morcillo, A. (2003). Utilité, utilisabilité, acceptabilité: interpréter les relations entre trois dimensions de l'évaluation des EIAH. In Environnements informatiques pour l'apprentissage humain. ATIEF / INRP éditions.

ADDITIONAL READING

Kats, Y. (2010). *Learning Management Systems Technologies and Software Solutions for Online Teaching: Tools and Applications.* IGI/Information Science Research. doi:10.4018/978-1-61520-853-1

Kats, Y. (2013). *Learning Management Systems and Instructional Design: Metrics, Standards and Applications.* IGI/Information Science Research. doi:10.4018/978-1-4666-3930-0

Ouadoud, M., Chafiq, T., Rida, N., & Chkouri, M. Y. (2019). Generate a Meta-Model Content for Collaboration Space of Learning Management System Compatible with IMS-LD. *International Journal of Interactive Mobile Technologies, 13*(01), 37–52. doi:10.3991/ijim.v13i01.9440

Ouadoud, M., & Chkouri, M. Y. (2019). Generate a Meta-Model Content for Communication Space of Learning Management System Compatible with IMS-LD. In M. Ezziyyani (Ed.), *Advanced Intelligent Systems for Sustainable Development (AI2SD'2018), Advances in Intelligent Systems and Computing* (pp. 24–39). Springer International Publishing., doi:10.1007/978-3-030-11928-7_3

Ouadoud, M., & Chkouri, M. Y. (2019). Designing an IMS-LD Model for Communication Space of Learning Management System. In M. Ezziyyani (Ed.), *Advanced Intelligent Systems for Sustainable Development (AI2SD'2018), Advances in Intelligent Systems and Computing* (pp. 40–54). Springer International Publishing., doi:10.1007/978-3-030-11928-7_4

KEY TERMS AND DEFINITIONS

HSI: Human-computer interaction

ODL: Open and distance learning.

SCORM: The SCORM® (Sharable Content Object Reference Model) was created to address these interoperability, reusability, and durability challenges. As a reference model, it was intentionally designed to leverage standard web technologies as well as existing learning technology specifications that already existed. SCORM® is comprised of a collection of interrelated technical specifications and guidelines designed to meet the DoD's high-level requirements for creating interoperable, plug-n-play, browser-based e-learning content. It consists of three different technical specifications "books" that collectively address challenges associated with interoperability, portability, reusability, and the instructional sequencing of self-paced e-learning content (Available at https://www.adlnet.gov/adl-research/scorm).

Chapter 3
Comparative and Evaluative Study of Free Learning Management Systems

ABSTRACT

LMSs are constantly changing; they have transformed the lives of teachers and students. In this chapter, the authors propose a comparative study of free LMSs, from a methodical and systemic approach, that identifies the dimensions, the specifications, and the essential criteria for evaluating LMSs. They evaluate the most recognized LMSs to measure the matching degree between technological possibilities that they offer and the pedagogical assumptions to facilitate the choice of the most suitable LMS to help the users in their choice to benefit the potential offered by technologies in pedagogy.

INTRODUCTION

In the digital age, universities and companies are increasingly concerned about the quality of the training they offer their students or employers to ensure their integration into the labor market or in the company. Moreover, distance learning helps students and teachers in their research, in the exploration, and the deepening knowledge content. Thus, it helps to communicate and interact without taking the spatial or temporal constraints between tutors and learners into consideration. Universities contribute widely to ensure the quality of courses, and help to solve the problem of overcrowding in terraces. Especially, Moroccan and international universities suffer from overpopulation

DOI: 10.4018/978-1-7998-4021-3.ch003

between student ranks, and this is due to the schooling high rate in recent years. In this respect, national and international reflections are looking for a new smart LMS that can diffuse innovative training in the context of teaching and learning where a large place is given to the distance and hybrid learning, mobile learning, to using the web tools and social networks.

Any LMS choice must meet specific requirements. This is both to present courses on the web, do homework, provide communication interfaces and be able to follow the learners through scheduled pedagogical tasks.

In such a proliferation context of the LMSs, the choice becomes difficult. Therefore, we conducted a comparative study of the existing free LMSs in use in teaching and learning to choose the most suitable LMS.

On the one hand, the process of choosing a free LMS is linked to the benefit it can bring to the training of learners. It is at the level of the quality of medialization of the didactic and educational resources and of the access to distance training which was only possible in face-to-face. On the other hand, it should be noted that if the technology is supposed to respond to the spatial and temporal constraints between tutors and learners, it should not hinder the learning process. This double constraint pushed us to issue the following questions:

- On one hand, how can we choose an LMS that meets the norms and standards as they are acknowledged in the distance education system?
- On the other hand, what norms and standards do the requirements meet in the evaluation of these LMSs? Which approach in terms of pedagogical multimedia engineering should we use to assess these LMSs?

These issues are the subject of the investigations as part of our study, to put the item on the question of the provisions. What we are proposing is an approach that allows us to make the right choice of the LMS from an evaluative comparative study, technical and pedagogical of its LMSs. To our knowledge, there is no kind of study that has been conducted. What makes this important for the educational community, which works for the development of approaches, methods, and tools, to advance research in the education context. This chapter mainly consists of five sections:

- In the first section, we present a general introduction to our chapter.

- The second section presents the definition and benefits of LMSs.
- The third section presents the selected LMSs and the approach used for the evaluation. Then, it specifies the chosen rating method and describes each rating score.
- In the fourth section, we put the selected LMSs in comparison.
- In the fifth section, we are putting the obtained results in contribution.

LEARNING MANAGEMENT SYSTEMS

1. Definition

An LMS is software, including a range of services that assist teachers with the management of their courses. It offers many services allowing the management of content, particularly by creating, importing, and exporting learning objects. The set of available tools in the LMS represents all these services that help in managing the teaching process and the interaction between users such as the access control services, synchronous and asynchronous tools of communication, and user administration services.

Moreover, as defined by the OVAREP, the LMS, especially LMS, is a computing system that groups several tools and ensures the educational lines. Across dedicated LMSs to the ODL, all conduits are preserved and expanded for the learner, tutor, coordinator, and administrator within the LMS (OVAREP, 2000).

It should be mentioned, that a free LMS is a software, which they use, the study, the modification, and the duplication to release or diffuse it are permitted, technically and legally (Free Software Foundation, 2017). This is to ensure certain freedoms that are induced, which include the program's control by the user and the sharing possibility between individuals (Stallman, 2017). These rights may simply be available or established by a license, called "free" based on copyright.

Figure 1 illustrates the general principle of the operation of an LMS by presenting the key features associated with the main actors: learners, teachers, tutors, coordinators, and administrators. The learner can consult and/or download the resources placed at his/her disposal by the teacher, he/she can create his/her learning activities while following his/her progress in training. The teacher, who is responsible for one or more modules, can create and manage the educational content he/she wishes to broadcast via the LMS.

The tutor accompanies and monitors each learner by providing the tools of communication and collaboration. Concerning the coordinator, they ensure the management of the overall system. Finally, the administrator is responsible for the customization of the LMS having the rights of the administration deriving from it (system installation, maintenance, access management...).

Figure 1. The general architecture of an LMS

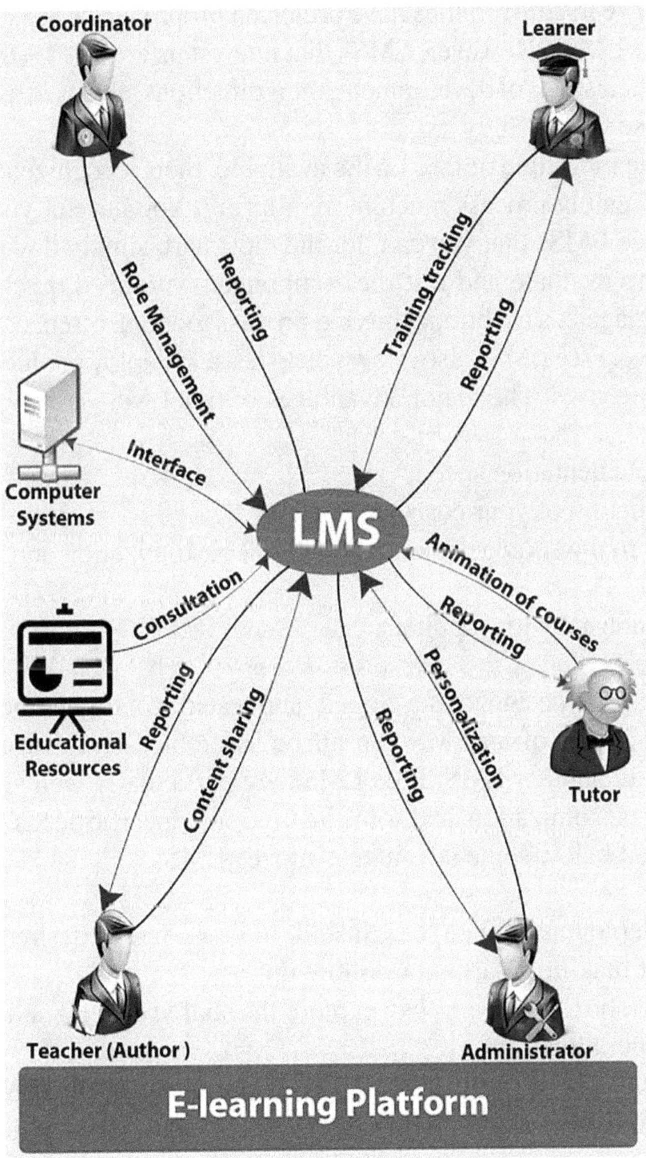

2. Benefits of Free LMSs

LMSs on which we count increasingly as a means of learning have considerable potential in knowledge building and skills development. Through the various services that these LMSs offer, individuals can access and use multiple sources of information, available interactively at anytime and anywhere, compose personalized training paths, and therefore develop the higher-level skills according to their needs (Gilbert, 2002; Marquet, 2005).

For many years, universities have preferred proprietary LMSs to meet the needs of new LMSs. However, LMSs that interest us are free LMSs, because their costs, their states of development, their directions, and used technologies are very close to this study axis.

Today, the multitude of free LMSs available, their recognized robustness make the assembly process much more alluring. You have at your disposal dozens of free LMSs that you can, for the most part, simply download. This allows you to evaluate and test the components you need quickly without having to engage in a traditional buying process too long often, constraining, and expensive. Free LMSs also allow you to test and deploy a solution without purchasing licenses. The major advantages of free LMSs are:

- the implementation speed,
- the reduction of your costs,
- Access to the source code allowing total customization and facilitating support,
- Independence with suppliers.

Free LMSs are designed, developed, and tested in a highly modular way. The different parts of an LMS can all be assembled and disassembled at your leisure in another LMS. Free LMSs are particularly well suited to the unique case, customization, and some institutions' specific needs. Therefore, we have listed below some advantages of free LMSs.

- Easy deployment. You can install it in as many desired locations without making a particular follow-up.
- No black box. The teams can explore the source code to understand the LMS operation.
- Independence towards editors. The evolutions of a free LMS, like its updates, rely on a community of developers and not a single editor.

- Access to the source code. Your institution maintains control of the program code lines. It can adapt it to their needs. According to the license affixed to the free and open-source LMS, institutions and developers are required or not to share the changes of the source code.
- Unlike to proprietary model. The open-source license is free and defines the LMS use terms.
- Community development. Communities develop each part of the free and open-source LMSs. The latter promotes responsiveness when it comes to fixing a bug or a security flaw.
- Economy. A null cost for the LMS in the majority case of the free LMSs downloadable on the internet.

LMS EVALUATION METHODOLOGY

1. Selection of LMSs

In this chapter, we take care of four free LMSs, which were selected in detail on 27 LMSs. These LMSs were selected from 650 LMSs listed in the THOT CURSUS directory.

Other LMSs like Elgg, Dokeos, and WIMS..., are "encountered" in the work and are not cited as counted because they are tools and not LMSs in the sense of this study. Besides, their costs, their development status, orientation, and the used technologies are too far from the axis of this study. We did the first filter on free LMSs currently used in University or training structures. Next, we have elaborated a second filter according to the following criteria:

- Be operational and have been used by learners as part of lessons,
- Rely on new internet technologies, and meet the standards in force,
- Allow managing several types of pedagogical activities (reading, exercises, collaboration, communication…),
- It can manage a large number of users.
- Enable the teachers and learners to create, organize and propose different types of activities (forum, wiki, blog…) as they like.
- Enable the teachers and learners to access and manage their interactions via these activities where and when they want according to their needs and objectives in terms of learning.
- Relies on well-founded and proven learning theories.

After applying the two filters, the study had focused on four listed LMSs, namely: ATutor, Claroline Connect, Chamilo Connect, Efront, Formagri, Ilias, Moodle, Opigno, and Sakai.

It should be recalled that this study was conducted in two stages:

- a census of LMSs that matches the type of LMSs, including the requested filters,
- Then, a detailed comparative study of the selected LMSs.

Thus, to achieve our study, we opted for a qualitative approach consisting to realize an analysis by product exploration, analysis of documentation, collection of user opinions, discussions with publishers, and simulation tests that we carried on the selected LMSs. We present thereafter a common table (see table 1) we used to evaluate its LMSs.

Table 1. Evaluation approach of the LMSs quality

Assessment and Analysis Grid of the LMSS Quality
LMS Identification
o LMS's name:
o LMS designer:
o LMS type:
o LMS genre:
o LMS's pedagogical model:
o LMS license:
o Description:
o Version & Edition:
o Used technology:
o Language:
o Website:
Utility Specifications
Functional suitability tools
Performance efficiency tools
Compatibility tools
Security tools
Maintainability tools
Portability tools
Usability Specifications
Usability criteria

(Ouadoud and al., 2016)

2. Evaluation Approach of LMSs

To be used effectively, the selected LMSs need an overall evaluation of the utility and usability specifications to be well exploited and used in the best conditions. Several evaluation methods of the LMSs were encountered in the literature (Lablidi and al., 2009; Aska and al., 2000). However, they have not been chosen, because these studies focus mainly on the functional aspect, forgetting other aspects very important such as security, maintainability, portability, compatibility, performance efficiency, and usability. For this reason, we have realized our evaluation approach of the LMSs' quality. Table I present an overview of our approach with measures and criteria adopted for the evaluation of the LMSs.

This approach sets up tags for the exploration of LMSs. It organized and prepared our comparative study to assess LMSs and allowed us to live the experience of distance training via a suitable LMS on which we built our judgment of the relevance of the teaching and technological choices and meeting most of our expectations. Before applying this approach, we try to explain how to use it.

3. Quality Metric

To verify that each LMS meets the various criteria mentioned in the evaluation approach of the LMSs quality.

We have mentioned in this study, that the metric for measuring the quality of an LMS will be the IS0 9126's conformity index (ISO/IEC 9126-3, 2003). Furthermore, we have implemented a rating system that gives a score ranging from 0 to 4 for each criterion, instead of 0 to 1 will, therefore, be adapted as follows: ∀ A, B, X, Y ∈ ℕ

$$CI = \frac{A}{B} = \frac{\sum x}{\sum y} = \frac{\sum functional\,suitability\,scores}{\sum functional\,suitability\,attributes}$$

With A ∈ [0, 116], x = 2n ∀ n ∈ [0, 2]

Or

$$CI = \frac{A}{B} = \frac{\sum x}{\sum y} = \frac{\sum performance\,efficiency\,scores}{\sum performance\,efficiency\,attributes}$$

With A ∈ [0, 12], x = 2n ∀ n ∈ [0, 2]

Or

$$CI = \frac{A}{B} = \frac{\sum x}{\sum y} = \frac{\sum compatibility\, scores}{\sum compatibility\, attributes}$$

With A ∈ [0, 36], x = 2n ∀ n ∈ [0, 2]

Or

$$CI = \frac{A}{B} = \frac{\sum x}{\sum y} = \frac{\sum security\, scores}{\sum security\, attributes}$$

With A ∈ [0, 32], x = 2n ∀ n ∈ [0, 2]

Or

$$CI = \frac{A}{B} = \frac{\sum x}{\sum y} = \frac{\sum maintainability\, scores}{\sum maintainability\, attributes}$$

With A ∈ [0, 20], x = 2n ∀ n ∈ [0, 2]

Or

$$CI = \frac{A}{B} = \frac{\sum x}{\sum y} = \frac{\sum portability\, scores}{\sum portability\, attributes}$$

With A ∈ [0, 20], x = 2n ∀ n ∈ [0, 2]

Or

$$CI = \frac{A}{B} = \frac{\sum x}{\sum y} = \frac{\sum usability\, scores}{\sum usability\, attributes}$$

With A ∈ [0, 32], x = 2n ∀ n ∈ [0, 2]

CI is the conformity index to the functional suitability, performance efficiency, compatibility, security, maintainability, portability, or usability requirements.

A is some of the functional suitability, performance efficiency, compatibility, security, maintainability, portability, or usability scores.

X is the functional suitability, performance efficiency, compatibility, security, maintainability, portability, or usability scores. Each score has a value selected in our case between 0 and 4 is defined according to the following scale:

- 4: This means that the LMS fully satisfies this characteristic (or sub-characteristic).
- 2: This means that the LMS partially satisfies this characteristic (or sub-characteristic).
- 0: This means that the LMS does not satisfy this characteristic (or sub-characteristic).

B is the number of functional suitability, performance efficiency, compatibility, security, maintainability, portability, or usability attributes.

Y is the functional suitability, performance efficiency, compatibility, security, maintainability, portability, or usability attributes.

Given that $0 \leq CI \leq 4$, the more the CI value is near to its maximum 4, and more the CI index will comply with the standard requirements for the investigated characteristic. This index can also be expressed as a percentage rather than an absolute value (between 0 and 4) because the relative value in percentage makes it easier index interpretation. For example, if CI = 3 then, we can say that the CI conformity index meets 75% (3/4) of the standard requirements for the given characteristic or sub-characteristic. Consequently, the quality measuring metric of an LMS will be calculated as the following:

$$Qm = \frac{\sum utility\ and/\ or\ usability\ scores}{\sum utility\ and/\ or\ usability\ attributes}$$

4. The Quality Level of the Scores

In this study, we are assessing the overall quality level of the designed LMSs to be integrated into the distance-learning field. The following evaluation type allows having a general idea about the quality level of the evaluated LMSs (see table 2).

Table 2. Description of the appropriate quality level for each obtained score note

Overall Score	Overall Capacity (%)	Quality Level
217 ⇨ 268	From 81% to 100%	**Very good**: This score level allows us to achieve an excellent level of quality for educational use since it meets the required quality criteria.
163 ⇨ 216	From 61% to 80%	**Good**: The LMS is sufficient and adequate for educational use, although it does not allow pedagogical exploitation to full potential.
109 ⇨ 162	From 41% to 60%	**Average**: The LMS can be used in teaching and learning, but it does not allow a sufficiently significant educational use.
0 ⇨ 108	From 0% to 40%	**Substandard**: The LMS is far from being used in a teaching and learning context since it does not meet the criteria expressed.

The selected LMSs are presented in the next section, with their identification, their general characterization, their strong and weak points. Moreover, this, using a critical analysis based on the evaluation approach of the LMSs quality presented in table 1.

LMSS' COMPARISON

In this section, we will do a comparison of the selected LMSs by using critical analysis, based on an evaluation approach presented in table 1. The latter presents an overview of the utility and usability dimensions with the measurements and adapted criteria for the LMSs' evaluation.

1. Identification of LMSs

Before proceeding to a global evaluation, we begin with identifying the selected LMSs to get an idea about their quality levels and the ability to be used in distance learning (see Table 3).

2. Utility Analysis

In the development of interactive software, the best-known utility criteria were presented in this section. Moreover, in the following, we present the essential criteria for the utility analysis, as well as the analyzed LMSs.

2.1 Functional Suitability

Functional suitability means the degree to which a product or system provides functions that meet stated and implied needs when used under specified conditions (ISO/IEC 25010, 2011). Table 4 (Appendix) projects the essential functionalities for functional suitability analysis, as well as the analyzed LMSs.

2.2 Performance Efficiency

Performance efficiency, which means the performance relative to the number of resources used under stated conditions (ISO/IEC 25010, 2011). In table 5 (Appendix), we project the essential functionalities for performance efficiency analysis, as well as the analyzed LMSs.

2.3 Compatibility

Compatibility signifies the degree to which a product, system, or component can exchange information with other products, systems or components, and/or perform its required functions, while sharing the same hardware or software environment (ISO/IEC 25010, 2011). Table 6 (Appendix) presents the essential functionalities for compatibility analysis, as well as the analyzed LMSs.

2.4 Security

Security means the degree to which a product or system protects information and data so persons or other products or systems have the degree of data access appropriate to their types and levels of authorization (ISO/IEC 25010, 2011). Table 7 (Appendix) shows the essential functionalities for security analysis, as well as the analyzed LMSs.

2.5 Maintainability

Maintainability. It means the degree of effectiveness and efficiency with which a product or system can be modified by the intended maintainers (ISO/IEC 25010, 2011). In table 8 (Appendix), the essential functionalities for maintainability analysis, as well as the analyzed LMSs.

Table 3. Identification of the selected LMSs

LMS's name	**Atutor***	**Claroline Connect***	**Chamilo Connect***	**Efront***	**Formagri***	**Ilias***	**Moodle***	**Opigno***	**Sakai***
LMS designer	*Inclusive Design Research Centre, OCAD Université*	*UCL / IPM / ECAM*	*Communauté Chamilo and Partenaires professionnels*	*Société grecque Epignosis*	*AGROSUP DijonEDUTER / Eduter CNERTA*	*Alexander Killing*	*Martin Dougiamas and Moodle Community*	*Société Connect-i.*	*Sakai Community*
LMS type	LMS	LMS	LCMS	LMS	LMS	LMS	CMS, VLE, LCMS	LMS	LMS
LMS genre	Online learning LMS	Online learning LMS	Online learning LMS	Online learning LMS	Online learning LMS	Online learning LMS	Online learning LMS	Online learning LMS	Online learning LMS
LMS's pedagogical model	traditional pedagogy	social constructivist	social constructivist	traditional pedagogy	traditional pedagogy	social constructivist	social constructivist	traditional pedagogy	Constructivism
LMS license	GPL	GPL	GNU/GPL V3+	GPL V2	GPL	GPL	GPL	GNU/GPL V2+	Educational Community License
Version & Edition	V. 2.2.4 (20 Jun 2018)	V. 12.5 (17 Dec. 2019)	V. 1.11.10 (05 Aug. 2019)	V. 3.6.15.5 15/06/ 2015	V. 2.8 (12 Oct 2018)	V. 5.4.2 (06 Jan. 2019)	V. 3.8+ (03 Jan. 2019)	V. 2.9 (19 Dec. 2019)	V. 19.0 (March 21, 2019)
Used Technology	PHP (5.6.3)	PHP (5.5+)	PHP (>=5.3+)	PHP (5.2+)	PHP	PHP (5.3+)	PHP (5.4.4+)	PHP (5.3+)	JAVA
Language	Multi-language support, more than 21 languages	Multi-language support, limited languages number (fr, en, es)	Support multi-langue, more than 57 languages	Multi-language support, more than 45 languages	Multi-language support, limited languages number, 3 languages	Multi-language support, more than 28 languages	Multi-language support, more than 135 languages	Multi-language support, limited languages number, 5 languages	Multi-language support, more than 20 languages
Website	www.atutor.ca	www.claroline.net	www.chamilo.org	www.efrontlearning.net	www.formagri.fr	www.ilias.de	www.moodle.org	www.opigno.org	www.sakaiproject.org
User institutions	Srinakharinwirot university, softaculous, Nursing Course Server, Ubicomp Courses, etc.	High School of Namur-Liège-Luxembourg, Neuchâtel university, campus: Belfort & Lyon 'esta', LaSalle Beauvais, etc.	Atlassian Bitbucket, Makina Corpus, etc.	Francisco Partners 'FP', Softaculous, les Echos, SiteGround, Glassdoor, eLearning Industry, ECHO STATTION, Prezi, etc.	Forestry and vocational training in Midi-Pyrénées EPLEFPA VIC, Web space of professionals in French agricultural education 'ChloroFil', etc	Konstanz university, Freiburg university, zu Köln university, Tubingen university, Stuttgart university, HOHENHEIM university, etc.	Toulouse III 'Paul Sabatier' university, Louvain Catholic university, Lille 1 & Lille 3 university, Jean Moulin university, etc.	Plateforme d'apprentissage en ligne 'IT-Connect', Training Industry, An Upwork Company 'Elance', CityWizz, Cogicube, etc.	Baltimore university, Duke university, GHANA university, Brock university, Washington & Lee university, Collège Washington & Jefferson, etc.

2.6 Portability

Portability signifies the degree of effectiveness and efficiency with which a system, product, or component can be transferred from one hardware, software, or other operational or usage environment to another (ISO/IEC 25010, 2011). Table 9 (Appendix) shows the essential functionalities for portability analysis, as well as the analyzed LMSs.

3. Usability Analysis

Usability refers to means the degree to which a product or system can be used by specified users to achieve specified goals with effectiveness, efficiency, and satisfaction in a specified context of use (ISO/IEC 25010, 2011). Table 10 (Appendix) projects the essential functionalities for usability analysis, as well as the analyzed LMSs.

LMSS' EVALUATION

After applying the proposed approach and analyzing the selected LMSs by assigning a score for each criterion. We obtained the following results.

1. Study of LMSs

We achieved overall scores between 180 and 252, which means that the LMSs have reached between 67% and 94% of the criteria. The percentages that reflect the LMSs' quality levels regarding the analysis and evaluation of each dimension. Consequently, we obtained the presented results in Table 11 (Appendix) and figure 2.

Analyzed LMSs, present each with a philosophy, interesting pedagogical conceptual references, different benefits, and special characteristics, all offering a set of functionalities allowing educational institutions to put online training courses.

1. Moodle, Sakai, Opigno, and Atutor are LMSs that present a very good utility and usability degree.
    a. Moodle provides, operationally, the greatest functional and pedagogical wealth for learners and teachers as is shown in table

11 (Appendix). This LMS offers a plagiarism detection module, as well as other important educational tools.

The LMS is centered on social constructivism it is extremely modular, and the LMS is suitable for all structures. Thus, we obtained the following results:

Figure 2. The utility and usability degree for analyzed LMSs, turn by turn, in each figure, the x-axis represents certain conformities indices to the utility and usability requirements for each LMS. These preliminary indices are presented in the Subfigures by numbers from 1 to 7. Thus, the y-axis represents the values of these indices. In our study, these values are between 0 and 4.

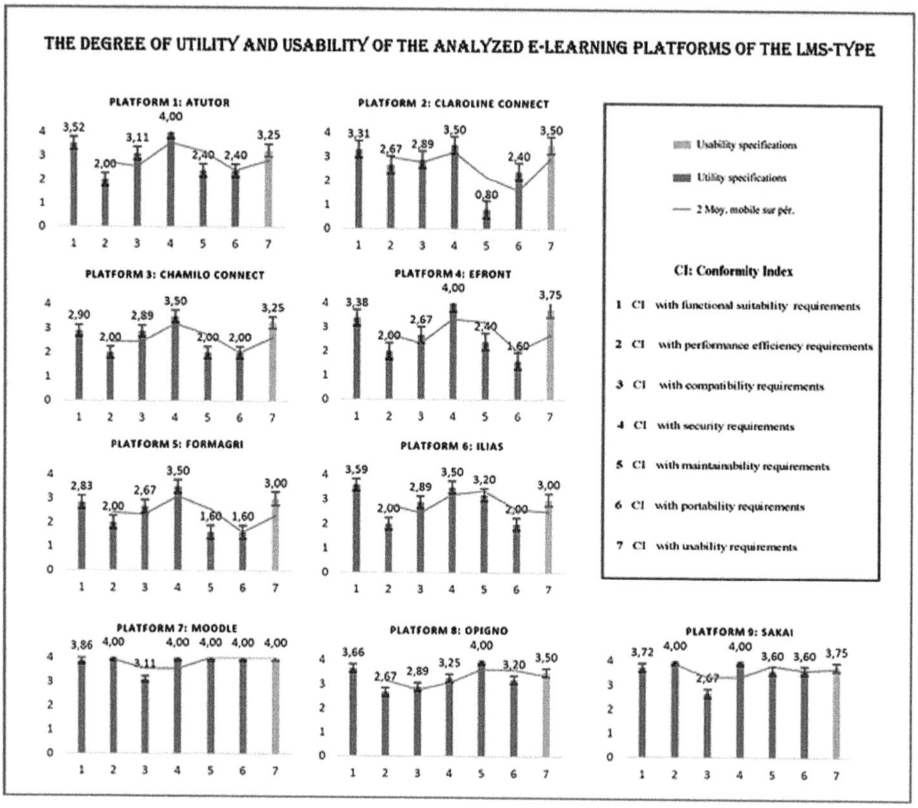

We got a 4 (100%) compliance index regarding maintainability, security, and usability. Besides, this reflects that Moodle's specifications are fully satisfied for educational use. Moreover, we got a: 3.86 (97%) functional suitability,

3.6 (90%) portability, 3.33 (83%) compatibility, and 2.67 (67%) effective performance compliance index. This reflects that Moodle's specifications are sufficient for good pedagogy. Consequently, we obtained a 252 overall score, which means that the LMS has 94% reached criteria, a percentage that reflects the LMS quality level. This level allows Moodle to achieve an excellent quality level for educational use.

b. Sakai offers a very important functional and pedagogical wealth. The LMS is centered on constructivism and it is extremely modular. Notably, we obtained the following results:

We got a: 3,75 (94%) usability and security, 3,66 (92%) functional suitability, 3,6 (90%) maintainability, 3,2 (80%) portability, and 2.67 (67%) compatibility and effective performance compliance index. This reflects that Sakai's specifications are sufficient for good pedagogy. Consequently, we obtained a 232 overall score, which means that the LMS has 87% reached criteria, a percentage that reflects the LMS quality level. This level allows Sakai to achieve a very good quality level for educational use.

c. Opigno offers a very important pedagogical wealth, for the learning support and the design and the conduct of the teachings. Opigno is centered on traditional pedagogy, it is extremely modular. Notably, we obtained the following results:

We got a 4 (100%) compliance index regarding maintainability. Also, this reflects that this Opigno's specification is fully satisfied for educational use. Moreover, we got a: 3,66 (92%) functional suitability, 3,5 (88%) usability, 3,25 (81%) security, 2,89 (72%) compatibility, 2,8 (70%) portability, and 2,67 (67%) effective performance compliance index. This reflects that these Opigno's specifications are sufficient for good pedagogy. Consequently, we obtained a 228 overall score, which means that the LMS has 85% reached criteria, a percentage that reflects the LMS quality level. This level allows Opigno to achieve a very good quality level for educational use.

d. ATutor offers a very important functional wealth. The LMS is centered on traditional pedagogy, it is extremely modular. Notably, we obtained the following results:

We got a 4 (100%) compliance index regarding security. Besides, this reflects that this Atutor's specification is fully satisfied for educational use. Moreover, we got a: 3,52 (88%) functional suitability, 3,25 (81%) usability, 3,11 (78%) compatibility, and 2,4 (60%) portability and maintainability compliance index. This reflects that these Atutor's specifications are sufficient for good pedagogy. Furthermore, we got a 2 (50%) effective performance compliance index. This reflects that this Atutor's specification is partially sufficient for educational use. Consequently, we obtained a 218 overall score, which means that the LMS has 81% reached criteria, a percentage that reflects the LMS quality level. This level allows ATutor to achieve a very good quality level for educational use.

2. Ilias, Efront, Claroline Connect, Chamilo Connect, and Formagri are LMSs that present a good utility and usability degree.
    a. Ilias allows some sharing of tasks between teachers and offers important functionalities. The LMS is centered on social constructivism. It is extremely modular. Notably, we obtained the following results:

We got a: 3,59 (90%) functional suitability, 3,5 (88%) security, 3,2 (80%) maintainability, 3 (75%) usability, and 2,89 (72%) compatibility compliance index. This reflects that Ilias's specifications are sufficient for good pedagogy. Moreover, we got a 2 (50%) effective performance and portability compliance index. This reflects that these Ilias' specifications are partially sufficient for educational use. Consequently, we obtained a 214 overall score, which means that the LMS has 80% reached criteria, a percentage that reflects the LMS quality level. This level allows Ilias to achieve a good quality level for educational use.

    b. Efront offers important functionalities. The LMS is centered on the traditional pedagogy. It is extremely modular. Notably, we obtained the following results:

We got a 4 (100%) compliance index regarding security. Also, this reflects that this Efront's specification is fully satisfied for educational use. Moreover, we got a: 3,75 (94%) usability, 3,45 (86%) functional suitability, 2,67 (67%) compatibility, and 2,4 (60%) maintainability compliance index. This reflects that these Efront's specifications are sufficient for good pedagogy. Furthermore, we got a: 2 (50%) effective performance, and 1,6 (40%)

portability compliance index. This reflects that these Efront's specifications are partially sufficient for educational use. Consequently, we obtained a 212 overall score, which means that the LMS has 79% reached criteria, a percentage that reflects the LMS quality level. This level allows Efront to achieve a good quality level for educational use.

c. Claroline Connect offers important functionalities. The LMS is centered on social constructivism. It allows some sharing of tasks between teachers, as well as interconnection and exchange of information with several Claroline Connect LMS. Notably, we obtained the following results:

We got a: 3,5 (88%) usability and security, 3,24 (81%) functional suitability, 2,89 (72%) compatibility, and 2,67 (67%) effective performance compliance index. This reflects that these Claroline's specifications are sufficient for good pedagogy. Moreover, we got a 2 (50%) portability compliance index. This reflects that this Claroline's specification is partially sufficient for educational use. Furthermore, we got a 0,8 (20%) maintainability compliance index. This reflects that this Claroline's specification is not sufficient for good pedagogy. Consequently, we obtained a 198 overall score, which means that the LMS has 74% reached criteria, a percentage that reflects the LMS quality level. This level allows Claroline Connect to achieve a good quality level for educational use.

d. Chamilo Connect offers important functionalities. The LMS is centered on social constructivism. It allows some sharing of tasks between teachers. Notably, we obtained the following results:

We got a: 3,25 (81%) security and usability, 2,9 (73%) functional suitability, and 2,89 (72%) compatibility compliance index. This reflects that these Chamilo Connect specifications are sufficient for good pedagogy. Furthermore, we got a: 2 (50%) effective performance, portability, and maintainability compliance index. This reflects that these Chamilo's specifications are partially sufficient for educational use. Consequently, we obtained a 188 overall score, which means that the LMS has 70% reached criteria, a percentage that reflects the LMS quality level. This level allows Chamilo Connect to achieve a good quality level for educational use.

e. Formagri offers important functionalities. The LMS is centered on the traditional pedagogy. Notably, we obtained the following results:

We got a: 3,25 (81%) security, 3 (75%) usability, 2,90 (73%) functional suitability, and 2,67 (67%) compatibility compliance index. This reflects that these Formagri specifications are sufficient for good pedagogy. Moreover, we got a: 2 (50%) effective performance, and 1,6 (40%) maintainability and portability compliance index. This reflects that these Formagri's specifications are partially sufficient for educational use. Consequently, we obtained a 180 overall score, which means that the LMS has 67% reached criteria, a percentage that reflects the LMS quality level. This level allows Formagri to achieve a good quality level for educational use.

2. Classification of LMSs

Figure 3 presents the general classification results of the analyzed LMSs, according to utility and usability degree falling within our critical analysis of free LMSs. The latter is based on ISO 9126's quality measurement index (ISO/IEC 9126-3, 2003).

These analyzed LMSs offer an important pedagogical and functional wealth, for the learning support and designing. They also offer an improvement in the conduct of teachings, the construction, and the organization of elaborate formations. Besides, these LMSs implement interoperability management between multimedia teaching resources and LMS.

These LMSs offer many options and authorize diverse usage scenarios, of which we see that the Moodle LMS has overcome the list of LMSs. Notably, it presents a very good utility and usability degree. Moodle can host thousands of learners, teachers, and tutors. It is one of the most used free LMSs in the world, with its large francophone and the international community; it is clear, well-structured, and useful documentation. Its many discussion forums focusing on all problems generated by distance learning complexity. The Moodle LMS is based on the creation of learners' communities around with content and pedagogical activities. Moodle favors human exchanges, builds communities of practices, and promotes mutual help and support between learners such as between teachers and tutors. Despite the utility and usability degree reached by the analyzed LMSs, the result of each LMS evaluation shows that each has its strengths and weaknesses. However, they have all unsatisfied needs on the pedagogical side, especially concerning pedagogical conceptual references adopted by the LMSs.

In the next section, we present our study results in the form of a recommendation system of free LMSs according to the objectives and the specificities of any institution.

Figure 3. Figure 3. The general classification of the analyzed LMSs, according to utility and usability degree

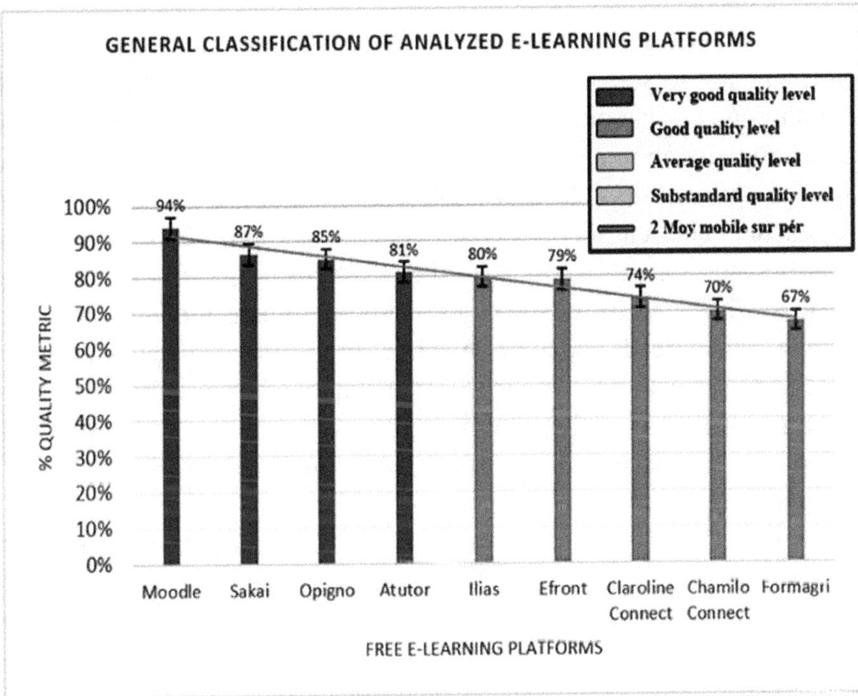

CONCLUSION

The subject of this chapter is very important. The free LMSs are, on the one hand, a topical domain in Software Engineering and Pedagogical Engineering Multimedia. On the other hand, the application of these LMSs in e-learning reaches a vast clientele. Moreover, academically, it seems that it is interesting to apply for the first time an inspired approach of software engineering to evaluate the LMSs' quality.

Indeed, LMSs quality analysis, according to our approach led to very interesting results. We see that most of the analyzed LMSs were initially developed a decade ago, based on a classical training model. The teacher is the one who holds the knowledge and transmits it, according to different modalities, to future learners to the learning foster of these latter. They are mostly TMS, which is to say tools at the teacher service to create and manage courses rather than at the learner service and the learning process. They are always part of logic, uniform, techno-centric, and cantoned architecture in a reduced learning conception, which advocates a particular pedagogical theory independently of others.

An LMS choice, pledge of success, and sustainability for the pedagogical system, which also seems inadequate with the free LMSs' philosophy and their community dynamic. Consequently, constructed a new LMS, we seem ideal for implementing a first one of distance training systems centered on the user and his activity. The new LMS we are looking at implementing will allow teachers and learners to create, organize and propose different types of activities (forum, wiki, blog…) as they like. Furthermore, they can access and manage their interactions via these activities where and when they want according to their needs and their objectives in learning terms. Our LMS will be based on the idea that we should give equal action possibilities to both teachers and learners of distributing their control on the LMS. The latter will also give the place to the learner to learn and make himself an actor in his learning.

In the next chapters, an experiment is therefore indispensable to validate what has been developed in the context of this chapter. Indeed, the latter will be based on the implementing results of a teaching and learning system in Moroccan university, based on a platform known as intelligent and anthropocentric relying on reduced learning design, to enhance distance learning.

REFERENCES

Aska, Le Préau, & Klr.fr. (2000). *Choisir une solution de téléformation: 2000 study*. l'offre de plates-formes et de portails de téléformation.

Claroline, C. O. M. M. (2016). *Introduction*. Claroline Connect Documentation. https://claroline.gitbooks.io/claroline-connect-documentation/en/

Connect-i society. (2016). *Opigno User Manual.* https://www.opigno.org/160707_Opigno_User-Manual.pdf

Dooremont, F. (2014). *Sakaï | Fiche logiciel validé PLUME.* www.projet-plume.org/fiche/sakai

Free Software Foundation. (2017). http://www.gnu.org/philosophy/free-sw.fr.html

Gilbert, P. (2002). *L'ingénierie pédagogique.* Pour construire l'apprentissage en réseau.

ISO/IEC 25010, 2011. Systems and software engineering -- Systems and software Quality Requirements and Evaluation (SQuaRE) -- System and software quality models

ISO/IEC 9126-3, 2003. Software Engineering - Software product quality - Part 3: Internal Metric

Knoop, A. P., & Groen, R. (2012). *SCORM - Contrib: SCORM Player – Confluence.* https://confluence.sakaiproject.org/display/SCORMPLAYER/SCORM

Lablidi, A., Abourrich, A., & Talbi, M. (2009). *Démarche préconisée pour évaluer une plate-forme.* Association EPI. www.epi.asso.fr/revue/articles/a0912b.htm

Marquet, P. (2005). Lorsque le développement des TIC et l'évolution des théories de l'apprentissage se croisent. *Savoirs*, 105–121. doi:10.3917avo.009.0105

Moodle, C. O. M. M. (2019). *Fonctionnalités — MoodleDocs.* https://docs.moodle.org/3x/fr/Fonctionnalités

Ouadoud, M., Chkouri, M. Y., Nejjari, A., & El Kadiri, K. E. (2016). Studying and Analyzing the Evaluation Dimensions of LMSs Relying on a Software Engineering Approach. *International Journal of Emerging Technologies in Learning*, *11*, 11–20. doi:10.3991/ijet.v11i01.4924

Stallman, R. (2017). *gnu.org.* http://www.gnu.org/gnu/thegnuproject.html

The OVAREP (Observatoire des ressources multimédias). (2000). *Étude comparative technique et pédagogique des plateformes pour la formation ouverte et à distance.* Academic Press.

Vucic, V. (2007). *A Tutor Getting Started, An Overview of interface and functionality*. https://www.researchgate.net/publication/28806580_ATutor_Getting_Started_An_Overview_of_interface_and_functionality

Whyte, A., & Federico, J. (2018). *Home – Contrib: bigbluebutton – Confluence*. https://confluence.sakaiproject.org/display/BBB/Home

ADDITIONAL READING

Ouadoud, M., Chafiq, T., Rida, N., & Chkouri, M. Y. (2019). Generate a Meta-Model Content for Collaboration Space of Learning Management System Compatible with IMS-LD. *International Journal of Interactive Mobile Technologies, 13*(01), 37–52. doi:10.3991/ijim.v13i01.9440

Ouadoud, M., & Chkouri, M. Y. (2019). Generate a Meta-Model Content for Communication Space of Learning Management System Compatible with IMS-LD. In M. Ezziyyani (Ed.), *Advanced Intelligent Systems for Sustainable Development (AI2SD'2018), Advances in Intelligent Systems and Computing* (pp. 24–39). Springer International Publishing. doi:10.1007/978-3-030-11928-7_3

Ouadoud, M., & Chkouri, M. Y. (2019). Designing an IMS-LD Model for Communication Space of Learning Management System. In M. Ezziyyani (Ed.), *Advanced Intelligent Systems for Sustainable Development (AI2SD'2018), Advances in Intelligent Systems and Computing* (pp. 40–54). Springer International Publishing. doi:10.1007/978-3-030-11928-7_4

KEY TERMS AND DEFINITIONS

Constructivism: Is a learning pedagogy based on the idea that the learner himself builds knowledge based on mental activity. Constructivism is based on the assumption that, by reflecting on our experiences, we construct our vision of the world in which we live.

LMS: Learning management system.

ODL: Open and distance learning.

OVAREP: Observatoire des Ressources Multimédias.

SCORM: The SCORM® (Sharable Content Object Reference Model) was created to address these interoperability, reusability, and durability challenges. As a reference model, it was intentionally designed to leverage standard web technologies as well as existing learning technology specifications that already existed. SCORM® is comprised of a collection of interrelated technical specifications and guidelines designed to meet the DoD's high-level requirements for creating interoperable, plug-n-play, browser-based e-learning content. It consists of three different technical specifications "books" that collectively address challenges associated with interoperability, portability, reusability, and the instructional sequencing of self-paced e-learning content (Available at https://www.adlnet.gov/adl-research/scorm).

Social Constructivism: Is centered on the learner. The learner learns through its representations. The construction of knowledge although personal is carried out in a social setting. The context and come from both what we think and what others bring as interactions.

THOT CURSUS: Is a directory of LMSs, LCMSs, and other systems for content and learning management.

TMS: Teaching management systems.

Traditional Pedagogy: Is that of the transmissive model. This pedagogy privileges the relationship between the teacher and the knowledge. In other words, the teacher exposes a knowledge in the form of lecturing, usually followed by exercises and/or lessons to be learned. The learner must integrate and apply the exposed knowledge by the teacher.

APPENDIX

Table 4. Functional suitability analysis of the selected LMSs

Resource Management (course)	Partial, sharing courses for the groups (Vucic, 2007) and not in activity spaces	Yes, share resources of activity spaces (community, 2016)	Yes, The integration of multimedia teaching resources	Yes. The integration of teaching resources	Yes. Multi-format teaching resource management	Yes, 'Course' tool	Yes, course management plugin (Moodle, 2019)	Yes, The integration of multimedia teaching resources (Connect-i, 2016)	Yes, integration of multimedia in the course.
Support of multiple authors	Yes, the teacher has the right to create and manage his course	Yes, the teacher has the right to create and manage his / her course	Yes, the teacher has the right to create and manage his / her course	Yes, the teacher has the right to create and manage his / her course	Yes, the teacher has the right to create, manage, and giving access right to tutors in his / her course	Yes, the teacher has the right to create and manage his / her course	Yes, the teacher has the right to create, manage, and giving access right to tutors in his / her course	Yes, the teacher has the right to create and manage his / her course	Yes, the teacher has the right to create and manage his / her course (Dooremont, 2014).
FUNCTIONAL CORRECTNESS									
Management of working time of learners and teachers	No, the LMS does not manage the learners' working time	No, the LMS does not manage the learners' working time	No, the LMS does not manage the learners' working time	No, the LMS does not manage the learners' working time	No, the LMS does not manage the learners' working time	No, the LMS does not manage the learners' working time	No, the LMS does not manage the learners' working time	No, the LMS does not manage the learners' working time	No, the LMS does not manage the learners' working time
Results and notes	Yes, ' Tests and Surveys' module	Yes	Yes, Hotspot, matrix, and correspondance questions tools…	Yes, 'Gradebook' tool which managing of students' notes	Yes, solution of sending and correcting homework	Yes, using 'Test and assessment' tool	Yes. All given notes in forums and tests (Moodle, 2019)	Yes, 'Quiz certificates' module	Yes (Dooremont, 2014)
Notes display	Yes	Yes	Yes	Yes	Yes	Yes	Yes	Yes	Yes
Tracking statistics of course	Yes, ' tests and surveys' tool	Yes, monitoring tools of the learners' activities (Claroline, 2016).	Yes	Partial, 'Reports' space to tracking user statistics, courses and lessons.	Yes, a statistic tracking module of the LMS users.	Yes, 'Statistics and Learning Progress' space	Yes, activity reports are available with graphs (Moodle, 2019)	Yes, 'Statistics ' and 'Quiz Statistics' module	Yes, statistics of learner visits (Knoop and Groen, 2012; Dooremont, 2014].
Control Connections (learners' tracking)	Yes, module ' Tests and Surveys'	Yes, monitoring tools, statistics; + dashboard (Claroline, 2016)	Yes	Yes, 'Reports' space to tracking user statistics.	Partial, supervisory tools to tracking of learners / missing dashboard	Partial, supervisory tools to tracking of learners / missing dashboard	Yes, supervision tools (groups, activities, etc.); + dashboard.	Yes, Monitoring the result of the class or the course (Connect-i, 2016)	Yes (Dooremont, 2014)
Report on the test results	Yes, ' tests and surveys' tool	No	Yes	Yes, tracking student progress via 'Lesson reports' interface.	No	Yes. 'Statistics and Learning Progress' interface	Yes, Interface for viewing reports of test results.	Yes, visualization via the report interface and scoring quizzes	Yes
Glossary	Yes, 'Glossary' tool	No	Yes	No	No	Yes	Yes, Glossary Module	Yes	Yes, Glossary Module
Report on the frequency or the use of a course	Yes, 'My Tracker' tool	Yes, through a tracking interface	No	Yes, tracking student progress via 'Course reports' interface	Yes	Yes, 'Statistics and Learning Progress' tool	Yes, «*Rapports d'activités*» tool	Yes	Yes, 'Statistics' tool
FUNCTIONAL APPROPRIATENESS									
Certification	Yes (Vucic, 2007)	Yes	No	Yes, 'Certificates per Lesson' plugin	No	Yes, Certificate of completing course objectives	Yes, 'Certificate' plugin	Yes, Certificate of completing the course (Connect-i, 2016)	Yes
Foyer (family group)	Yes, creating a discussion forum	Yes, creating a discussion forum	Yes, creating a home forum	Yes, creating a home forum	Yes, free discussion forum	Yes. free discussion forum	Yes, discussion forum by user (Moodle, 2019)	Yes, discussion forum by user	Yes, creating a discussion forum
Registration chat	Yes (Vucic, 2007)	Yes	Yes (+réseau social)	Yes	Yes	Yes	Yes, All sessions are recorded (Moodle, 2019)	Yes	Yes
Messaging	Yes, mail (Vucic, 2007)	Yes, internal messaging (Claroline, 2016)	Yes, internal e-mail and mailing	Yes, Using the 'Quick mails' tool	Yes	Yes, internal e-mail and mailing	Yes, messaging has existed since Moodle	Yes, internal e-mail and mailing (Connect-i, 2016)	Yes
Plagiarism detection tools	No	No	No	No	No	No, currently in production	Yes, plagiarism plugin 'Turnitin'	No	No
RSS / podcast	No	Yes	Yes, RSS (reading and emission)	Yes, RSS feed inside the lesson dashboard	Yes, RSS	Yes, RSS (reading and emission) and podCast	Yes	Yes, RSS (reading and emission)	Yes, Display the news contents via RSS (Whyte and Federico, 2018)

Resource Management (course)	Partial, sharing courses for the groups (Vucic, 2007) and not in activity spaces	Yes, share resources of activity spaces (community, 2016)	Yes, The integration of multimedia teaching resources	Yes. The integration of teaching resources	Yes. Multi-format teaching resource management	Yes, 'Course' tool	Yes, course management plugin (Moodle, 2019)	Yes, The integration of multimedia teaching resources (Connect-i, 2016)	Yes, integration of multimedia in the course.
Support of multiple authors	Yes, the teacher has the right to create and manage his course	Yes, the teacher has the right to create and manage his / her course	Yes, the teacher has the right to create and manage his / her course	Yes, the teacher has the right to create and manage his / her course	Yes, the teacher has the right to create, manage, and giving access right to tutors in his / her course	Yes, the teacher has the right to create and manage his / her course	Yes, the teacher has the right to create, manage, and giving access right to tutors in his / her course	Yes, the teacher has the right to create and manage his / her course	Yes, the teacher has the right to create and manage his / her course (Dooremont, 2014).
FUNCTIONAL CORRECTNESS									
Management of working time of learners and teachers	No, the LMS does not manage the learners' working time	No, the LMS does not manage the learners' working time	No, the LMS does not manage the learners' working time	No, the LMS does not manage the learners' working time	No, the LMS does not manage the learners' working time	No, the LMS does not manage the learners' working time	No, the LMS does not manage the learners' working time	No, the LMS does not manage the learners' working time	No, the LMS does not manage the learners' working time
Results and notes	Yes, ' Tests and Surveys' module	Yes	Yes, Hotspot, matrix, and correspondance questions tools…	Yes, 'Gradebook' tool which managing of students' notes	Yes, solution of sending and correcting homework	Yes, using 'Test and assessment' tool	Yes. All given notes in forums and tests (Moodle, 2019)	Yes, 'Quiz certificates' module	Yes (Dooremont, 2014)
Notes display	Yes	Yes	Yes	Yes	Yes	Yes	Yes	Yes	Yes
Tracking statistics of course	Yes, ' tests and surveys' tool	Yes, monitoring tools of the learners' activities (Claroline, 2016).	Yes	Partial, 'Reports' space to tracking user statistics, courses and lessons.	Yes, a statistic tracking module of the LMS users.	Yes, 'Statistics and Learning Progress' space	Yes, activity reports are available with graphs (Moodle, 2019)	Yes, 'Statistics ' and 'Quiz Statistics' module	Yes, statistics of learner visits (Knoop and Groen, 2012; Dooremont, 2014].
Control Connections (learners' tracking)	Yes, module ' Tests and Surveys'	Yes, monitoring tools, statistics; + dashboard (Claroline, 2016)	Yes	Yes, 'Reports' space to tracking user statistics.	Partial, supervisory tools to tracking of learners / missing dashboard	Partial, supervisory tools to tracking of learners / missing dashboard	Yes, supervision tools (groups, activities, etc.); + dashboard.	Yes, Monitoring the result of the class or the course (Connect-i, 2016)	Yes (Dooremont, 2014)
Report on the test results	Yes, ' tests and surveys' tool	No	Yes	Yes, tracking student progress via 'Lesson reports' interface.	No	Yes. 'Statistics and Learning Progress' interface	Yes, Interface for viewing reports of test results.	Yes, visualization via the report interface and scoring quizzes	Yes
Glossary	Yes, 'Glossary' tool	No	Yes	No	No	Yes	Yes, Glossary Module	Yes	Yes, Glossary Module
Report on the frequency or the use of a course	Yes, 'My Tracker' tool	Yes, through a tracking interface	No	Yes, tracking student progress via 'Course reports' interface	Yes	Yes, 'Statistics and Learning Progress' tool	Yes, «*Rapports d'activités*» tool	Yes	Yes, 'Statistics' tool
FUNCTIONAL APPROPRIATENESS									
Certification	Yes (Vucic, 2007)	Yes	No	Yes, 'Certificates per Lesson' plugin	No	Yes, Certificate of completing course objectives	Yes, 'Certificate' plugin	Yes, Certificate of completing the course (Connect-i, 2016)	Yes
Foyer (family group)	Yes, creating a discussion forum	Yes, creating a discussion forum	Yes, creating a home forum	Yes, creating a home forum	Yes, free discussion forum	Yes. free discussion forum	Yes, discussion forum by user (Moodle, 2019)	Yes, discussion forum by user	Yes, creating a discussion forum
Registration chat	Yes (Vucic, 2007)	Yes	Yes (+réseau social)	Yes	Yes	Yes	Yes, All sessions are recorded (Moodle, 2019)	Yes	Yes
Messaging	Yes, mail (Vucic, 2007)	Yes, internal messaging (Claroline, 2016)	Yes, internal e-mail and mailing	Yes, Using the 'Quick mails' tool	Yes	Yes, internal e-mail and mailing	Yes, messaging has existed since Moodle	Yes, internal e-mail and mailing (Connect-i, 2016)	Yes
Plagiarism detection tools	No	No	No	No	No	No, currently in production	Yes, plagiarism plugin 'Turnitin'	No	No
RSS / podcast	No	Yes	Yes, RSS (reading and emission)	Yes, RSS feed inside the lesson dashboard	Yes, RSS	Yes, RSS (reading and emission) and podCast	Yes	Yes, RSS (reading and emission)	Yes, Display the news contents via RSS (Whyte and Federico, 2018)

Table 5. Performance efficiency analyis of the selected LMSs

LMS's name	Atutor*	Claroline Connect*	Chamilo Connect*	Efront*	Formagri*	Ilias*	Moodle*	Opigno*	Sakai*
RESOURCE UTILIZATION									
Is that LMS functionalities tools meet the distance requirements Learning	Partial. functionalities tools partially meet to the distance learning requirements	Partial. functionalities tools partially meet to the distance learning requirements	Partial. functionalities tools partially meet to the distance learning requirements	Partial. functionalities tools partially meet to the distance learning requirements	Partial. functionalities tools partially meet to the distance learning requirements	Partial. functionalities tools partially meet to the distance learning requirements	Partial. functionalities tools partially meet to the distance learning requirements	Partial. functionalities tools partially meet to the distance learning requirements	Partial. functionalities tools partially meet to the distance learning requirements
CAPACITY									
Is that the LMS meets all the distance requirements learning	Partial, the LMS does not meet all the distance learning requirements	Partial, the LMS does not meet all the distance learning requirements	Partial, the LMS does not meet all the distance learning requirements	Partial, the LMS does not meet all the distance learning requirements	Partial, the LMS does not meet all the distance learning requirements	Partial, the LMS does not meet all the distance learning requirements	Partial, the LMS does not meet all the distance learning requirements	Partial, the LMS does not meet all the distance learning requirements	Partial, the LMS does not meet all the distance learning requirements
Assistance quality	Partial	Yes	Partial	Partial	Partial	Partial	Yes	Yes	Yes

Table 6. Compatibility analysis of the selected LMSs

LMS's name	Atutor*	Claroline Connect*	Chamilo Connect*	Efront*	Formagri*	Ilias*	Moodle*	Opigno*	Sakai*
CO-EXISTENCE									
Course transfer from one LMS to another	Yes, transfer of SCORM courses to an adapted LMS	Yes, transfer of SCORM courses to an adapted LMS	Yes, transfer of SCORM courses to an adapted LMS	Yes, transfer of SCORM courses to an adapted LMS	Yes, transfer of SCORM courses to an adapted LMS	Yes, transfer of SCORM courses to an adapted LMS	Yes, transfer of SCORM courses to an adapted LMS	Yes, transfer of SCORM courses to an adapted LMS	Yes, transfer of SCORM courses to an adapted LMS
SCORM	Yes. SCORM V.1.2/2004	Yes (Claroline, 2016)	Yes, SCORM V.1.2 -/2004 import-/export	Yes, SCORM V. 1.2 -/2004	Yes, SCORM V. 1.2 -/2004	Yes, SCORM V. 1.2 -/2004	Yes, SCORM V. 1.2 import-/2004	Yes, 2004 (Connect-i, 2016)	Yes (Knoop and Groen, 2012)
IMS QTI	Yes, QTI–V.1.2 and V.2.1	Partial, QTI being finalized	Yes, QTI–V.1.2 and V.2.0	No	Yes	No	Partial, QTI 2.0 export is still unfinished	Yes, QTI–V.1.2 and V.2.0	Yes
AICC	No	No	Partial	No	Yes	Yes	Yes	Partial	No
IMS XML	Yes, C/I/E CC-CP	No	No	Yes	No	No	Yes	No	No
INTEROPERABILITY									
Information and application sharing	Yes, via Dropbox and EWiki collaboration tools	Yes, via Wiki (Claroline, 2016), and shared files.	Yes, via the shared files, wiki and portfolio.	Yes, via 'Shared files' and 'eFront Wiki' tools	Yes, via the shared folders and "WikiDocs".	Yes, via the Wiki and portfolio, + the "Dropbox" tool	Yes, via Wiki collaboration (Moodle, 2019), + "Dropbox" tool	Yes, Wiki collaboration space	Yes, Wiki collaboration space
Interconnection LMS	No	Yes, LMSs exchange information (Claroline, 2016)	No	No	No	No	No	No	No
Import and export of resources	Yes, the LMS offers the ability to import and export of resources	Yes, the ability to import and export of resources	Yes, possibility to import and export resources	Yes, possibility to import and export resources	Yes, possibility to import and export resources	Yes, possibility to import and export resources	Yes, possibility to import and export resources	Yes, possibility to import and export resources	Yes, possibility to import and export resources
Using plugins	Yes	Yes	Yes	Yes	No	Yes	Yes	Yes	Yes

Table 7. Security analysis of the selected LMSs

LMS's name	Atutor*	Claroline Connect*	Chamilo Connect*	Efront*	Formagri*	Ilias*	Moodle*	Opigno*	Sakai*
CONFIDENTIALITY									
Secured by login / password	Yes, the user name and the password allow the system to authenticate each user's access	Yes, the user name and the password allow the system to authenticate each user's access	Yes, the user name and the password allow the system to authenticate each user's access	Yes, the user name and the password allow the system to authenticate each user's access	Yes, the user name and the password allow the system to authenticate each user's access	Yes, the user name and the password allow the system to authenticate each user's access	Yes, the user name and the password allow the system to authenticate each user's access	Yes, the user name and the password allow the system to authenticate each user's access	Yes, the user name and the password allow the system to authenticate each user's access
Assigning access rights	Yes, assign different access levels to the system based on the predefined roles	Yes, assign different access levels to the system based on the predefined roles	Yes, assign different access levels to the system based on the predefined roles	Yes, assign different access levels to the system based on the predefined roles	Yes, assign different access levels to the system based on the predefined roles	Yes, assign different access levels to the system based on the predefined roles	Yes, assign different access levels to the system based on the predefined roles	Yes, assign different access levels to the system based on the predefined roles	Yes, assign different access levels to the system based on the predefined roles
INTEGRITY									
Ability to use SSL	Yes, SSL protocol, certificates and TLS are supported via OpenSSL/1.0.1i toolbox	Yes, the protocol SSL, certificates and TLS are supported by the LMS	Yes, the protocol SSL, certificates and TLS are supported by the LMS	Yes, the protocol SSL, certificates and TLS are supported by the LMS	Yes, the protocol SSL, certificates and TLS are supported by the LMS	Yes, the protocol SSL, certificates and TLS are supported by the LMS	Yes, the protocol SSL, certificates and TLS are supported by the LMS	Yes, the protocol SSL, certificates and TLS are supported by the LMS	Yes, the protocol SSL, certificates and TLS are supported by the LMS
NON-REPUDIATION									
Tracking system	Yes, the LMS allows teachers to track learner progress via the 'My Tests and Surveys', and 'My Tracker' tools	Yes. Tracking learner progress via the dashboard, statistics and tracking of badges (Claroline, 2016)	Yes	Yes, the LMS allows teachers to track learner progress via the 'Reports' interface	Yes, the LMS allows teachers to track learner progress via statistical tracking module of the usages	Yes. Tracking learner progress via the 'Statistics and Learning Progress' tool	Yes, the LMS allows teachers to track learner progress.	Yes, the LMS allows teachers to track learner progress.	Yes, the LMS allows teachers to track learner progress.
Backup system	Yes, backup and restore of copies via the 'Backup Manager' tool.	No	No	Yes, Data backup via 'Backup - Restore' tool.	Yes, the LMS offers a data backup solution	No	Yes, the possibility of making backup copies and restore these copies.	No	Yes
ACCOUNTABILITY									
Barrier of security	Yes, a well secured workspace. Management of access rights and anti spam	Yes, a well secured workspace. Management of access rights (Claroline, 2016).	Partial, via the error detection tool using the log files / the workspace is not well secured	Yes, plugin 'Security' which manages a number of self-control	Partial, lack of error detection tools	Yes, via the 'Privacy and Security' tool + data are validated, cookies are encrypted	Yes, The forms are checked against an LDAP server, of a mail or newsgroup server.	Partial, lack of error detection tools	Partial, self register possible / lack of error detection tools
AUTHENTICITY									
Assigning username and password	Yes, assignment with login and password	Yes, assignment with login and password, + LDAP authentication (Claroline, 2016)	Yes, the system or course access is protected by username and password	Yes, the system or course access is protected by username and password	Yes, the system or course access is protected by username and password, + LDAP authentication, Sso-cas, etc.	Yes, the system or course access is protected by username and password	Yes, the system or course access is protected by username and password	Yes, the system or course access is protected by username and password	Yes, the system or course access is protected by username and password
Identity card	Yes (profile)	Yes (badge) (Claroline, 2016)	Yes (profile)	Yes (profile)	No	Yes (profile)	Yes (visit card)	Yes, dashboard (Connect-i, 2016)	Yes. Profile + social networks

Table 8. Maintainability analysis of the selected LMSs

LMS's name	Atutor*	Claroline Connect*	Chamilo Connect*	Efront*	Formagri*	Ilias*	Moodle*	Opigno*	Sakai*
MODULARITY									
Is that the LMS contains of discrete plugins	Yes	No	No	Yes	No	Yes	Yes	Yes	Yes
REUSABILITY									
Interaction with other operating systems (multi-operating systems)	Partial, interaction with Linux, Windows / and not with other operating systems	Partial, interaction with Linux, Windows / and not with other operating systems	Yes, Unix, GNU /Linux, FreeBSD, Windows, Mac OS X	No	Partial, interaction with Linux, Windows / and not with other operating systems	Yes, interaction with Linux, Mac OS X, Microsoft Windows	Yes, interaction with Unix, Linux, FreeBSD, Windows, Mac OSX, NetWare,	Yes, interaction with Unix, GNU /Linux, FreeBSD, Windows, Mac OS X	Yes, interaction with Unix, Linux, FreeBSD, MS Windows, Mac OS X
Interaction with other databases (multi-database)	No	No	No	No	No	No	Yes, MariaDB 5.5.31 ; MySQL 5.5.31 ; PostGreSQL 9.1 ; Oracle 10.2 ; MS SQL	Yes, MySQL 5.0.15 ; MariaDB 5.1.44 ; Percona Server 5.1.70 ; PostgreSQL ; SQLite	Yes, MySQL, Oracle DB, MariaDB, (IBM DB 2 only for Sakai 2.7x)
MODIFIABILITY									
Modifiability of the system without errors	Yes, the new version of the LMS is stable	No, the new version of the LMS is not stable yet	Yes, the new version of the LMS is stable	Yes, the new version of the LMS is stable	Yes, the new version of the LMS is stable	Yes, the new version of the LMS is stable	Yes, the new version of the LMS is stable	Yes, the new version of the LMS is stable	Yes, the new version of the LMS is stable
TESTABILITY									
Maintenance and updating	Yes, last updated 20 Jun. 2018	Yes, last updated 12 Dec. 2019	Yes, last updated 05 Aug. 2019	No, last updated 15 Jun. 2015	Yes, last updated 12 Oct 2018	Yes, last updated 06 Jan. 2019	Yes, last updated 03 Jan. 2019	Yes, last updated 19 Dec. 2019	Partial, last updated March 21, 2019

Table 9. Portability analysis of the selected LMSs

LMS's name	Atutor*	Claroline Connect*	Chamilo Connect*	Efront*	Formagri*	Ilias*	Moodle*	Opigno*	Sakai*
ADAPTABILITY									
Adaptation to mobiles terminals	Partial, interface adapted to responsive design	Partial, interface adapted to responsive design (Claroline, 2016)	Partial, interface adapted to responsive design	No	No	Partial, interface adapted to responsive design	Yes, interface adapted to responsive design (+ Moodle mobile App).	Partial, interface adapted to responsive design	Partial, interface adapted to responsive design
Compatibility with common browsers	Yes, the LMS is compatible with common browsers	Yes, the LMS is compatible with common browsers	Yes, the LMS is compatible with common browsers	Yes, the LMS is compatible with common browsers	Yes, the LMS is compatible with common browsers	Yes, the LMS is compatible with common browsers	Yes, the LMS is compatible with common browsers	Yes, the LMS is compatible with common browsers	Yes, the LMS is compatible with common browsers
Adapting to different training devices	Partial, the design of the LMS is adapted to the xMOOC, the SPOC and not to the cMOOC	Partial, the design of the LMS is adapted to the xMOOC, the SPOC and not to the cMOOC	No, the design of the LMS is not adapted to MOOC / SPOC	No, the design of the LMS is not adapted to MOOC / SPOC	No, the design of the LMS is not adapted to MOOC / SPOC	No, the design of the LMS is not adapted to MOOC / SPOC	Partial, the design of the LMS is adapted to the xMOOC, the SPOC and not to the cMOOC	Partial, the design of the LMS is adapted to the xMOOC, the SPOC and not to the cMOOC	Partial, the design of the LMS is adapted to the xMOOC, the SPOC and not to the cMOOC
INSTALLABILITY									
Instability of without errors LMS	Yes, easy installation of the LMS and without errors	Partial, some difficulties during the installation under Windows	Yes, easy installation of the LMS and without errors	Yes, easy installation and without errors	Yes, easy installation and without errors	Yes, easy installation of the LMS and without errors	Yes, easy installation of the LMS and without errors	Partial, blocking during installation	Yes, easy installation of the LMS and without errors
REPLACEABILITY									
Replaceability with the new LMS version	No	No, migration from Caroline is in realization progress (Claroline, 2016)	No	No	No	No	Yes, the LMS offers the possibility of replacing the old version	Yes, the LMS offers the possibility of replacing the old version	Yes, the LMS offers the possibility of replacing the old version

Table 10. Usability analysis of the selected LMSs

LMS's name	Atutor*	Claroline Connect*	Chamilo Connect*	Efront*	Formagri*	Ilias*	Moodle*	Opigno*	Sakai*
Appropriateness recognizability	Yes, the LMS is very intuitive	Yes, the LMS is very intuitive	Yes, the LMS is very intuitive	Yes, the LMS is very intuitive	Yes, the LMS is very intuitive	Yes, the LMS is very intuitive	Yes, the LMS is very intuitive	Yes, the LMS is very intuitive	Yes, the LMS is very intuitive
Learnability	Partial, the LMS is partially easy to handle	Yes, the LMS is easy to handle	No, the LMS is not easy to handle	Yes, the LMS is easy to handle	Yes, the LMS is easy to handle	Partial, the LMS is partially easy to handle	Yes, the LMS is easy to handle	Yes, the LMS is easy to handle	Yes, the LMS is easy to handle
Operability	Partial, the LMS is dynamic and almost easy to apprehend	Yes, the LMS is dynamic and easy to apprehend	Yes, the LMS is dynamic and easy to apprehend	Yes, the LMS is dynamic and easy to apprehend	Partial, the LMS is dynamic and almost easy to apprehend	Partial, the LMS is dynamic and almost easy to apprehend	Yes, the LMS is dynamic and easy to apprehend	Yes, the LMS is dynamic and easy to apprehend	Yes, the LMS is dynamic and easy to apprehend
User error protection	Yes, haute protection contre les erreurs utilisateur	Partial, average protection against user errors	Yes, high protection against user errors	Yes, high protection against user errors	Yes, high protection against user errors	Yes, high protection against user errors	Yes, high protection against user errors	Partial, average protection against user errors	Yes, high protection against user errors
User interface aesthetics	Yes, typography, graphic design and chosen colors correspond to the aesthatic requirements	Yes, typography, graphic design and chosen colors correspond to the aesthetic requirements	Yes, typography, graphic design and chosen colors correspond to the aesthetic requirements	Yes, typography, graphic design and chosen colors correspond to the aesthetic requirements	Partial, typography, graphic design and chosen colors do not all correspond to the aesthetic requirements	Partial, typography, graphic design and chosen colors do not all correspond to the aesthetic requirements	Yes, typography, graphic design and chosen colors correspond to the aesthetic requirements	Yes, typography, graphic design and chosen colors correspond to the aesthetic requirements	Yes, typography, graphic design and chosen colors correspond to the aesthetic requirements
Accessibility	Yes, extremely readable and incentive LMS	Yes, extremely readable and incentive LMS	Yes, extremely readable and incentive LMS	Yes, extremely readable and incentive LMS	Partial, partially readable and incentive LMS	Yes, extremely readable and incentive LMS	Yes, extremely readable and incentive LMS	Yes, extremely readable and incentive LMS	Yes, extremely readable and incentive LMS
Reliability	Partial, the LMS does not respond to all distance training expectations	Partial, the LMS does not respond to all distance training expectations	Partial, the LMS does not respond to all distance training expectations	Partial, the LMS does not respond to all distance training expectations	Partial, the LMS does not respond to all distance training expectations	Partial, the LMS does not respond to all distance training expectations	Yes, the LMS does respond to all distance training expectations	Partial, the LMS does not respond to all distance training expectations	Partial, the LMS does not respond to all distance training expectations
Guidance / Feedback	Yes, Immediate feedback	Yes, Immediate feedback	Yes, Immediate feedback	Yes. Immediate feedback	Yes. Immediate feedback	Yes. Immediate feedback	Yes. Immediate feedback	Yes. Immediate feedback	Yes. Immediate feedback

LMS's name	Atutor*	Claroline Connect*	Chamilo Connect*	Efront*	Formagri*	Ilias*	Moodle*	Opigno*	Sakai*
Appropriateness recognizability	Yes, the LMS is very intuitive	Yes, the LMS is very intuitive	Yes, the LMS is very intuitive	Yes, the LMS is very intuitive	Yes, the LMS is very intuitive	Yes, the LMS is very intuitive	Yes, the LMS is very intuitive	Yes, the LMS is very intuitive	Yes, the LMS is very intuitive
Learnability	Partial, the LMS is partially easy to handle	Yes, the LMS is easy to handle	No, the LMS is not easy to handle	Yes, the LMS is easy to handle	Yes, the LMS is easy to handle	Partial, the LMS is partially easy to handle	Yes, the LMS is easy to handle	Yes, the LMS is easy to handle	Yes, the LMS is easy to handle
Operability	Partial, the LMS is dynamic and almost easy to apprehend	Yes, the LMS is dynamic and easy to apprehend	Yes, the LMS is dynamic and easy to apprehend	Yes, the LMS is dynamic and easy to apprehend	Partial, the LMS is dynamic and almost easy to apprehend	Partial, the LMS is dynamic and almost easy to apprehend	Yes, the LMS is dynamic and easy to apprehend	Yes, the LMS is dynamic and easy to apprehend	Yes, the LMS is dynamic and easy to apprehend
User error protection	Yes, haute protection contre les erreurs utilisateur	Partial, average protection against user errors	Yes, high protection against user errors	Yes, high protection against user errors	Yes, high protection against user errors	Yes, high protection against user errors	Yes, high protection against user errors	Partial, average protection against user errors	Yes, high protection against user errors
User interface aesthetics	Yes, typography, graphic design and chosen colors correspond to the aesthetic requirements	Yes, typography, graphic design and chosen colors correspond to the aesthetic requirements	Yes, typography, graphic design and chosen colors correspond to the aesthetic requirements	Yes, typography, graphic design and chosen colors correspond to the aesthetic requirements	Partial, typography, graphic design and chosen colors do not all correspond to the aesthetic requirements	Partial, typography, graphic design and chosen colors do not all correspond to the aesthetic requirements	Yes, typography, graphic design and chosen colors correspond to the aesthetic requirements	Yes, typography, graphic design and chosen colors correspond to the aesthetic requirements	Yes, typography, graphic design and chosen colors correspond to the aesthetic requirements
Accessibility	Yes, extremely readable and incentive LMS	Yes, extremely readable and incentive LMS	Yes, extremely readable and incentive LMS	Yes, extremely readable and incentive LMS	Partial, partially readable and incentive LMS	Yes, extremely readable and incentive LMS	Yes, extremely readable and incentive LMS	Yes, extremely readable and incentive LMS	Yes, extremely readable and incentive LMS
Reliability	Partial, the LMS does not respond to all distance training expectations	Partial, the LMS does not respond to all distance training expectations	Partial, the LMS does not respond to all distance training expectations	Partial, the LMS does not respond to all distance training expectations	Partial, the LMS does not respond to all distance training expectations	Partial, the LMS does not respond to all distance training expectations	Yes, the LMS does respond to all distance training expectations	Partial, the LMS does not respond to all distance training expectations	Partial, the LMS does not respond to all distance training expectations
Guidance / Feedback	Yes, Immediate feedback	Yes, Immediate feedback	Yes, Immediate feedback	Yes. Immediate feedback	Yes, Immediate feedback	Yes. Immediate feedback	Yes. Immediate feedback	Yes. Immediate feedback	Yes. Immediate feedback

Table 11. Critical analysis results of analyzed LMSs

LMSs Utility and Usability Degree			ATutor	Claroline Connect	Chamilo Connect	Efront	Formagri	Ilias	Moodle	Opigno	Sakai
Utility specifications	Functional suitability	Score = ∑ Scores	102	94	84	100	84	104	112	106	106
		CI = ∑ Scores / 29	3,52	3,24	2,90	3,45	2,90	3,59	3,86	3,66	3,66
	Performance efficiency	Score = ∑ Scores	6	8	6	6	6	6	8	8	8
		CI = ∑ Scores / 3	2,00	2,67	2,00	2,00	2,00	2,00	2,67	2,67	2,67
	Compatibility	Score = ∑ Scores	28	26	26	24	24	26	30	26	24
		CI = ∑ Scores / 9	3,11	2,89	2,89	2,67	2,67	2,89	3,33	2,89	2,67
	Security	Score = ∑ Scores	32	28	26	32	26	28	32	26	30
		CI = ∑ Scores / 8	4,00	3,50	3,25	4,00	3,25	3,50	4,00	3,25	3,75
	Maintainability	Score = ∑ Scores	12	4	10	12	8	16	20	20	18
		CI = ∑ Scores / 5	2,40	0,80	2,00	2,40	1,60	3,20	4,00	4,00	3,60
	Portability	Score = ∑ Scores	12	10	10	8	8	10	18	14	16
		CI = ∑ Scores / 5	2,40	2,00	2,00	1,60	1,60	2,00	3,60	2,80	3,20
	Results	Total Score = ∑ Scores	192	170	162	182	156	190	220	200	202
		% Qm = ∑ Scores / 236	81,36%	72,03%	68,64%	7,12%	66,10%	80,51%	93,22%	84,75%	85,59%
Usability specifications	Usability criteria	Score = ∑ Scores	26	28	26	30	24	24	32	28	30
		CI = ∑ Scores / 8	3,25	3,50	3,25	3,75	3,00	3,00	4,00	3,50	3,75
	Results	Total Score = ∑ Scores	26	28	26	30	24	24	32	28	30
		% Qm = ∑ Scores / 32	81.25%	87,50%	81,25%	93,75%	75,00%	75,00%	100%	87,50%	93,75%
General results		Total Score = ∑ Scores	218	198	188	212	180	214	252	228	232
		% Qm = ∑ Scores / 268	81%	74%	70%	79%	67%	80%	94%	85%	87%
Quality Level			Very good	Good	Good	Good	Good	Good	Very good	Very good	Very good

Chapter 4
A New Smart Recommendation System of Learning Management Systems

ABSTRACT

This chapter presents the functional and technical architecture of a recommendation system of free learning management systems that the authors have implemented to facilitate the choice of the most suitable LMS to meet the objectives, specifications, and criteria chosen by the institution. Thus, any random choice entails a loss of money, effort, and time loss for porters and device designers, and this is for various reasons (cost, utility, usability, etc.). Notably, this system takes into account more than 20 LMSs. The choice of these LMSs is based on a methodical and systemic approach that identifies the adequate criteria to the objectives and specifications chosen by the institution, depending on the objects and pedagogical tools related to the recommended teaching and learning device, to retain the most suitable LMS. This chapter is motivated by the desire to clarify and support users in their choice of the most suitable LMS to meet their needs and to get maximum benefit from the potential offered by technologies in pedagogy.

DOI: 10.4018/978-1-7998-4021-3.ch004

INTRODUCTION

E-learning is a fast and efficient way of providing and sharing knowledge with learners in different parts of the world. According to (Liu, 2010; Karim and al., 2013), it is defined as the following: "E-learning uses the Internet or other digital content for learning and education activities, that takes full advantage of modern educational technology to provide a new mechanism for communication and learning environment rich in resources to achieve a new way of learning."

In the 20th century, there was an international movement in favor of e-learning integration in higher education. This movement has been operationalized due to the variety of the educational offer by universities, which most have opted to diversify knowledge dissemination means (sounds, images, animations ... etc.) to meet the needs of their target public. If access to knowledge was previously conditioned by the physical presence in the classroom, technology enables its learners to exceed this condition of presence and be opened towards other learning modalities today. We can say that e-learning provides solutions in the context of distance learning without claiming to represent the solution to all educational dysfunctions. Among these solutions, distance learning seems to be the challenge ahead to face the new training requirements in the digital era.

In the case of our study, the e-learning solutions that interest us are free LMSs, because their costs, their states of development, their directions, and used technologies rendered them very close to the axis of this study.

During the last decade, LMSs have evolved a lot. However, several comparative studies have been developed previously (Dimet, 2006; Menasri, 2004; DOGBE-SEMANOU and al., 2007; Kaddouri and Bouamri, 2010; EL MAWAS and al., 2014; OVAREP, 2000; Graf and List, 2005; Galloy and al., 2002; Caro Dambreville and al., 2008), but they have been abandoned because their life cycle is changing apace. In such a context of proliferation of the training, the choice becomes difficult.

Consequently, any random choice causes a loss of money, effort, and time.

Thereby, we developed a recommendation system of LMSs, based on a comparative and analytical study of the free LMSs (Ouadoud and al., 2016); to facilitate the choice of the most suitable LMS according to the objectives and specifications of any institution, and this is based on an evaluation approach of the LMSs quality (Ouadoud and al., 2016).

For our study, in section 3, we present the functional architecture of the recommendation system of used LMSs. This section mainly consists of three subsections:

1. The system will facilitate the selection of the LMS and will allow choosing the one that suits best your training ecosystem.
2. The system gives you the possibility to choose the characteristics and pedagogical tools adapted to your specifications.
3. The system does the analysis and treatment of the choices obtained, to recommend the most suitable LMS to institutional goals.

LEADERTICE.COM RECOMMENDATION SYSTEM

LeaderTICE.com is a recommendation system of free LMSs, under the GNU / GPL V3 (Ouadoud, 2019), that we implemented (Ouadoud, 2019) to facilitate the choice of LMSs, seeing that any random choice entails money, effort, and time loss to porters and systems designers, and this is for various reasons (cost, utility, usability ...). Notably, this system takes into account several LMSs selected among 600 LMSs listed by the THOT CURSUS directory (LMSs directory, LMS, and LCMS LMSs).

The LeaderTICE.com system is mainly based on our evaluation approach of the LMSs' quality (Ouadoud and al., 2016). Several LMSs evaluation approaches were encountered in the literature (Lablidi and al., 2009; Aska and al., 2000). However, they have not been adopted, because these studies are focusing on the functional aspect mainly, forgetting other very important aspects such as security, maintainability, portability, compatibility, performance efficiency, and usability. For this reason, the implementation of the system is based on a methodical and systemic approach (Ouadoud and al., 2016) taking into account the software engineering aspects, learning theories, and current educational tools. Our main goal is to propose the most suitable LMS, which meshes with the objectives and contexts of teaching and learning of any institution.

FUNCTIONAL ARCHITECTURE OF THE SYSTEM

Figure 1 illustrates the general principle of the LeaderTICE.com system functioning by presenting the main functionalities associated with the main actors. This figure represents the articulation between learning objects and pedagogical tools that might underlie your pedagogical scenario when exploring the recommendation system (of LMSs) LeaderTICE.com.

Figure 1. LeaderTICE.com recommendation system of LMSs

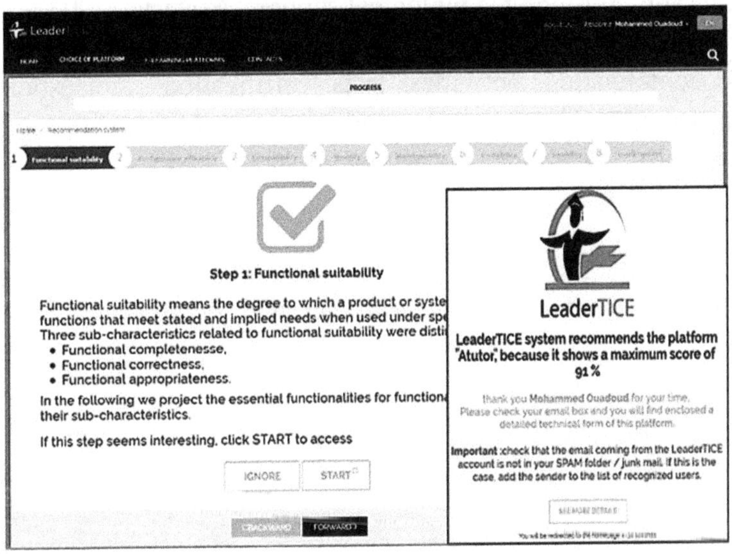

LeaderTICE.com allows you to choose the most suitable LMS for your objects and your requested pedagogical tools. Moreover, this is according to three main steps that have been distinguished according to the circuit shown in figure 2. These steps are the formalization of needs, the choice of pedagogical tools, the analysis, and the processing of the results.

1. Formalization of Needs

In the choice process, the formalization of needs will facilitate the selection of the LMS that will allow the dissemination of training. To choose the one that will be best integrated with our training ecosystem, we, therefore, must arbitrate between:

- The pedagogical situation, which presents a genuine assumed, of simultaneous and complementary way, that a certain destabilization same time is a chosen fulcrum (Astolfi, 1992), after determining the objectives, specifying the pedagogical used method (expositive, interrogative, collaborative work ...) and the used supports (documents, video, image ...).

- Learning Objects, which present the smallest information units or smallest information processing tools (applications or tutorials) used in a teaching context with a pedagogical intention aiming at facilitating the learning through technological support (Novasys, 2003).
- Functional or organizational pedagogical tools... such as forum, wiki, videoconferencing, activities, tests, certification... corresponding to your pedagogical expectations and your teaching/learning situation.
- Financial implications, any wrong choice of LMS will have financial repercussions.

Figure 2. Functional architecture of the LeaderTICE.com recommendation system of free LMSs

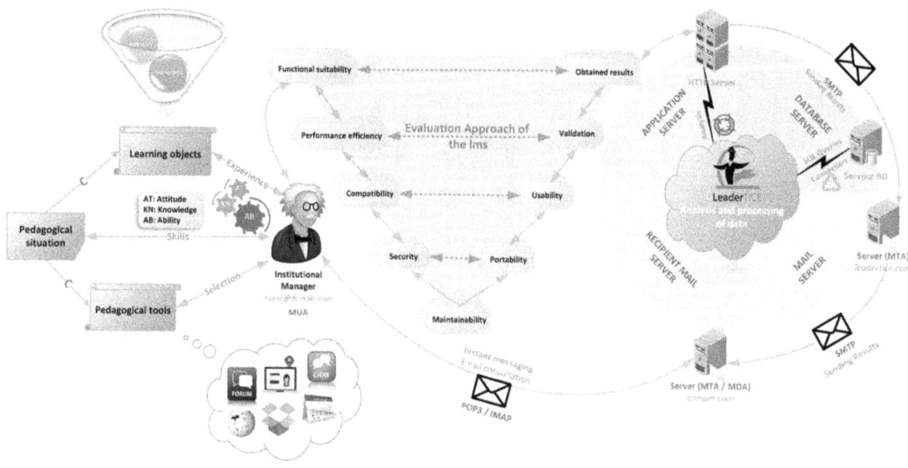

2. Choice of Pedagogical Tools

After the formalization of the needs, the institutional manager has to choose the characteristics and pedagogical tools adapted to the institutional specificities, according to a questionnaire based on an evaluation approach of the LMSs quality (Ouadoud and al., 2016). The latter presents an overview of the utility and usability dimensions with their adapted measures and criteria to evaluate LMSs. This approach is mainly composed of seven characteristics:

- Functional suitability means the degree to which a product or system provides functions that meet stated and implied needs when used under specified conditions.
- Performance efficiency, which means the performance relative to the number of resources used under stated conditions.
- Compatibility signifies the degree to which a product, system, or component can exchange information with other products, systems or components, and/or perform its required functions while sharing the same hardware or software environment.
- Security means the degree to which a product or system protects information and data so persons or other products or systems have the degree of data access appropriate to their types and levels of authorization.
- Maintainability. It means the degree of effectiveness and efficiency with which a product or system can be modified by the intended maintainers.
- Portability signifies the degree of effectiveness and efficiency with which a system, product, or component can be transferred from one hardware, software, or other operational or usage environment to another.
- Usability refers to the degree to which a product or system can be used by specified users to achieve specified goals with effectiveness, efficiency, and satisfaction in a specified context of use.

Thus, it should be mentioned that you have the right to choose just the adapted characteristics and sub-characteristics to your institutional needs, your technical imperatives, and your functional and organizational expectations.

Finally, before having validated your choices, you can do a general verification of your chosen characteristics by pressing the back button.

3. The Results Analysis and Processing

After validating your choices, the LeaderTICE.com system does the analysis and processing of results obtained by algorithmic programs interpreted in PHP language via an "Apache HTTP Server" application server, who took charge of the PHP language interpretation, the analysis and processing of the code, and interconnection to the MySQL database. To display the treatment result and recommend the most suitable LMS to your institutional goals, according to the criteria and specifications that you have expressed. Thereafter, the

"Apache HTTP Server" application server sends the results obtained in the previous step by mailing way via the SMTP communication protocol, used to transfer the electronic mails towards the mail server. Furthermore, the MTA mail server responsible for transport, by its turn, returns the mail of received results by the application server "Apache HTTP Server" by mailing way via the SMTP communication protocol toward the MTA recipient's mail server. Lastly, the latter delivers, then, the mail that contains the result obtained in the incoming electronic mail server (named MDA for Mail Delivery Agent), which then stores the mail in the meantime, via the POP3 / IMAP protocol which allows you to retrieve the electronic mail containing the result.

Figure 3. The quality model selected for choosing an LMS-type e-learning platform

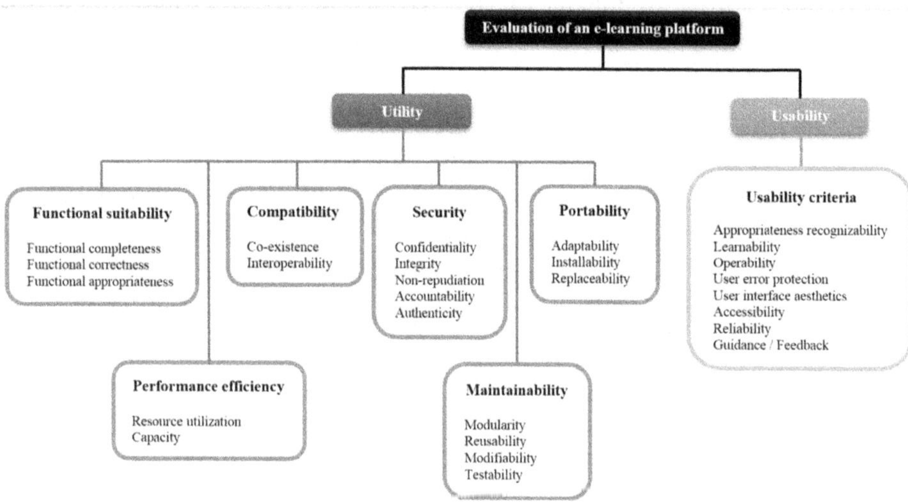

CONCLUSION

The subject of this chapter is very important because the free LMSs are, on the one hand, an actuality domain in Software Engineering and Pedagogical Engineering Multimedia. On the other hand, the application of these LMSs in e-learning reaches a vast clientele.

An LMS choice, pledge of success, and sustainability for the pedagogical system also seem inadequate with the free LMSs' philosophy and their community dynamic. Furthermore, academically, it seemed interesting to apply for the first time a recommendation system of the free LMSs based on a methodical and systemic approach inspired by software engineering to facilitate the choice of the most suitable LMS to the objectives and institutional specifications.

In a later phase, two important functionalities will be added to the system to facilitate recommending LMSs, namely:

- Implementation System. The system will offer the possibility to automatically install option the recommended LMS.
- Personalization system. The recommended LMS will be installed in a personalized manner according to the needs you have expressed.

In the next chapters, an experiment is therefore indispensable to validate what has been developed in the context of this chapter. Indeed, the latter will be based on the results of the establishing of a teaching/learning system in Moroccan university, based on an LMS known as intelligent and anthropocentric relying on reduced learning design, to enhance distance learning.

REFERENCES

Aska, L. P., & Klr.fr. (2000). *Choisir une solution de téléformation: 2000 study: l'offre de plates-formes et de portails de téléformation*. Academic Press.

Caro Dambreville, S. (2008). Evaluer un dispositif de formation à distance Principes et retour d'expérience. *Revue des Interactions Humaines Médiatisées, 19*(2). Accessed: http://europia.org/RIHM/V9N2/RIHM9(2)-3CaroDemberville.pdf

Dimet, B. (2006). *Etude comparative technique et pédagogique des plates-formes pour la formation ouverte et à distance*. Available: https://www.portices.fr/formation/Res/ Formation/Plateformes/Pf1Resume.html

Dogbe-Semanou, Koffi, D.A., Durand, A., Leproust, M., & Vanderstichel, H. (2007). Etude comparative de plates-formes de formation à distance. *le cadre du Projet@ 2L*. https://www.projet-plume.org/files/Choix_plateforme_a2l.pdf

El Mawas, N., Oubahssi, L., & Laforcade, P. (2014). *Étude comparative de plateformes de formation à distance*. GRAPHIT-D2.5&2.2. Available: http://www-lium.univ-lemans.fr/~laforcad/graphit/wp-content/uploads/2014/08/GRAPHIT-D2.52.2-V6.pdf

Galloy, S., Haas, C., & Lodewijck, M. (2002). *Analyse d'environnements de formation à distance*. CIFoP – Le Centre Interuniversitaire de Formation Permanente. Accessed: http://www.formahetice.ulg.ac.be/upload/wiki/b/b5/Document2.pdf

Graf, S., & List, B. (2005). An evaluation of open source e-learning platforms stressing adaptation issues. In Fifth IEEE International Conference on Advanced Learning Technologies (ICALT'05). https://dx.doi.org/10.1109/ICALT.2005.54

Kaddouri, M., & Bouamri, A. (2010). Usage de plateformes d'enseignement à distance dans l'enseignement supérieur marocain : avantages pédagogiques et difficultés d'appropriation. *Questions Vives. Recherches en éducation, 7*(14), 107–118.

Karim, F., & Goodwin, R. (2013, October-December). Using Cloud Computing in Elearning Systems. *International Journal of Advanced Research in Computer Science & Technology, 1*(1), 66–67.

Lablidi, A., Abourrich, A., & Talbi, M. (2009). *Démarche préconisée pour évaluer une plate-forme*. Association EPI. Available: www.epi.asso.fr/revue/articles/a0912b.htm

Menasri, S. (2004). *Etude comparative de plateformes d'enseignement en ligne (e-learning) utilisées dans un contexte universitaire*. Available: http://urfist.enc.sorbonne.fr/anciensite/archives/gremi/gremi10juin04/comparatif.htm#

Ouadoud, M. (2019). *LeaderTICE – Choosing e-learning platform*. Available: http://leadertice.com/ChoixDePlateforme

Ouadoud, M., Chkouri, M. Y., Nejjari, A., & El Kadiri, K. E. (2016). Studying and Analyzing the Evaluation Dimensions of LMSs Relying on a Software Engineering Approach. *International Journal of Emerging Technologies in Learning, 11*, 11–20. doi:10.3991/ijet.v11i01.4924

Ouadoud, M., Chkouri, M. Y., Nejjari, A., & El-Kadiri, K. E. (2016). Studying and comparing the free e-learning platforms. In 2016 4th IEEE International Colloquium on Information Science and Technology (CiSt). https://dx.doi.org/10.1109/CIST.2016.7804953

OVAREP (Observatoire des ressources multimédias). (2000). *Étude comparative technique et pédagogique des plateformes pour la formation ouverte et à distance*. Author.

ADDITIONAL READING

Kats, Y. (2010). *Learning Management Systems Technologies and Software Solutions for Online Teaching: Tools and Applications*. IGI/Information Science Research. doi:10.4018/978-1-61520-853-1

Kats, Y. (2013). *Learning Management Systems and Instructional Design: Metrics, Standards and Applications*. IGI/Information Science Research. doi:10.4018/978-1-4666-3930-0

Ouadoud, M., Chafiq, T., Rida, N., & Chkouri, M. Y. (2019). Generate a Meta-Model Content for Collaboration Space of Learning Management System Compatible with IMS-LD. [iJIM]. *International Journal of Interactive Mobile Technologies*, *13*(01), 37–52. doi:10.3991/ijim.v13i01.9440

Ouadoud, M., & Chkouri, M. Y. (2019). Generate a Meta-Model Content for Communication Space of Learning Management System Compatible with IMS-LD. In M. Ezziyyani (Ed.), *Advanced Intelligent Systems for Sustainable Development (AI2SD'2018), Advances in Intelligent Systems and Computing* (pp. 24–39). Springer International Publishing. doi:10.1007/978-3-030-11928-7_3

Ouadoud, M., & Chkouri, M. Y. (2019). Designing an IMS-LD Model for Communication Space of Learning Management System. In M. Ezziyyani (Ed.), *Advanced Intelligent Systems for Sustainable Development (AI2SD'2018), Advances in Intelligent Systems and Computing* (pp. 40–54). Springer International Publishing. doi:10.1007/978-3-030-11928-7_4

KEY TERMS AND DEFINITIONS

HTTP: Hypertext transfer protocol.

MTA: Mail transfer agent.

SMTP: Simple mail transfer protocol.

THOT CURSUS: Is a directory of LMSs, LCMS, and other systems for content and learning management.

Chapter 5
Educational Modeling of a New Smart Learning Management System

ABSTRACT

The problems of most LMSs are first of all of a pedagogical nature and then of a technical one. Studying these interrelated problems provides a useful conceptual reference that enables us to design a new model for a more relevant solution. In this chapter, a new conceptual model of an LMS is presented. The model, which stems from a methodological and systemic approach, is based on the hybridization between four learning theories, namely the traditional pedagogy, behaviorism, cognitivism, and social constructivism. The authors present at first each of these learning theories by discussing both their advantages and limits. The main principles of these learning theories and the technical functionalities of the proposed LMS that result from the hybridization of these principles are outlined. They finally discuss the implications of the new conceptual model for how to design and develop a new LMS that fits the needs of their final users, in particular learners.

INTRODUCTION

In light of our studies (Ouadoud, Feb. 2016; Ouadoud, 2017; Ouadoud, Jan. 2018) and the previous (Poulova and al., 2015; El-Mawas and al., 2014; Kaddouri and Bouamri, 2010; Dambreville, 2008; Dogbe-Semanou and al., 2007; Dimet, 2006; Graf and List, 2005; Itmazi and Megías, 2005; Menasri,

DOI: 10.4018/978-1-7998-4021-3.ch005

2004; Paulsen and al., 2003; Galloy and al., 2002; The OVAREP, 2000) ones we think that most of the free and commercial e-learning platforms, including the LMS, were initially developed a decade ago, based on a classical training model. The teacher is considered as the one who holds knowledge and transmits it, according to different modalities, to learners to foster their learning. Most e-learning platforms that are developed are mostly TMS (Teaching Management System), which is to say tools at the teacher's service to create and manage courses rather than in the service of learners and the learning process. They are always part of a uniform and techno-centric logic and architecture that reduced the learning conception to a particular pedagogical theory independently of others (Ouadoud, 2016). Therefore, we have decided to work on a new conceptual model that combines learning theories to promote both the teaching and learning processes.

The proposed LMS which results from our new conceptual model and which we plan to implement at a later stage is software-based on collaborative learning. Both teachers and learners can create, organize, and propose different types of activities (forum, wiki, blog…) as they like. Furthermore, they can access and manage their interactions via these activities where and when they want according to their needs and objectives in terms of learning.

Our LMS will be modeled on the idea that we should give the same possibilities of action to both teachers and learners of distributing their control on the platform. For example, a personal office and different spaces of activities will make available to all users of the proposed LMS in a way that enables them to personalize them using a variety of web services. This is what ensures more interactivity and knowledge sharing. Moreover, tracking services will provide to track users' activities and interactions with different tools.

The use of any tool in the field of education must be justified according to its pedagogical support and its capacity to address the real needs of its final users, particularly learners. However, it should be noted that although seen as an effective solution for overcoming space-time restrictions, the platforms might be an obstacle for the learning process to the extent that the pedagogical principles are neglected during their design. Thus, when designing our LMS we have tried to answer at first the following questions:

- How an LMS should be modeled to fit better the requirements of standards and norms of e-learning programs?

- To what degree of specificity could the LMS respond as an innovative technical system? And on what engineering methods should the modeling of an LMS be based?
- To what degree of specificity, the learning theories could promote online learning?

These and many other questions were investigated within our conceptual model. Our objective was to test and to check if our proposed model is worthy and useful for the design, development, and diffusion of e-learning systems, particularly the LMS.

The present study attempts to bring some light into the questions above by exposing at first the four learning theories that were judged the most important and relevant to our modeling, namely the traditional pedagogy, behaviorism, cognitivism, and social constructivism. Then, these learning theories which have inspired for a long time the design of computer applications are combined and put into perspective with several emergent pedagogical functionalities to build original modeling for our new LMS. Reveals that this proposed modeling that is presented to readers here looks for ways to leverage technology for learning by considering users as being human actors and not human factors (Henri, 2007).

THE MAIN THEORETICAL CURRENTS

Educational sciences draw their theoretical foundations of psychology, sociology, philosophy, and cognitive science, among others. This diversity of theoretical fields at the base of the different approaches to teaching and learning can sometimes be confusing, insofar as some authors may find themselves inside of more than one theoretical current. Currently, the majority of educational theorists agree to group teaching and learning models according to four currents: traditional pedagogy, behaviorist, cognitivist and social constructivist.

This chapter describes the four previously mentioned currents, in a synthetic way that identifies the main characteristics and technologically adapted tools. Besides, it contains examples that illustrate the underlying key concepts and make the link with the LMS e-learning platform. Addressed from a historical perspective, this document intends to nourish the reflection of teachers who want to situate their educational practices inside a conceptual framework and to appreciate the complexity and impact of their pedagogical actions.

Figure 1. History and evolution of the theoretical currents of learning adapted from Minier (In Kozanitis) (Kozanitis, 2005)

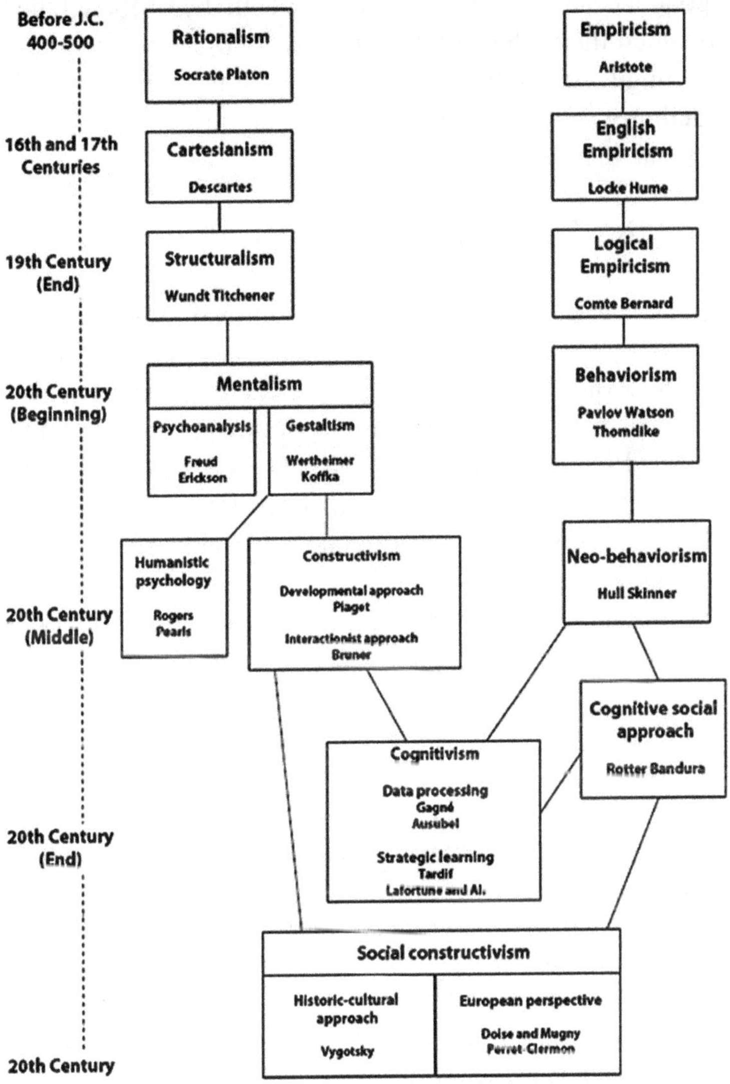

LMS AND THE UNDERLYING LEARNING THEORIES

Although the considerable potential of the LMS in the construction of knowledge and competence development, the latter can generate a real pedagogical success only if, their use relies on solid and proven learning theories (Paquette, 2002).

In the next part, we will evoke the transposition of the use of four learning theories in the design and development of LMS. For that purpose, we will do the correspondence between the tools available in the LMS and the learning theories to which they refer. As the latter part will show, the hybridization of these learning theories that we have judged more important and relevant to our modeling work can only be a source of enrichment to improve the quality of online learning.

1. LMS and the Traditional Pedagogy

The conception of learning as supported by traditional pedagogy is essentially relying on a direct and systematic mode of transmission. Indeed, we put forward the authoritarian role of the teacher who must deliver fixed and unchanging knowledge, evaluate and involve learners by following the different stages of a pre-established scenario. From this perspective, learners are only passive recipients of the information who respond ideally to external factors provided by their teacher in advance in a particular environment. In this way, they develop their knowledge.

Among the main ideas that are associated with the traditional pedagogy (Morandi, 2006), we mention:

- Lecture-based teaching: this idea generally refers to the teaching-centered pedagogy in which the teacher is the main provider of subject content to learners. The acquisition of knowledge is assessed through various operations of reproduction such as recitation, examination, and practical exercises.
- The idea of transmission and reception: we consider that the teacher delivers knowledge in ways that are clear, concise, and transparent and the learner receives it without any difficulty of memorizing understanding, and reproduction.
- Individualism: the learner is a part of a group, but still works individually. No exchange between learners is allowed. This implies an absence of debate, dialogue, and communication. Everything is centralized around and by the teacher.
- The sanction: the role of the teacher is to identify errors. Learners are classified to generate a spirit of competition between them. Those who fail to learn are those who commit one or many errors.

These main ideas from the traditional pedagogy have had an impact on the design and development of LMS, which focuses on learning by the reception. Indeed, this kind of software integrates different spaces to allow teachers to organize, structure, exposing their knowledge, and particularly assessing the learning progress. Thus, a central place is given to teachers, who do have the necessary tools to deliver knowledge and engage learners in the proposed learning activities of reproduction, consultation, and execution.

In general, we think that the contribution of the traditional pedagogy is so valuable to the extent that it allows teachers to facilitate and assist learners by making at their disposal well-structured information based on over-prescriptive scenarios. However, traditional pedagogy has its limits that rely very much on the fact that learners who are considered as the main actors in the teaching-learning process are widely neglected. Their needs are not taken into consideration and they are only seen as passive receivers of knowledge.

2. LMS and the Behaviorism

Behaviorism is a learning theory concerned with the study of human observable behavior (Tavris, 1999) without recourse to inner mental states (Good, 1995). It is built on the assumption that the brain is only a black box that no one can access.

The term "behaviorism" appeared at the beginning of the 20th century in parallel with the works of the American psychologist John Watson. This latter is considered the pioneer of behaviorism. He proposed making general psychology a scientific discipline by using experimental laboratory methods to set exploitable results that can then statistically evaluated (Watson, 1972). Works of the physiologist Ivan Pavlov on the conditioning of animals influenced Watson. This leads him to admit that all behavior operates on a principle of "stimulus-response" or what is called "classical conditioning".

In the same vision, Fechner comparing an individual to a black box, which we do not know what is going inside it, but may help us to predict certain behavior. Indeed, by providing specific stimuli we always get the same output results (Raynal, 1997; Chekour, 2015).

Behaviorist theories consider that learning consists of acquiring a new behavior or modifying an existing one. From a psychological viewpoint, Fablet defines learning as: *"a more or less durable effects process whereby new behaviors are acquired or already existing ones are modified the environment" [The translation is ours]* (Fablet, 2007).

For the advocates of behaviorism (such as Pavlov and Skinner), the learning process is perceived in a very simplistic way as an external change in human behavior that results from specific instrumental conditioning. This means that the confrontation of any individual with a discriminative stimulus inevitably leads usually to the emergence of constructing responses over time. To teach a certain skill, the behaviorist approach proposes to break it down into sub-objectives, which have to be simultaneously assimilated and mastered. In this perspective, the teacher should be able to present information to learners under restricted stimulus associated with reinforcement. The learners' role here is to respond to these stimuli by adopting the expected behavior. The teacher also proposes progressive practical exercises that allow checking the acquisition of knowledge while giving positive and/or negative feedback based on the responses provided. The type of pedagogical scenario that prevails, in that case, is the one, which highlights learning by the reception-exercises-test (see Figure 2).

The mark of behaviorism can be found in the LMS which displays systematic exercises allowing learning by repetition (trial and error) and in which the principles of conditioning are integrated.

Although behaviorism had focused more broadly on supporting the change of superficial behavior by allowing the development of certain procedural knowledge in an individual and progressive way, a deeper understanding of notions is not attainable from this perspective.

Behaviorism as a theory of learning to many advantages because:

- It is learner-centered.
- It streamlines the preparation of courses (objectives, evaluation).
- Students have sown path of success, until knowledge.
- This is a very good theory to promote the acquisition of automatisms.
- Beyond that, behaviorism seems to be criticized because:
- Intermediate objectives can be achieved without reaching the overall goal.
- There is a difficulty in transferring knowledge to a new situation (too much guiding).
- The student finds it difficult to make sense of the knowledge taught.

3. LMS and the Cognitivism

Cognitivism was born at the same time as Artificial Intelligence, in 1956. Miller and Bruner proposed it in reaction to Behaviorism. The focus was put on the ways of thinking and solving problems. The main idea was that learning cannot be limited to a conditioned recording, but should rather be considered as a complex process of knowledge acquisition. Memory has its structure, which involves the organization of information and the use of management strategies (Crozat, 2002).

Cognitive psychology considers that there are three broad categories of knowledge: declarative, procedural, and conditional knowledge. This invites the teacher to develop different strategies to facilitate the integration of each of them because they are represented differently in memory; the declarative knowledge answers to the "WHAT", the procedural knowledge to the "HOW" and the conditional knowledge to the "WHEN" and to the "WHY" (In Chekour and al.) (Chekour, 2015).

There are different categories of cognitive strategies, namely: the cognitive strategies and the metacognitive ones. These strategies can be used in systematic teaching. The authors (Pressley, 1990; Weinstein, 1986) insist on the fact that teaching these strategies is important for the learning process. Indeed, using them as a part of the curriculum helps learners to acquire knowledge and so achieve their objectives in terms of learning. However, the quality of education is not about telling learners what to do in a transmissivity way; but it concerns showing them how to learn effectively.

With an LMS based on the cognitivist approach (see figure 3), the learner is an active information-processing system, like a computer: it perceives information that comes from the outside world, recognizes them, stores them in memory, and then recovers them to understand the environment or resolve problems (Bibeau, 1996). The teacher is the learning manager. He/she guides, animates, directs, advises, explains, regulates, and remedies. Knowledge becomes an external reality that the learner must integrate into his/her mental patterns and reuse rather than acquire observable behaviors (Bibeau, 2007). The best teaching method is the one that takes into consideration individual variables particularly the learning styles. Therefore, the cognitivist teacher is the one who uses ICTs that promote high interactivity with learners, such as simulators, experiments, and intelligent tutorials. However, the cognitivist model has an important limit, related to the fact that a well-structured material is not sufficient to ensure learning. The motivation of learners is a crucial factor because it provides the required energy to perform learning.

Figure 2. LMS and underlying Behaviorism model

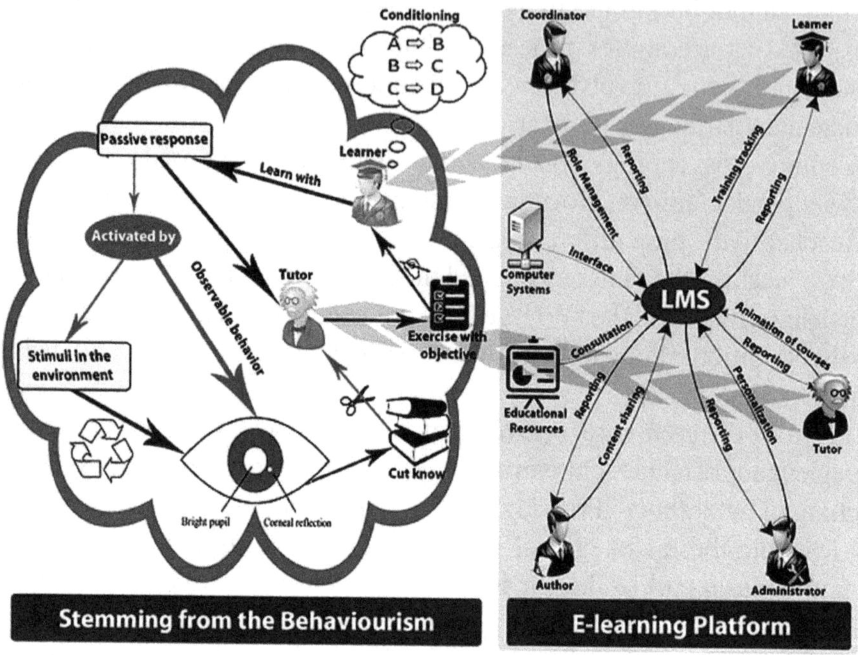

Figure 3. LMS and underlying Cognitivism model

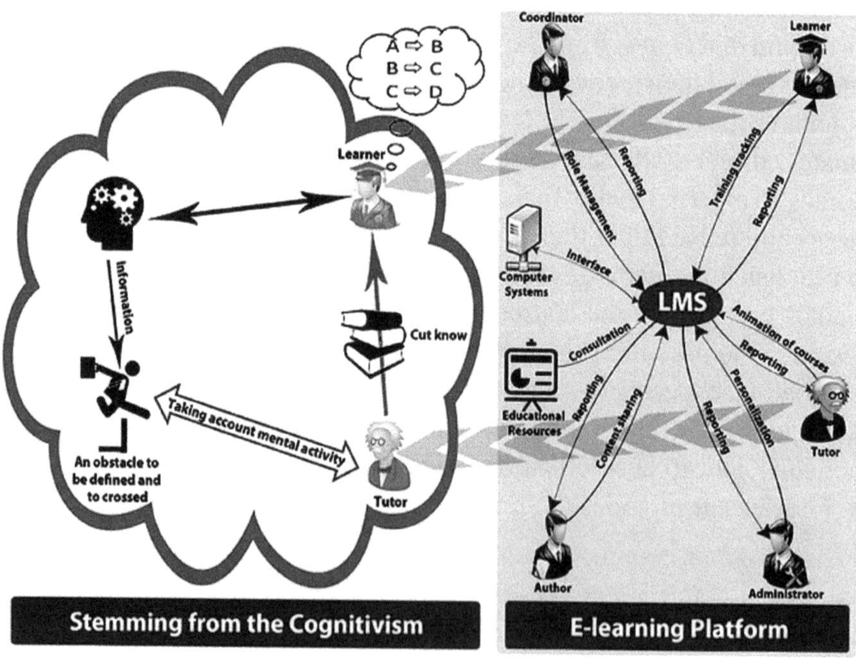

4. LMS and the Social Constructivism

Social constructivism is the fruit of the development of learning theories under the influence of some researchers, particularly Lev Vygotski in 1934 (In El-Mhouti and al.) (Chekour, 2015; El-Mhouti, 2013), who wanted to depart from behaviorism by integrating other factors that can positively influence the knowledge acquisition. Thus, new ideas emerged in connection with the possible interaction of individuals with the environment.

Social constructivism outlines learning by construction in a community of learners. In this light, learners are expected to interact with the available human resources (teachers, tutors, other learners…) in the proposed learning environment. In this way, the learners' psychological functions increase through social-cognitive conflicts that occur between them. These conflicts lead to the development of the zone of proximal development (WAKE, 2001) and thus facilitate the acquisition of knowledge.

Learning is seen as the process of acquisition of knowledge through the exchange between teachers and learners or between learners. These latter learn not only through the transmission of knowledge by their teacher but also through interactions (Doise, 2012).

The teacher's role is to define precisely this zone to design suitable exercises for learners. Furthermore, designing collaborative tasks, which involve discussions and exchange (social-cognitive conflicts) between learners is so important in this model. Errors are considered as a point of support for the construction of new knowledge.

The contribution of Bruner (Bruner, 1996) in the social constructivist theory is so valuable. Indeed, this author explained that the traditional model considers the teacher as a single operator, which prevents learners from being autonomous. According to him, the teacher should propose the most agreeable tasks to be achieved under his/her guidance by avoiding the dependence of learners on him/her. Keeping learners motivated and involved in learning is required to ensure the quality of both teaching and learning.

Based on the social constructivist approach (see figure 4), the design and development of LMS were oriented towards integrating online communication and collaboration tools. In practice, a wide range of platforms, particularly the social constructivist ones, proposes a set of tools, which allow sharing, exchanging, and interacting in a synchronous and asynchronous mode such as blogs, wikis, forums…

Figure 4. LMS and underlying Social Constructivism model

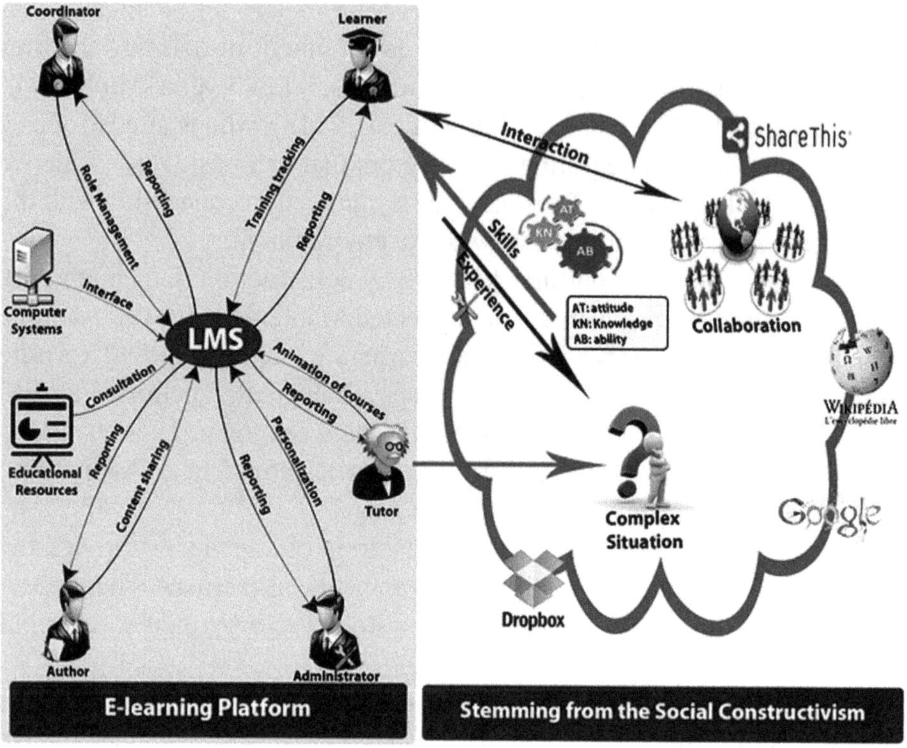

In summary, the ideas of social constructivist authors have highlighted the social nature of learning. Other authors have taken one step further by emphasizing the distribution of intelligence between individuals and the environment. Furthermore, considering that learning occurs in a social context is no longer enough to ensure deep learning. Indeed, working in groups can affect negatively the quality of learning if the following conditions are not taken into consideration:

- Learning styles,
- The way groups are formed,
- The interaction modality,
- The characteristics of tasks.

Besides, a wide range of researchers considered Connectivism as a branch of social constructivism. It is not necessarily a learning theory, but rather a pragmatic concept of participatory teaching and learning (Haug, 2013).

This concept relies on the assumptions of Latours Actor-Network-Theory (Anderson and Dron, 2011). If viewed as a theory by itself, it would also overlap with the social constructivist paradigm in terms of the importance of interaction in social structures.

George Siemens and Stephen Downes have developed a new learning theory (cf. figure 6) they have called "Connectivism" since it is based on the principles of connection, online networking and thus interactions between objects of the world (material or symbolic). According to these researchers, other learning theories have been developed in a time in which learning was not widely affected by the presence of technologies (Siemens, 2005). They stated that Connectivism is based on the use of a network composed of nodes and connections as a central metaphor of learning (Duplàa, 2012). In this metaphor, a node can be information, data, feelings, pictures, or simulations. Learning is the process of making connections, including the neural ones, the connection between humans, computers, and the interconnections between different fields of knowledge (Siemens, 2005).

Figure 5. Siemens's connectivism model (In Chekour and al.) (Chekour, 2015; Siemens, 2005)

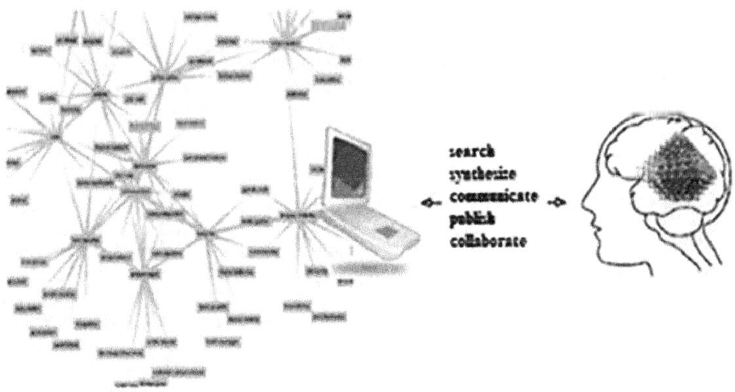

Connectivism has given birth to many learning environments, particularly LMS, offering mainly what we call open massive online courses (MOOCs). These courses, which include a set of online resources, are connectivists. In other words, they highlight the creation and genesis of knowledge and not the reproduction of this latter. This is not the case in xMOOCs, which are designed based on traditional pedagogy. Therefore, a wide range of tools has been integrated with most LMS to ensure interactivity and so to allow online exchange and collaboration. Among these tools, we mention online social networks, sharing-resource websites, forums… and any other tool that can connect learners.

The benefits of Connectivism as a new learning theory reside in the importance given to the principle of connection which leads to the understanding of the learning process by describing how and why connections are formed at different levels: neural, cognitive/conceptual, and social.

Beyond that, Connectivism seems to be widely criticized since it does not describe in detail how individuals learn in a particular technological environment, whereas this constitutes the core problem of each learning theory.

EDUCATIONAL MODELING OF AN LMS

The problems of most Learning Management Systems (LMS) are first of all of a pedagogical nature and then of a technical one. Studying these interrelated problems provides a useful conceptual reference that enables us to design a new model for a more relevant solution. This solution can only be a new learning management system (LMS) that has to be developed to address the needs of all its users, particularly learners.

The modeling presented here tries to propose a relevant solution to some of these problems based on the following three principles:

- Describing the type of learning activities proposed and their paths (free, sequential, conditional…),
- Identifying different actors and/or groups of actors according to their roles and the tasks they have to achieve,
- Describing different spaces of activities in the learning system. Each space includes various resources such as multimedia documents, forums, wikis, video conferencing, mind maps, exercises…

1. The Conceptual Model

The modeling of our LMS that will be presented in detail here offers both pedagogical and technical richness in terms of functionalities. It allows not only supporting the learning process but also the teaching process by facilitating the design and development of online training systems.

Our LMS is based on an original pedagogical reference that combines four learning theories and their emerging functionalities aiming to improve users' teaching and learning processes.

As seen in Figure 6, each of the four theories of learning involved in our modeling brings benefits in terms of the teaching-learning process and contributes to the enrichment of our LMS.

Figure 6. The conceptual model of an LMS

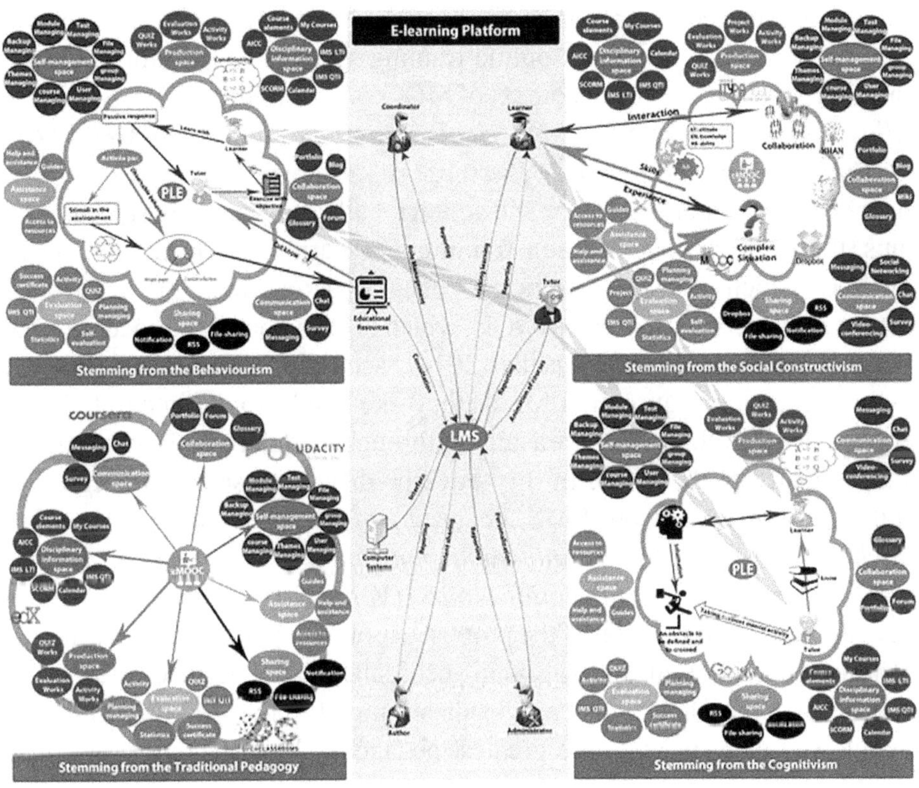

Based on behaviorism, the LMS that we propose is broken down into learning units, which offers the possibility to present structured knowledge and learning activities (progressive application exercises) and assistance. Social constructivism allowed us to justify the integration of services, allowing the installation of internal and external applications, enabling communication and collaboration between educational actors. In this manner, the knowledge building in a group outweighs the individualization of the learning path.

Also, cognitivism opened the door for the use of multiple learning pathways to take into account individual variables that may influence how learners process information. The cognitivist teacher is invited to use ICTs that promote high interactivity with learners, such as simulators, experiments, and intelligent tutorials. This does not prevent the development of personal learning environments in parallel to the services offered according to the needs of each of the actors involved in the training system.

Thus, the modeling that we propose in this chapter makes at the disposal of its users a wide range of spaces for information, production, assessment, communication, collaboration, assistance, and self-management to enable them to manage well various online training systems (e-learning, blended learning, MOOCs…). In the context of MOOCs which *"refer […] to massive online training[s] relying on numerical technologies and social web" [The translation is ours] (Jézégou, 2015),* these spaces are presented in a way that ensures more freedom of choice and action for all users, particularly learners. Thus, the latter can control their training and learning. Indeed, whether in xMOOC, which relies on traditional pedagogy (Rosselle, 2013), and thus focuses on the content, or in cMOOC, which is based on the connection that means network-oriented (Rosselle, 2014), according to our modeling all final users can configure the LMS as they like thanks to the integrated web services. These web services are available through modular interfaces designed independently of the LMS. In this way, the different users can access the malleability offered by our LMS. *According to Hoogstoel, this malleability which "allows improving the individual motivation of actors and promoting their engagement" [The translation is ours] (Varga, 2010)* is possible through the automatic configuration of the proposed tools, adaptation to the proposed interfaces, and their customization in accordance to the defined roles.

It is therefore clear that the hybridization of the four learning theories has allowed us to provide the greatest pedagogical and technical richness for both learners and teachers.

The principle of reusability and interoperability were taken into consideration when working on the proposed modeling. Therefore, we applied the focused-resources approach, which is mainly based on the notion of *"bricks"* and *"aggregates"* (Burgos, 2005). This approach aims to allow the use and re-use of the learning objects in different contexts, regardless of the mobilized pedagogical approaches and the designed scenarios. Another approach that has also inspired us is the one developed by Rob Koper (In Burgos and al.) (Burgos, 2005), which outlines the notions of learning units and pedagogical activities. In practice, the final users of our LMS can model their needs and the type of activities they like per the assumed roles in the proposed learning environment. The latter provides various services, resources, and relevant tools to achieve the objectives in terms of learning.

Finally, it is worth noting that the modeling proposed here ensures the best management of online interactions; reinforces the learner autonomy, and sustains their motivations.

2. The Modular Approach

Adopting a modular approach when designing and developing a new LMS allows us to derive from it a granular structure that can adapt to different contexts. Thus, we have decided to comply with this approach by proposing a learning system based on the needs of all its users regardless of their roles and the tasks they have to achieve.

The platform LMS that we plan to implement at a later stage will promote sharing experiences through the following technological advances:

- Activity spaces and generic tools: access to pedagogical resources (texts, videos, webography…) per different contexts of use: MOOCs, SPOCs, e-learning projects, blended learning…
- Resources and/or activities: text editors, files for download…
- Shared models of activity spaces and pedagogical paths.
- A complete redesign of self-corrected exercises tool for more interactivity and usable offline.
- A range of functionalities for the administrative management of training: management of training catalogs, registration, management of resources (local training, materials…).
- Improving the tracking services of the pedagogical activities and the integration of graphic exercises.
- A chat plug-in (text, audio, video) allowing the organization of webinars and virtual classrooms.
- The "inter-LMS" connection, allowing exchanges between several LMS platforms.
- Improving the tracking of users via a dashboard system allowing tracking a user or a user group in a centralized way.
- Finally, integrated error management and user tracking problems through integrated support Ticketing system for detecting bugs reported by the platform users.

When studying several LMS, we realized that most of them are arborescent, linear, and are part of a logic of closed course-by-course. They focus on teaching instead of highlighting the learner and the learning process. Most of these LMSs are TMSs, which is to say tools at the service of the teacher and not in the service of the learning process. Thus, our modeling reflects our intention of centering the user around the following two concepts, allowing the entire transversality and the desired personalization:

- Customizable personal office,
- Activity spaces and generic tools.

Therefore, the user will have a personal office that he/she can be customized and personal activity space, in which he/she is the manager. He/she can register in the activity spaces or even create them if he/she possesses the rights.

3. Customizable Personal Office

All are centered on the customized personal office that each user can customize to his/her requirements through a widget system. Moreover, each user can also create learning spaces, aggregate, produce resources…, and further: like the comment on, and tag them… Thus, our LMS will allow freedom of action to all its users regardless of their roles (teachers, learners, tutors…) to ensure more activity, creativity, and re-appropriation of the learning process.

For more customization of the proposed LMS, a rapid start with it, and more ease of its use, we will develop:

- Graphic interfaces, which can be configured to fit the needs of users and be adapted to the used peripherals (responsive design),
- Dashboards and customized statistics,
- A user "office" that aggregates information flows and customized home pages (tabs, texts, and widgets).

Particularly other more important ideas seem to be at the heart of human motivations within a personal office such as:

- Distinctive behavior, which can be identified when someone tries to be objective, factual and struggles to advocate his/her ideas using the logic of finding holes in other's ideas.

- Connected behavior, which refers to a subjective individual who listens and asks questions to understand other's views.
- Constructed behavior refers to someone who is conscious of his/her approaches and mobilizes them per the situation encountered.

In general, learning can be stimulated through a good quantity of interconnected behaviors within a learning community. Indeed, not only individuals are brought together, but also their psychological functions are developed and promoted by replacing the existing beliefs.

4. Activity Spaces and Generic Tools

Our LMS was modeled, in light of a particular vision that aims to accelerate the teaching and learning rhythm by using various activity spaces and generic tools.

In the proposed LMS, the learner has a personal space like that of the teacher. Both of them can create forums. Thus, the focus is put on making the user, regardless of his/her roles, more active by enabling him/her to customize his/her office, create various activity spaces, aggregate, copy and share resources in each activity space.

The proposed LMS will make at the disposal of its final users a set of resources and tools for creating and managing online training systems such as MOOCs (e.g., badges, peer assessment, management of groups…).

Our LMS is focused on the user and his/her activity. It allows creating and organizing activity spaces, proposing various types of learning activity, creating forums, blogs, and managing the interactions within it. It also allows the management of resources per users' needs. Therefore, the same possibilities of action were given to both teachers and learners, for more distribution of the platform control.

Furthermore, other tools were integrated into our LMS such as courses, quizzes, forums, instant messenger, and blogs. A wide range of external and internal tools was provided and configured to adapt to different supports (computers, tablets, or smartphones).

Finally, some web services were displayed in a single location (public profile, portfolios, wikis, forums, blogs, RSS feeds, widgets, information sharing, notifications, commentaries, notes…) aiming at:

- Creating communities of teachers and learners,
- Facilitating interactions and information sharing,

- Promoting openness to lifelong learning.

Furthermore, the traditional pedagogy, behaviorism, cognitivism, and social constructivism have allowed us to propose a personal office, which consists of different spaces for activities of teaching and learning within the LMS (see figure 6). In these spaces, both teachers and learners can:

- Transmit and present structured information in different formats: biography, text, video... (disciplinary information space);
- Communicate with one or more actors (communication space);
- Share resources with one or more actors (sharing space);
- Interact and collaborate with other actors (collaboration space);
- Evaluate themselves and other resources (evaluation space);
- Produce information (production space);
- Select and use various tools according to their needs (self-management space);
- Propose and/or receive personalized assistance (assistance space).

4.1 Disciplinary Information Space

Teachers or tutors can export content from the LMS as IMS/SCORM conformant Content Packages that can be viewed offline, or imported into the LMS. Content packages can be imported and exported with QTI Tests, and AccessForAll adapted content together in a single package. Teachers and tutors can create disciplinary information through the following technological advances:

- My Courses. Teachers, tutors, or learners can manage the LMS courses they teach and/or are enrolled in. When learners register, they are automatically logged into My Courses.
- IMS LTI. Support for IMS Learning Tool Integration (LTI) for simple, standards-based integration with third-party tools running outside LMS The basic use case behind the development of the LTI specification is to allow the seamless connection of web-based, externally hosted applications, and content, or learning tools to platforms that present them to users (IMS Global Learning Consortium, 2017).

- SCORM. Upload and configure SCORM packages, enabling interoperability and accessibility of web-based learning content.
- IMS QTI. Import and export interoperable QTI test packages or question banks.
- Course elements provide pre-shaped pedagogic bricks that can be used as resources in a course. The latter provide high semantic level objects that are commonly used in written learning content, such as Important, local goals, reminders, work description, tips, and tricks... Other course elements provide a pre-styled constant way of course headings, section, block, and sequence headings.
- Calendar. View a weekly or monthly summary of scheduled events, either for a course or work site or for an active individual in one or more LMS
- AICC publishes recommendations and a set of specifications for managing the loading of content into a distance-learning platform (LMS), standardizing communication between the content and the LMS, and adapting the pedagogical content according to the learner.

Figure 7. Benefits of IMS Learning Tools Interoperability (IMS Global Learning Consortium, 2017)

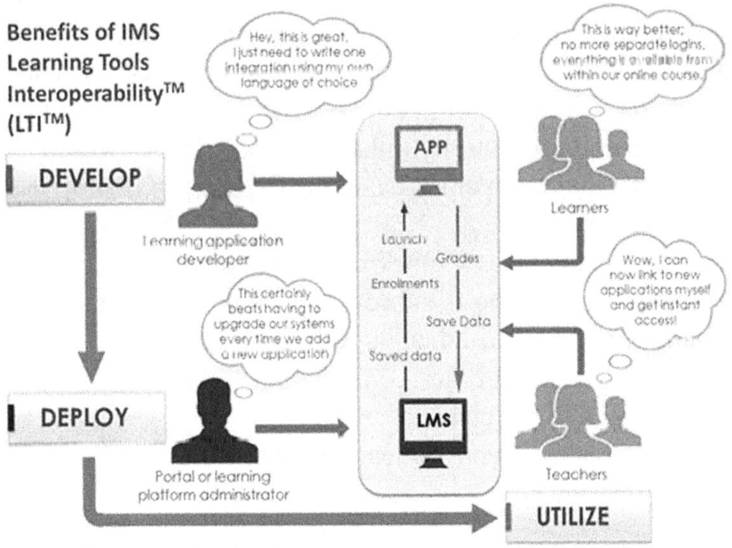

4.2 Communication Space

Communication is the act of conveying intended meanings from one entity or group to another using mutually understood signs and semiotic rules. Learners can communicate with others through their Inbox using LMS's private mail, through the discussion forums, the chat rooms. Teachers, tutors, and learners can promote sharing experiences through the following technological advances:

- Social Networking. All LMS users can develop a network of contacts, create and join interest groups, set up a network profile, and link any of the thousands of remote gadget applications into their networking environment. Photos can be shared across courses, or through the social networking area.
- Messaging. Teachers, tutors, and learners can send bulk messages to course members, assistants, or both. Insert tokens to customize messages for each user.
- Survey. This module provides an Amazon-style 5-star rating system for courses. Each user can give a rating and the total is displayed in the block. Administrators can connect to survey module instances on the same course from the block, to add a "Review" survey.
- Videoconferencing is a web conferencing system for distance education. The goal of the module is to enable universities, and colleges to deliver a high-quality learning experience to remote learners. The latter supports real-time sharing of slides, audio, video, chat, and desktops. It also records all content for later playback. This module enables you to:
    - Create multiple activity links to online sessions within a course,
    - Specify join open/close dates for the session that appears in the LMS's calendar.
- Chat. This module uses a block to list all online users that are part of all courses. A user who is subscribed can open a chat window at the bottom of the page. The advantages of the chat are:
    - Establish a real-time conversation with other online users subscribed to the course;
    - Collaborate with your colleagues, or ask questions to your teachers or tutors.

4.3 Sharing Space

Sharing space or exchange space allows discussion, to define and to follow the implementation of collaborative projects of one or several courses. Teachers and learners can promote sharing experiences through the following technological advances:

- File sharing. Use the file-sharing tool to gather and distribute course documents. Learners can gather their files in a personal workspace, and hand in assignments from there. Create group workspaces for private file sharing within workgroups.
- Notification. This notification block implements a solution that periodically notifies learners about new content or activities included in an LMS course. This solution will act as a sentinel that detects whether new content or new activities have been included in the LMS course, and notifies learners, the teachers, and/or the tutors about that.
- RSS. The RSS Plugin offers you the possibility to load multiple feeds into a block. The RSS block allows authorized users to configure multiple RSS feeds per instance.
- Assignment DropBox. Extending the File Storage. Teachers, tutors, or learners can create file folders for collecting assignment submissions, collected from all course members, from group members, or individuals.

4.4 Collaboration Space

Collaboration is the process of two or more people or organizations working together to realize or achieve something successfully (Martinez-Moyano, 2006). Collaboration requires leadership, although the form of leadership can be social within a decentralized and egalitarian group (Spence, 2005). Teams that work collaboratively can obtain greater resources, recognition, and reward when facing competition for finite resources. Teachers, tutors, and learners can promote collaboration experiences through the following technological advances:

- Forum. Teachers, tutors, or learners can create and manage multiple forums for each of their courses. Messages can be edited, deleted, locked for reading and/or replying, and “stuck” if a message is important. Administrators or coordinators can create forums shared across multiple courses.

- Glossary. Words and phrases added to the glossary by the teacher, the tutors, or the learner, can be accessed from terms embedded within content pages or viewed alphabetically in their entirety using the glossary tool.
- Blog. Provide collaborative blogging and/or online journaling capability of your course or project team.
- Wiki is a module that provides the collaborative modification of its content and structure. The key intention of this wiki is to provide a simple collaborative teaching tool suitable for learners to use.
- Portfolio. This module allows learners to create portfolio contributions, with a structure set by the teacher. The course teacher(s) can create an overall structure for the learners' work via a series of chapters. The learners of the course are then able to add their contributions based on this structure, which can then be commented on by the course teacher(s).

4.5 Evaluation Space

Evaluation is a process where learners are assessed to determine their suitability to take a course. The learners' aptitudes are determined by a variety of techniques including interviews, group exercises, presentations, examinations, and psychometric testing. Teachers, tutors, and learners can promote sharing experiences through the following technological advances:

- Statistics. The main goal of this module is to facilitate the work of the learning plan tutors. It provides an overview of learner learning plans (such as rating in courses, user evidence). It also offers statistics by learning plans and competencies for learning plan templates.
- Self-evaluation and Quizzes. Create and manage online assessments using a robust toolset: closed and open-ended questions, matching, setpoint value, auto-grading, statistics, timed assessments, audio recording, etc.
- Planning management. Schedule and maintain deadlines, activities, and events related to a course, project, or worksite; assignments, assessments, materials, etc.
- Success certificate. This module allows for the dynamic generation of certificates based on predefined criteria set by the teacher.

- Project and activity. This module intended to give a complete project and activity-driving tool in a pedagogical environment, allowing teaching the first principles of pragmatic project or activity management to learners.

4.6 Production Space

The teacher or tutor can create notifications, and assess the productions undertaken by learners. Teachers and learners can promote sharing experiences through the following technological advances:

- Self-evaluation and Quizzes production. Create and manage the production of online assessments with a robust toolset determined by the teacher: closed and open-ended questions, matching, question pools, auto-grading, statistics, timed assessments or audio recording, etc.
- Project and activity production. Intended to give a complete project and activity-driving tools in a pedagogical environment, allowing learners to produce projects and activities that meet the principles of pragmatic project or activity management.

The goal through the integration of these tools is to fit the LMS with a fully-featured project management tool that could be used to manage real projects or drive learner's projects as a project based pedagogy.

4.7 Self-Management Space

Self-management is the management of an LMS by the administrators themselves. The customizations are decentralized as much as possible and the sharing of tasks between all the users (administrators, coordinators, teachers, tutors, and learners) is done equitably. Teachers and tutors can promote sharing experiences through the following technological advances:

- Test managing. Teachers or tutors can create tests with multiple-choice, multiple answers, true/false, Likert, ordering, matching, drag and drop, and several open-ended question types. M/C, M/A, ordering, matching, and T/F questions are marked automatically. Moreover, these tests enable learners to add questions to a Question Bank, then select questions from it to assemble a test or quiz.

- Course managing. Courses on a system can be sorted, their authors modified, and their teachers or tutors managed. We can create new courses and assign them to teachers or tutors. Besides, we can use course backups to generate initial content for a new course.
- Group managing. Teachers or tutors can manually create, or automatically generate workgroups for a variety of purposes. Groups might be used to provide a private area where learners can work.
- Backup managing. The entire content and structure of a course can be backed up and stored on the LMS server, or downloaded and saved to your local computer for safe-keeping.
- File managing. Teachers, tutors, or learners can upload and manage course-related files. Directories can be created to sort files; zip archives can be uploaded and unpacked. A popup file manager can be opened alongside the Content Editor or test question editors.
- Module managing. Administrators or coordinators can install modules, enable and disable them, and define a default set of modules and menu blocks for new courses.
- Themes managing. Easily create a custom version of LMS by modifying an existing theme, or creating a new one. Assign themes to categories of courses to give all related courses the same look.
- User managing. Users on a system can be sorted, personal information can be viewed, and access privileges can be modified. User accounts can be managed by adding, modifying, or deleting accounts.

4.8 Assistance Space

Assistance designates the action of bringing help or succor. It is about providing aid, support, or succor in all matters. Assistance may have different objectives that affect learners and institutions:

- Substitution of capacities. Use of assistance to undertake courses and assume duties that would normally be the responsibility of a learner.
- Capacity supplementation. Use of assistance to provide orientations and advice on training learners, often in particular areas.
- Capacity building. Using assistance to transfer skills and abilities to learners. Capacity building is often considered the most advanced form of assistance.

Learners can promote assistance through the following technological advances:

- Guides. Digital documents and videos that gather a set of information, which facilitate the use of modules and the technological advances of the LMS: generic activity spaces and tools, resources and/or activities, public profile, portfolios, wikis, blogs, forums, FluxRss, widgets, sharing Information, notifications, comments, notes, etc.
- Help and assistance. The learner asks for help when it is needed by sending a message to the teacher or tutor. To clarify a block, a section, a figure, a video, an image... or anything at the level of the course, to ensure a better understanding of the learners.

DISCUSSION

A great deal of research is focused in one way or another on the platform engineering for distance education, including LMS. For example, Chekour (Chekour, 2015), presented a synthesis of the main learning theories in the digital era, namely behaviorism, cognitivism, constructivism, and social constructivism. El-Mhouti (El-Mhouti, 2013) highlighted the ICT use in the service of active pedagogies, based on the social constructivist approach, the principles that structure the instructional design approaches, and the assessment of the social constructivist activities.

These works, among many others, emphasized the contribution of learning theories in the design and development of learning systems. The direct application of each of these theories allows particularly providing supporting methods for the design and development of LMS. The hybridization of the learning theories that we presented in this chapter as an original conceptual model has allowed us to design a new LMS whose benefit resides essentially in the richness of the proposed functionalities in a way that fits the needs of all its final users: teachers and learners.

Furthermore, multiple searches (Benslimane, 2016; Zoubaidi, 2014; Chemsi, 2011) had the goal to implement and present the functionalities of LMS platforms (such as Moodle) and their possibilities to effectively manage users' assessment approach (teachers and/or learners) within training institutions. Paquette (Paquette, 2000) elaborated e-learning portals editor that opens the way to more diverse and evolved pedagogical models on the pedagogical plan, focusing more on the quality of interactions. Moreover, in the framework of the European project Mediasite (Bechina, 2005); a reference model for the process for distance learning has been developed. This theoretical framework has led to the integration of several applications (video-conferencing, document manager, portal...) to define an electronic training platform for online communication and/or collaboration.

On the other hand, other research aimed at proposing the modeling of new units, approaches, architecture, or adaptive, flexible, and interactive e-learning systems. For example, Sadiq proposed the modeling of learning units on e-learning platforms, which relies on the application of the standard IMS Learning Design in the production of adaptive learning units (Sadiq, 2010). Tonye proposed a distance education model adapted to the African context (Tonye, 2011). Chouchane proposed the modeling of an adaptive agent-based approach to m-learning for an efficient and flexible mobile learning system (Chouchane, 2012). Moreover, Brunel proposed a modeling work based on the following five fundamental functions: organize learning, inform, collaborate, accompany, and produce. His modeling work shows that mastering the overall logic of functioning of these digital learning environments helps to avoid the focus on the tools and providing active pedagogy adapted to the context and the needs of all users (Brunel, 2015).

Despotović-Zrakić described in his paper, an approach to providing adaptivity in e-education courses to enhance an existing e-education system, namely Moodle LMS (Despotović-Zrakić and al., 2012). Aammou proposed implementing traditional features of adaptive hypermedia in an open environment, for describing learning objects and architectural models based on the use of ontologies (Aammou and al., 2010). Dahmani also presented ontology-based modeling for interactive learning. His work deals with interactive learning and focuses particularly on the possibility of using the results of ontological engineering in the modeling of educational domains as well as in the knowledge assessment of learners in the case of computer-assisted learning exercises (Dahmani, 2010).

Based on these various research works, which seemed to us incomplete, we proposed a modeling portrait of a new LMS platform. The latter is anthropocentric and relies on a learning conception that is located at the intersection of the most used learning theories. Indeed, the idea is to orient the design work research towards great and optimal compatibility between the services offered by e-learning platforms and the needs of all users, particularly learners, for better optimization of online learning.

CONCLUSION

In this chapter, we proposed the original conceptual modeling of an LMS platform based on the hybridization of four learning theories, namely traditional pedagogy, behaviorism, cognitivism, and social constructivism. Our first motivation was to provide a more learner-centric LMS while opening it up dynamically to the teacher. Indeed, the proposed LMS offers a range of customizable web services that fit users' needs. In this way, freedom of choice is left about teaching and learning concerning the creation, adaptation, and personalization of various components of the LMS.

One of the most important qualities of the proposed LMS, apart from the fact that it integrates several pedagogical functionalities, is allowing the concerned users (teachers and learners) to have the same possibilities of interactive intervention in the system through configuration interfaces that are easy to use. These interfaces include, in addition to a customizable personal office, various activity spaces. This ensures better optimization of online teaching and learning.

Technical modeling and development of the proposed LMS are still taking place. Thereafter, we are looking at the implementation of its prototype as part of university training with groups of teachers and learners. This will allow us to check the validity of our modeling work with the target audience and therefore take relevant decisions for better exploitation and wide dissemination of the LMS in the future.

REFERENCES

Aammou, S., Mohamed, K., Ahmed, I., & El-Kadiri, K. E. (2010). Adaptive hypermedia systems for e-learning. *IEEE EDUCON 2010 Conference*, 1799–1804. doi:10.1109/EDUCON.2010.5492421

Anderson & Dron. (2011). *Three Generations of Distance Education Pedagogy*. Academic Press.

Aska, Le Préau, & Klr.fr. (2000). *Choisir une solution de téléformation: 2000 study: l'offre de plates-formes et de portails de téléformation*. Academic Press.

Bechina, A., Keith, B., & Brinkschulte, U. (2005). *Mediasite: Une nouvelle plate-forme dédiée à l'enseignement à distance*. IRES.

Benslimane, M., Zine, O., Derouich, A., & Talbi, A. (2016). Proposition et implémentation sur moodle d'une approche de conception d'un cours en ligne: cas d'un cours d'algorithmique. *Workshop International sur les Approches Pédagogiques & E-Learning*.

Bibeau, R. (1996). École informatisée clés en main. Projet franco-québécois de recherche-action. *Revue de l'EPI (Enseignement Public et Informatique), 82*, 137–147.

Bibeau, R. (2007). Les technologies de l'information et de la communication peuvent contribuer à améliorer les résultats scolaires des élèves. *Revue de l'EPI*, (94).

Brunel, S., Girard, P., & Lamago, M. (2015). *Des plateformes pour enseigner à distance: vers une modélisation générale de leurs fonctions*. In AIP Primeca 2015, La Plagne, France. https://hal.archives-ouvertes.fr/hal-01128532

Bruner, J. S., & Bonin, Y. (1996). *L'éducation, entrée dans la culture: les problèmes de l'école à la lumière de la psychologie culturelle*. Retz.

Burgos, D., Arnaud, M., Neuhauser, P., & Koper, R. (2005). IMS Learning Design la flexibilité pédagogique au service des besoins de l'e-formation. *Revue de l'EPI (Enseignement Public et Informatique)*. https://www.epi.asso.fr/revue/articles/a0512c.htm

Caro Dambreville, S. (2008). Evaluer un dispositif de formation à distance Principes et retour d'expérience. Revue des Interactions Humaines Médiatisées, 9(2).

Chekour, M., Laafou, M., & Janati-Idrissi, R. (2015). L'évolution des théories de l'apprentissage à l'ère du numérique. *Revue de l'EPI (Enseignement Public et Informatique)*. http://www.epi.asso.fr/revue/articles/a1502b.htm

Chemsi, G., Radid, M., Sadiq, M., & Talbi, M. (2011). Une plate-forme d'évaluation des enseignements et des formations à distance: EVAL-EFD. *Revue de l'EPI (Enseignement Public et Informatique)*. http://www.epi.asso.fr/revue/articles/a1109b.htm

Chouchane, K. (2012). *"Modélisation et réalisation d'une approche pour le m-learning," Magister en Informatique Option Système d'Informatique et de Communication (SIC)*. Université Hadj Lakhdar – Batna – Algérienne.

Crozat, S. (2002). *Éléments pour la conception industrialisée des supports pédagogiques numériques* (Doctoral dissertation). Université de Technologie de Compiègne.

Despotović-Zrakić, M., Marković, A., Bogdanović, Z., Barać, D., & Krčo, S. (2012). Providing Adaptivity in Moodle LMS Courses. *Journal of Educational Technology & Society, 15*(1), 326-338.

Dimet, B. (2006). *Etude comparative technique et pédagogique des plates-formes pour la formation ouverte et à distance.* https://www.portices.fr/formation/Res/-Formation/Plateformes/Pf1Resume.html

Dogbe-Semanou, Koffi, Durand, Leproust, & Vanderstichel. (2007). Etude comparative de plates-formes de formation à distance. *le cadre du Projet@ 2L.*

Doise, W., & Mugny, G. (1981). *Le développement social de l'intelligence* (Vol. 1). Paris: Interéditions.

Duplàa, E. & Talaat, N. (2012). Connectivisme et formation en ligne. *Distances et savoirs, 9*(4), 541-564.

El-Mawas, N., Oubahssi, L., & Laforcade, P. (2014). *Étude comparative de plateformes de formation à distance.* GRAPHIT-D2.5&2.2.

El-Mhouti, A., Nasseh, A., & Erradi, M. (2013). Les TIC au service d'un enseignement-apprentissage socioconstructiviste. *Revue de l'EPI (Enseignement Public et Informatique).* http://www.epi.asso.fr/revue/articles/a1301g.htm

Fablet, D. (2007). *Professeur en sciences de l'éducation Éduquer, Enseigner, Former, Séminaire de cours l'éducation tout au long de la vie.* Université Paris Ouest Nanterre La Défense (Paris 10 University).

Galloy, S., Haas, C., & Lodewijck, M. (2002). *Analyse d'environnements de formation à distance.* CIFoP – Le Centre Interuniversitaire de Formation Permanente.

Good, T. L., & Brophy, J. E. (1995). Educational Psychology: A Realistic Approach (4th ed.). New York: Longman.

Graf, S., & List, B. (2005). An evaluation of open source e-learning platforms stressing adaptation issues. *Fifth IEEE International Conference on Advanced Learning Technologies (ICALT'05),* 163–165. doi:10.1109/ICALT.2005.54

Haug, S., & Wedekind, J. (2013). cMOOC – ein alternatives Lehr-/ Lernszenarium? In R. Schulmeister (Hrsg.), MOOCs – Massive Open Online Courses. Offene Bildung Oder Geschäftsmodell? Münster: Waxmann.

Henri, F., Rabardel, P., & Pastré, P. (Eds.). (2005). Modèles du sujet pour la conception. International Journal of E-Learning & Distance Education, 22(1), 101–106.

IMS Global Learning Consortium. (2017). *Learning Tools Interoperability*. https://www.imsglobal.org/activity/learning-tools-interoperability

Itmazi, J. A., & Megías, M. (n.d.). Survey: Comparison and evaluation studies of learning content management systems. *MICROLEARNING2005: Learning & Working in New Media Environments. International Conference*. https://www.researchgate.net/publication/267856221_SURVEY_COMPARISON_AND_EVALUATION_STUDIES_OF_LEARNING_CONTENT_MANAGEMENT_SYSTEMS

Jézégou, A. (2015). Diriger soi-même ses activités d'apprentissage par et dans un Mooc de type connectiviste. *International Journal of E-Learning & Distance Education, 30*(1). http://www.ijede.ca/index.php/jde/article/view/868

Kaddouri, M., & Bouamri, A. (2010). Usage de plateformes d'enseignement à distance dans l'enseignement supérieur marocain: avantages pédagogiques et difficultés d'appropriation. *Questions Vives. Recherches en éducation, 7*(14), 107–118. http://questionsvives.revues.org/642

Lablidi, A., Abourrich, A., & Talbi, M. (2009). Démarche préconisée pour évaluer une plate-forme. *Revue de l'EPI (Enseignement Public et Informatique)*. www.epi.asso.fr/revue/articles/a0912b.htm

Martinez-Moyano, I. J. (2006). Exploring the dynamics of collaboration in interorganizational settings. *Creating a Culture of Collaboration: The International Association of Facilitators Handbook*.

Menasri, S. (2004). *Etude comparative de plateformes d'enseignement en ligne (e-learning) utilisées dans un contexte universitaire*. http://urfist.enc.sorbonne.fr/anciensite/archives/gremi/gremi10juin04/comparatif.htm#

Morandi, F. (2006). *Introduction à la pédagogie*. Armand Colin.

Née Dahmani Farida, B. (2010). *Modélisation basée ontologies pour l'apprentissage interactif - Application à l'évaluation des connaissances de l'apprenant* (PhD dissertation). Computer Science Department, Mouloud Mammeri University of Tizi-Ouzou, Algeria.

Ouadoud, M., Chkouri, M. Y., Nejjari, A., & El-Kadiri, K. E. (2017). Exploring a Recommendation System of Free E-learning Platforms: Functional Architecture of the System. *International Journal of Emerging Technologies in Learning, 12*(2), 219-226. doi:10.3991/ijet.v12i02.6381

Ouadoud, M., Chkouri, M. Y., & Nejjari, A. (2018, January). LeaderTICE: A Platforms Recommendation System Based on a Comparative and Evaluative Study of Free E-learning Platforms. *International Journal of Online Engineering, 14*(1), 132–161. doi:10.3991/ijoe.v14i01.7865

Ouadoud, M., Chkouri, M. Y., Nejjari, A., & El-Kadiri, K. E. (2016, February). Studying and Analyzing the Evaluation Dimensions of E-learning Platforms Relying on a Software Engineering Approach. *International Journal of Emerging Technologies in Learning, 11*(1), 11–20. doi:10.3991/ijet.v11i01.4924

Ouadoud, M., Chkouri, M. Y., Nejjari, A., & El-Kadiri, K. E. (2016). Studying and comparing the free e-learning platforms. *2016 4th IEEE International Colloquium on Information Science and Technology (CiSt)*, 581–586. 10.1109/CIST.2016.7804953

Paquette, G. (2000). Construction de portails de téléapprentissage Explor@ - Une diversité de modèles pédagogiques. *Science et Techniques Educatives, 7*(1), 207-226.

Paquette, G. L (2002). *Ingénierie Pédagogique: Pour Construire l'Apprentissage en Réseau*. PUQ.

Paulsen, M. F. (2003). Experiences with Learning Management Systems in 113 European Institutions. *Journal of Educational Technology & Society, 6*(4), 134-148. http://www.jstor.org.eressources.imist.ma/tc/accept?origin=/stable/pdf/jeductechsoci.6.4.134.pdf

Poulova, P., Simonova, I., & Manenova, M. (2015). Which One, or Another? Comparative Analysis of Selected LMS. *Procedia - Social and Behavioral Sciences, 186*, 1302–1308. doi:10.1016/j.sbspro.2015.04.052

Pressley, M., & Harris, K. (1990). What we really know about strategy instruction. *Educational Leadership*, *48*(1), 31–35.

Raynal, F., Rieunier, A., & Postic, M. (1997). *Pédagogie: Dictionnaire des concepts clés: Apprentissages, formation, psychologie cognitive*. ESF.

Rosselle, M. (2013). *Les MOOC: des dispositifs d'enseignement-apprentissage à personnaliser Atelier MOOC*. EIAH.

Rosselle, M., Caron, P. A., & Heutte, J. (2014). *Prémisse d'une typologie et des principales dimensions d'un cadre de description pour les MOOC. Journées Communication et Apprentissage Instrumentés en Réseau*. JOCAIR.

Sadiq, M., & Talbi, M. (2010). Modélisation des unités d'apprentissage sur des plates-formes de formation à distance. *Revue de l'EPI (Enseignement Public et Informatique)*. https://www.epi.asso.fr/revue/articles/a1003e.htm

Siemens, G. (2005). Connectivism: A Learning Theory for the Digital Age. *International Journal of Instructional Technology and Distance Learning*, *2*(1), 3-10. http://www.itdl.org/Journal/Jan_05/article01.htm

Spence, M. U. (2005). Graphic Design: Collaborative Processes. A course on collaboration, theory, and practice. In *Art 325: Collaborative Processes. Fairbanks Hall*. Oregon State University.

Tavris, C., & Wade, C. (1999). *"Béhaviorisme: Approche qui met l'accent sur l'étude du comportement observable et du rôle de l'environnement en tant que déterminant du comportement, " Introduction à la psychologie - Les grandes perspectives*. Erpi.

The OVAREP (Observatoire des ressources multimédias). (2000). *Étude comparative technique et pédagogique des plateformes pour la formation ouverte et à distance*. Author.

Tonye, E. (2010). *Modeling a framework for open and distance learning in sub-Saharan African countries*. http://www.frantice.net/docannexe.php?id=339

Varga, R., Caron, P. A., & Hoogstoel, F. (2010). Adapter des environnements numériques malléables à des dispositifs de formation. In *Dispositifs de formation, quand le numérique s§en mêle. Une approche pluridisciplinaire*. Paris: Hermès, Lavoisier.

Wake, J. D. (2001). *Evaluating the Organising of a Collaborative Telelearning Scenario from an Instructor Perspective œ an Activity Theoretical Approach* (Ph.D. dissertation). Dept. of Information Science, University of Bergen.

Watson, J. (n.d.). *Le béhaviorisme*. Paris: Editions Cepi.

Weinstein, C., & Mayer, R. (1986). The teaching of learning strategies. In Handbook of Research on Teaching (3rd ed.). New York: Macmillan.

Zoubaidi, X., Ait Daoud, M., Namir, A., Talbi, M., & Nachit, B. (2014). La formation de formateurs d'éducateurs du préscolaire: mise en place d'un dispositif de formation à distance. *Revue de l'EPI (Enseignement Public et Informatique)*. http://www.epi.asso.fr/revue/articles/a1401d.htm

ADDITIONAL READING

Kats, Y. (2010). *Learning Management Systems Technologies and Software Solutions for Online Teaching: Tools and Applications*. IGI/Information Science Research. doi:10.4018/978-1-61520-853-1

Kats, Y. (2013). *Learning Management Systems and Instructional Design: Metrics, Standards and Applications*. IGI/Information Science Research. doi:10.4018/978-1-4666-3930-0

Ouadoud, M., Chafiq, T., Rida, N., & Chkouri, M. Y. (2019). Generate a Meta-Model Content for Collaboration Space of Learning Management System Compatible with IMS-LD. *International Journal of Interactive Mobile Technologies, 13*(01), 37–52. doi:10.3991/ijim.v13i01.9440

Ouadoud, M., & Chkouri, M. Y. (2019). Generate a Meta-Model Content for Communication Space of Learning Management System Compatible with IMS-LD. In M. Ezziyyani (Ed.), *Advanced Intelligent Systems for Sustainable Development (AI2SD'2018), Advances in Intelligent Systems and Computing* (pp. 24–39). Springer International Publishing. doi:10.1007/978-3-030-11928-7_3

Ouadoud, M., & Chkouri, M. Y. (2019). Designing an IMS-LD Model for Communication Space of Learning Management System. In M. Ezziyyani (Ed.), *Advanced Intelligent Systems for Sustainable Development (AI2SD'2018), Advances in Intelligent Systems and Computing* (pp. 40–54). Springer International Publishing. doi:10.1007/978-3-030-11928-7_4

KEY TERMS AND DEFINITIONS

AICC: Aviation Industry CBT Committee.

ICT: Information and communication technologies.

IMS: Instructional management systems.

LMS: Learning management system.

MOOC: Massive open online course.

SCORM: The SCORM® (Sharable Content Object Reference Model) was created to address these interoperability, reusability, and durability challenges. As a reference model, it was intentionally designed to leverage standard web technologies as well as existing learning technology specifications that already existed. SCORM® is comprised of a collection of interrelated technical specifications and guidelines designed to meet the DoD's high-level requirements for creating interoperable, plug-n-play, browser-based e-learning content. It consists of three different technical specifications "books" that collectively address challenges associated with interoperability, portability, reusability, and the instructional sequencing of self-paced e-learning content (Available at https://www.adlnet.gov/adl-research/scorm).

Social Constructivism: Is centered on the learner. The learner learns through its representations. The construction of knowledge although personal is carried out in a social setting. The context and come from both what we think and what others bring as interactions.

TMS: Teaching management system.

Chapter 6
Designing an IMS-LD Meta-Model of a New Smart Learning Management System

ABSTRACT

The context of this work is that of designing an IMS-LD metamodel of an LMS. The approach is to first think about the conditions for creating an LMS between learners and designing the IT environment that supports this system. In this chapter, the authors try to adapt the IMS-LD model with a metamodel for LMS based on the hybridization between learning theories. This adaptation will go through three stages: first, the development of the meta-model of LMS; second, the study of the correspondence between the developed meta-model and IMS-LD model; and finally, their transformation to IMS-LD meta-model.

INTRODUCTION

In the 20th century, there was an international movement in favor of e-learning integration in higher education. This movement has been operationalized due to the variety of the educational offer by universities, which most have opted to diversify knowledge dissemination platforms to meet the needs of their target public.

DOI: 10.4018/978-1-7998-4021-3.ch006

E-learning is promoted through educational platforms: integrated systems offer a wide range of activities in the learning process. Teachers use the platforms to monitor or evaluate the work of students. They use LMSs to create courses, tests, etc. However, the LMS e-learning platforms do not offer personalized services and therefore do not take into account the aspects of personalization such as the level of knowledge, interest, motivation, and goals of learners. They access the same resource set in the same way.

We present an easy meta-model of LMS to create and administer the educational content online. This tool allows the generation and editing structures of websites through a database rather than pedagogical models, with a variety of choices that ensures better adaptation to the teaching of the course and learning style. Therefore, it is necessary to find a method to model all LMS types. To model the LMS, we have based ourselves upon the IMS-LD specification focusing on learning theory that was judged the most important and relevant to our modeling, namely the traditional pedagogy, behaviorism, cognitivism, and social constructivism. Then, these learning theories which have inspired for a long time the design of computer applications are combined and put into perspective with several emergent pedagogical functionalities to build original modeling for our LMS. Reveals that this proposed modeling that is presented to readers here looks for ways to leverage technology for learning by considering users as being human actors and not human factors (Henri and al., 2007).

The IMS-LD specification or instructional design engineering uses pedagogical concepts, allowing to model learning units. IMS-LD takes into account a wide variety of teaching models it is there its flexibility. A course plan extract of a general or specific database can be modeled with IMS-LD, through the description of the different roles, activities, environments, methods, properties, conditions, and notifications. It is used to transform the course plans into formal learning units (UOL) that can be performed with an IMS-LD editor based on an engine such as Copper core (Alfanet project, 2008). These executable units can be designed from the beginning using an editor such as Reload (Bolton, 2005).

In this chapter, we propose a modeling portrait of designing an IMS-LD meta-model for the LMS platform. The latter is anthropocentric and relies on a learning conception that is located at the intersection of the most used learning theory. Indeed, the idea is to orient the design work research towards great and optimal compatibility between the services offered by e-learning platforms and the needs of all users, particularly learners, for better optimization of online learning.

To concretize our modeling work, we present in the section "Theoretical approach, concepts and related work" the different theories of learning used for the modeling of this space, namely the traditional pedagogy and social constructivism. We also present the e-learning specification Learning Management Systems - Learning Design (IMS-LD) and related work. Next, in the "transformation rules" section, we present the ATL transformation language to perform the transformation between the developed meta-model and the IMS-LD model. We also determine in this section, the reasons why we did not use the ATL language for the transformation of models. Finally, we present in the section "Model-driven engineering ", the modeling Driven Architecture (MDA). Thus, we try to adapt the proposed meta-model of the LMS to the equivalent IMS-LD model.

LMS AND ACTIVITY SPACES

The LMS consists of different activity spaces for activities of teaching and learning (Ouadoud and al., 2018; Ouadoud and al., 2017), in these spaces, both teachers and learners can have:

- Disciplinary information space. In the disciplinary information space, teachers or tutors can export content from the LMS as IMS/SCORM conformant Content Packages that can be viewed offline, or imported into the LMS. Entire courses or individual course units can be packaged for viewing or redistribution.
- Communication space. Communication is the act of conveying intended meanings from one entity or group to another using mutually understood signs and semiotic rules. Learners can communicate with others through their Inbox using LMS's private mail, through the discussion forums, or the chat rooms.
- Collaboration space. Collaboration is the process of two or more people or organizations working together to realize or achieve something successfully (WAKE, 2001). Collaboration requires leadership, although the form of leadership can be social within a decentralized and egalitarian group (Combemale and al., 2005). Teams that work collaboratively can obtain greater resources, recognition, and reward when facing competition for finite resources.

- Sharing space. Sharing space or exchange space allows discussion, to define and to follow the implementation of collaborative projects of one or several courses.
- Evaluation space. Evaluation is a process where learners are assessed to determine their suitability to take a course. The learners' aptitudes are determined by a variety of techniques including interviews, group exercises, presentations, examinations, and psychometric testing.
- Production space. In the production space, the teacher or tutor can create notifications, and assess the productions undertaken by learners.
- Self-management space. Self-management is the management of an LMS by the administrators themselves. The customizations decentralized as much as possible and the sharing of tasks between all the users (administrators, coordinators, teachers, tutors, and learners) done equitably.
- Assistance space. Assistance designates the action of bringing help or relief. It is about providing aid, support, or relief in all matters.

CONCEPTS AND RELATED WORK

1. Instructional Management Systems - Learning Design

IMS-LD was published in 2003 by the IMS/GLC. (Instructional Management Systems Global Learning Consortium: Consortium for global learning management systems with training, the original name when IMS was started in 1997 Instructional Management Systems project) (Lejeune, 2004; Burgos and al., 2005). Reminds us of its origins: the source (EML1) of the proposed language was assessed by the European Committee for Standardization (CEN) in a comparative study of different SRMS (CEN/ISS WS/LT, 2002), (Burgos and al., 2005), as best suited to satisfy the criteria definition of an EML. EML is defined by CEN / ISS as *"an information aggregation and semantic model describing the content and processes involved in a unit of learning from an educational perspective and to ensure the reusability and interoperability."* (Burgos and al., 2005; El-Moudden and al., 2015) In this context, the North American IMS consortium undertook a study and provided a specification of such a language, giving birth in February 2003, the Learning Design specification V1.0 (IMS-LD). She adds that the proposal, largely inspired by EML developed by (Koper, 2001), (Burgos and al., 2005) (OUNL) provides a conceptual framework for modeling a Learning Unit and claims to offer a good compromise between on the one hand to the generic implement a variety of instructional approaches and secondly, the power of expression that allows an accurate description of each learning unit.

This specification allows us to represent and encode learning structures for learners both alone and in groups, compiled by roles, such as *"learners"* and *"Team"* (see Figure 1) (Burgos and al., 2005). We can model a lesson plan in IMS-LD, defining roles, learning activities, services, and many other elements and building learning units. The syllabus is modeled and built with resources assembled in a compressed Zip file, then started by an executable *("player")*. It coordinates the teachers, students, and activities as long as the respective learning process progresses. A user takes a "role" to play and execute the activities related to achieve a satisfactory learning unit. In all, the unit structure, roles, and activities to build the learning scenario to be executed in a system compatible with IMS-LD.

Figure 1. The conceptual model of Instructional Management Systems - Learning Design (Burgos and al., 2005)

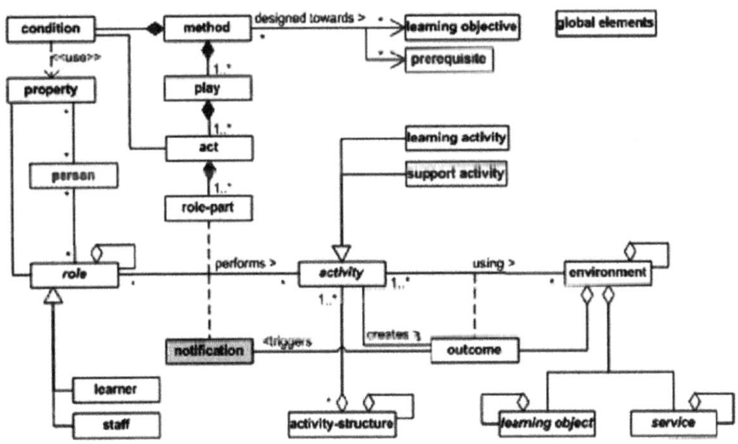

IMS-LD does not impose a particular pedagogical model but can be used with a large number of scenarios and pedagogic models, demonstrating its flexibility. Therefore, IMS-LD is often called a meta-pedagogic model. Previous eLearning initiatives claim to be pedagogically neutral, IMS-LS is not intended for pedagogical neutrality but seeks to raise awareness of eLearning on the need for a flexible approach.

IMS-LD has been developed for eLearning and virtual classes, but a course face to face can be done and integrated into a structure created by this specification, as an activity of learning or support activity. If the ultimate goal to create rich learning units, with support to achieve the learning objectives by providing the best possible experience, face-to-face meetings, and any other learning resource are permitted such as video conferencing, collaborative table, or any field action research.

IMS-LD uses the theatrical metaphor, which implies the existence of roles, resources, and learning scenarios themselves: one room is divided into one or more acts and conducted by several actors who can take on different roles at different times. Each role is to carry out some activities to complete the learning process. Besides, all roles must be synchronized at the end of each act before processing the next act.

2. Related Works

Many works emphasized the contribution of learning theories in the design and development of learning systems. The direct application of each of these theories allows particularly providing supporting methods for the design and development of LMS. The learning theory that we presented in this chapter for an original conceptual model of sharing has allowed us to design a new space of an LMS whose benefit resides essentially in the richness of the proposed functionalities in a way that fits the needs of all its final users: teachers and learners.

Furthermore, much work has been done in the field of collaborative learning and IMS-LD specification. For example, Dyke (Dyke and al., 2006) explains how models' socio-cognitive interactions related to the properties of collaborative tools. Ferraris (Ferraris and al., 2005) expresses collaborative learning scenarios by teachers animating virtual classrooms to promote re-use and share teaching practices. He proposes an approach led by the models following the recommendations of the Model Driven Architecture OMG. He presents a meta-model based on IMS-LD enhanced by the concepts of the participation model to capture the richness of the interactions inherent in collaborative activities. Moreover, El-Moudden (El-Moudden and al., 2015) proposes designing an IMS-LD model for collaborative learning. His approach is to first think about the conditions for creating a real collective activity between learners and designing the IT environment that supports these activities.

On the other hand, other research aimed at proposing the modeling of new units, approaches, architecture, or adaptive, flexible, and interactive e-learning systems. For example, Sadiq proposed the modeling of learning units on eLearning platforms, which relies on the application of the standard IMS-LD in the production of adaptive learning units (Sadiq and al., 2010).

Based on these various research works, which seemed to us incomplete, we proposed a modeling portrait of designing an IMS-LD meta-model for the LMS platform. For us, this is not the same case and the same vision as our modelization is more general, it aims one hand to create an LMS from which teachers can animate virtual groups for the re-use and sharing of teaching practices, and on the other hand, the re-use of the content created in other frameworks. Indeed, the idea is to orient the design work research towards great and optimal compatibility between the services offered by e-learning platforms (LMS) and the needs of all users, particularly learners, for better optimization of online learning.

TRANSFORMATION RULES

1. Atlas Language Transformation (ATL)

In their operational ATL, Canals use. (Canals and al., 2005; El-Moudden and al., 2015) State that to deal with the transformation of models; it is difficult and cumbersome to use object languages since we spend so much effort on the development of transformation definitions of Framework for the set work. The use of XSLT as a language if is more direct and adapted by rest against difficulty to maintain (Canals and al., 2005; El-Moudden and al., 2015). We follow their choice by focusing on the implementation of approaches centered on the MDA (Model Driven Architecture), MDE (Model Driven Engineering), and QVT (Queries View Transformation) tools. Query / View / Transformation (QVT) (OMG/RFP/QVT, 2002; El-Moudden and al., 2015) is a standard defined by the OMG. This is a standardized language to express model transformations. QVT is not advanced sufficiently now in its definition for Queries and View aspects. Against transformation by the appearance expressed by the MDA, the approach has resulted in various experiments (eg Triskell, ATL ...) at both academic and commercial levels. To determine the transformation, it is necessary to have tools of transformation. These are based on language transformations that must respect the QVT standard

(OMG/RFP/QVT, 2002; El-Moudden and al., 2015) proposed by the OMG (Bézivin and al., 2003; El-Moudden and al., 2015). There is an offer of free tools (ATL, MTF, MTL, QVTP, etc.) and commercial (eg MIA). We chose ATL (Atlas Transformation Language) from the provision of free tools to the extent that only ATL has a spirit consistent with OMG / MDA / MOF / QVT (Canals and al., 2005; El-Moudden and al., 2015).

2. ATL Description

Atlas Transformation Language (ATL) has been designed to perform transformations within the MDA Framework proposed by the OMG (ATLAS group LINA, 2006; Combemale and al., 2005; El-Moudden and al., 2015). The ATL language is mainly because the models are first-class entities. Indeed, the transformations considered models of transformation. Since the transformations considered themselves as models, we can apply their transformations. This possibility of ATL is considered an important point. Indeed, it provides the means to achieve higher-order transformations (HOT Higher-Order Processing) (Combemale and al., 2005; El-Moudden and al., 2015). A higher-order transformation is a transformation, including source and target models that are themselves transformations. As ATL is among the languages model transformation respecting the QVT (OMG/RFP/QVT, 2002) standard proposed by OMG (Bézivin and al., 2003), we describe its structure with this standard (QVT).

The study of the abstract syntax of the ATL language is to study two features provided by this language more than rules changes. The first feature, navigation, allows studying the possibility of navigation between meta-models sources and targets. The second feature, Operations, is used to describe the ability to define operations on model elements. Finally, the study of the transformation rules used to describe these types of rules, how they are called, and the type of results they return.

- Navigation (ATLAS group LINA, 2006; Bézivin and al., 2003; El-Moudden and al., 2015) this feature is offered by ATL language (Object Constraint Language). Navigation is allowed only if the model elements are fully initialized. The elements of the target model cannot be definitively initialized at the end of the execution of the transformation. Therefore, the navigation in the ATL can only be made between elements of the model (or meta-model) source and model (or meta-model) target.

- Operations: (ATLAS group LINA, 2006; El-Moudden and al., 2015) this feature ATL also provided by the OCL (Object Constraint Language). In OCL, operations can be defined on the elements of the model. ATL takes this opportunity to OCL to allow defining operations on elements of the source model and the transformation model (Bézivin and al., 2003; El-Moudden and al., 2015).

The transformation rules: there are several types of transformation rules based on how they are called and what kind of results they return (cf. Figure 2).

Figure 2. ATL Transformation rules (El-Moudden and al., 2015)

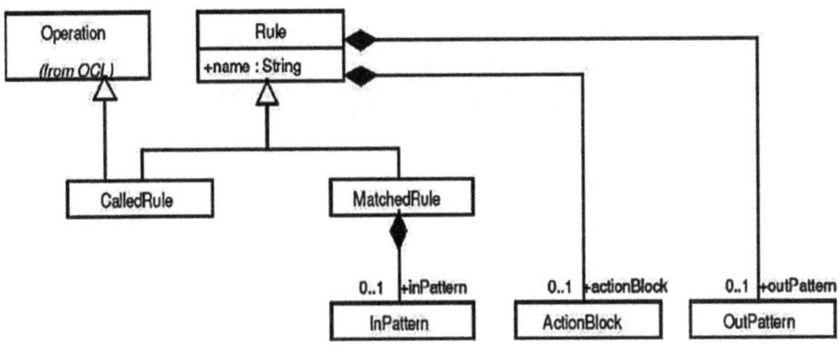

CalledRule (ATLAS group LINA, 2006) rule explicitly called by its name and by setting its parameters.

MatchedRule (ATLAS group LINA, 2006) rule executed when a person *(InPattern)* scheme recognized in the source model.

The result of a rule may be a set of predefined models *(OutPattern)* or a block of mandatory *(ActionBlock)*. If the rule is MatchedRule type and if its result is a set of elements of the target model *(OutPattern)*, it was named declarative. If it is CalledRule type whose result is a block of statements, it is then called procedure. Combinations of rules (declarative and imperative) are called hybrid rules (Bézivin and al., 2003).

3. Synthesis

In this research, we try to adapt the model IMS-LD with the LMS meta-model. This adaptation will go through three stages, first the development of an LMS meta-model; secondly, the study of the correspondence between the developed meta-model and IMS-LD model, and their transformation to the IMS-LD meta-model that reduced the MDA approach in a transformation that based on the rules implemented in the ATL language. However, we will talk about the IT design of our LMS meta-model without using the transformation that is based on the rules implemented in the ATL language, because we have detected the same problems as in El-Moudden's works (El-Moudden and al., 2015). In IMS-LD, we do not have the opportunity to build a course, which consists of several chapters. For this, there is at this level a semantic loss.

This led us to develop our proposal for an IMS-LD meta-model of a new smart LMS through the main lines of the diagrams in which we will finally identify the characteristics of the constituent entities of our activity spaces of our new smart LMS.

MODELING DRIVEN ARCHITECTURE (MDA)

In November 2000, the OMG in the field of software engineering consortium of over 1,000 companies, has initiated the process MDA [OMG MDA], the concepts-oriented models rather than object-oriented. The Model Driven Architecture MDA [OMG MDA] offers the power of abstraction, refinement, and different views of the models. This standard has to add a new way to design applications by separating business logic from business, any technical platform to increase the reuse of previously developed code, reducing development time, and facilitating the integration of new technology (Boulet and al., 2003). It allows developing independent model platforms and implementation (Thi-Lan-Anh and al., 2005) environment. MDA used to separate two extreme views of the same system (Clave, 2004):

- Its functional specifications on the one hand.
- Its physical implementation on the other hand.

Including several aspects of the life of the software, namely its tests, its quality requirements, the definition of successive iterations, etc. MDA architecture consists of four layers. In the center, there is a UML (Unified Modeling Language) standard MOF (Meta-Object Facility) and CWM (Common Warehouse Meta-model). The second layer contains the XMI (XML Metadata Interchange) standard for dialogue between the middleware (Java, CORBA, .NET, and Web services). The next layer refers to the services to manage events, transaction security, and directories. The last layer offers specific frameworks in scope (Telecommunications, medicine, electronic commerce, finance, etc.) A designer to create his application can use UML as it can use other languages. So, according to this architecture-independent technical context, MDA proposes to structure the front needs to engage in a transformation of this functional modeling technical modeling while testing each product model (Clave, 2004). This application model is to be created independently of the target implementation (hardware or software). This allows greater reuse of patterns. MDA considered an approach with the ambition to offer the widest possible view of the life cycle of the software, not content with only its production. Moreover, this is the intended overview described in a unified syntax. One of the assumptions underlying the MDA is that the operationalization of an abstract model is not a trivial problem. One of the benefits of MDA is to solve this problem (Caron and al., 2007). MDA proposes to design an application through a software chain divided into four phases with the aim of flexible implementation, integration, maintenance, and test:

- The development of a computer model without concern (CIM: Computer Independent Model).
- The manual transformation into a model in a particular technological context (PIM: Platform Independent Model).
- The automatic transformation into a pattern associated with the target implementation of the platform (PSM: Platform Specific Model) model to be refined,
- Its implementation in the target platform.

DESIGN OF AN IMS-LD META-MODEL OF A NEW SMART LMS

The new smart LMS consists of different activity spaces. Each IMS-LD meta-model represents a space, namely:

- IMS-LD meta-model of the disciplinary information space,
- IMS-LD meta-model of the collaboration space,
- IMS-LD meta-model of the communication space,
- IMS-LD meta-model of the sharing space,
- IMS-LD meta-model of the evaluation space,
- IMS-LD meta-model of the production space,

- IMS-LD meta-model of the self-management space,
- IMS-LD meta-model of the assistance space.

1. IMS-LD Meta-Model of the Disciplinary Information Space

We offer an IMS-LD meta-model for the disciplinary information space designed to meet the needs of learners who need to view educational content and the needs of teachers in terms of generating educational content. Consequently, we establish the following diagram (see Figure 3) as the first proposition of an IMS-LD meta-model of disciplinary information space.

Figure 3. IMS-LD conceptual meta-model of the disciplinary information space

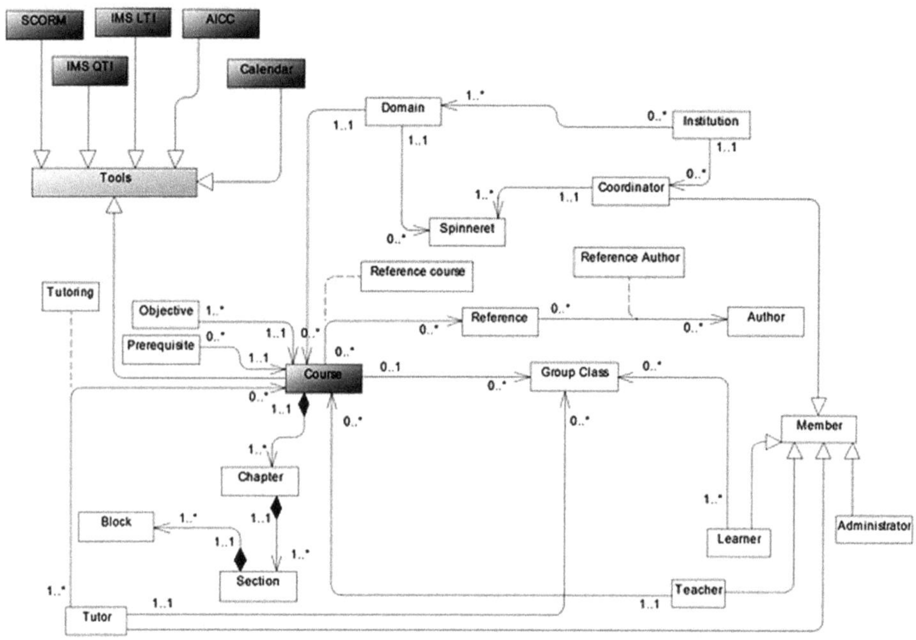

The majority of the classes designed in our IMS-LD meta-model of the disciplinary information space correspond perfectly to the IMS-LD model, which makes their transformations possible. The transformation of models is a technique aiming to put links between models to avoid unnecessary reproductions.

In Table 1, we have collected all the classes of the IMS-LD meta-model of the disciplinary information space and their equivalent to the IMS-LD model.

Table 1. Correspondence between the terminology of the IMS-LD and that of the IMS-LD meta-model of disciplinary information space

IMS-LD Meta-Model of the Disciplinary Information Space	IMS-LD Model
Prerequisite	Prerequisite
Phase	Play
The role, and features	Role
Members	Person
Coordinator, tutor, and teacher	Staff
Learner	Learner
Objective	Learning Objective
Disciplinary information space	Environment
Course, chapter, section, and block	Learning Object
Tools	Services

2. IMS-LD Meta-Model of the Collaboration Space

We offer an IMS-LD meta-model for the collaboration space designed to meet the needs of learners requiring online collaboration, and the needs of teachers in terms of the generation of collaborative educational content. Consequently, we establish the following diagram (see Figure 4) as the first proposition of an IMS-LD meta-model for collaborative learning.

The majority of the classes designed in our IMS-LD meta-model of the collaboration space correspond perfectly to the IMS-LD model, which makes their transformations possible. In Table 2, we have collected all the classes of the IMS-LD meta-model of the collaboration space and their equivalent to the IMS-LD model.

3. IMS-LD Meta-Model of the Communication Space

We offer an IMS-LD conceptual meta-model of the communication space designed to meet the needs of learners who require online communication and the needs of teachers in terms of the generation of collaborative educational content. Consequently, we establish the following diagram (see Figure 5) as the first proposition of an IMS-LD meta-model of communication.

Figure 4. IMS-LD conceptual meta-model of the collaboration space

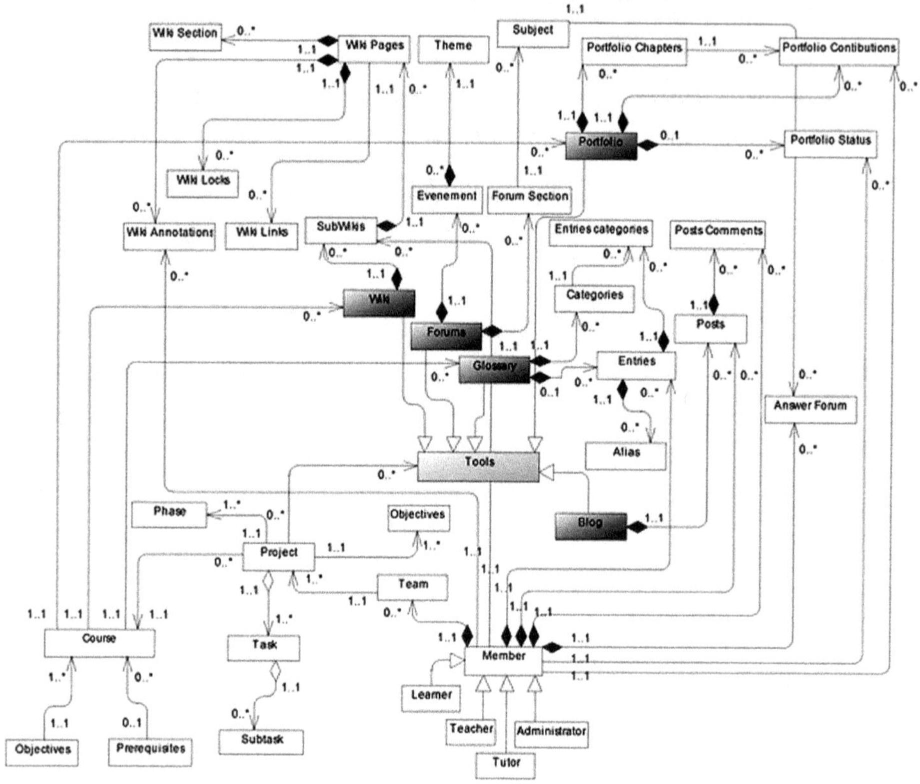

Table 2. Correspondence between the terminology of the IMS-LD and that of the IMS-LD meta-model of collaboration space

IMS-LD Meta-Model of the Collaboration Space	IMS-LD Model
Project	Activity
Task, and subtask	Activity structure
Phase	Play
The role, and features	Role
Members, and team	Person
Coordinator, teacher, and tutor	Staff
Learner	Learner
Collaboration space	Environment
Objective	Learning Objective
Course	Learning Object
Tools	Services

The majority of the classes designed in our IMS-LD meta-model of the communication space correspond perfectly to the IMS-LD model, which makes their transformations possible. In Table 3, we have collected all the classes of the IMS-LD meta-model of the communication space and their equivalent to the IMS-LD model.

Figure 5. IMS-LD conceptual meta-model of the communication space

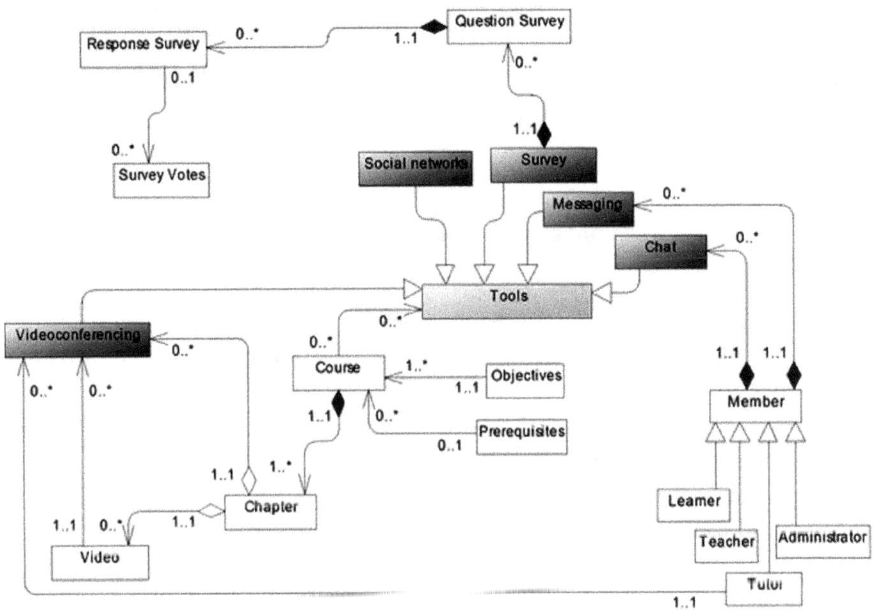

4. IMS-LD Meta-Model of the Sharing Space

We offer an IMS-LD meta-model for the sharing space designed to meet the needs of learners requiring online information sharing, and the needs of teachers in terms of the generation of shared educational content. Consequently, we establish the following diagram (see Figure 6) as the first proposition of an IMS-LD sharing meta-model.

The majority of the classes designed in our IMS-LD meta-model of the sharing space correspond perfectly to the IMS-LD model, which makes their transformations possible. In Table 4, we have tried to collect all the classes of the IMS-LD meta-model of the sharing space and their equivalent to the IMS-LD model.

Table 3. Correspondence between the terminology of the IMS-LD and that of the IMS-LD meta-model of communication space

IMS-LD Meta-Model of the Communication Space	IMS-LD Model
Activity	Activity
The role, and features	Role
Members	Person
Coordinator, teacher, and tutor	Staff
Learner	Learner
Objective	Learning Objective
Course and chapter	Learning Object
Tools	Services
Communication space	Environment

Figure 6. IMS-LD conceptual meta-model of the sharing space

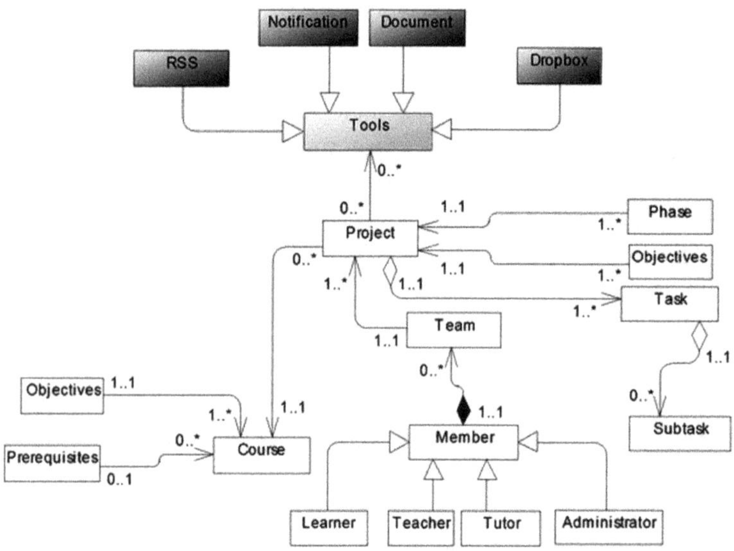

5. IMS-LD Meta-Model of the Evaluation Space

We offer an IMS-LD meta-model for the assessment space designed to meet the needs of learners requiring online assessment and the needs of teachers in terms of generating assessment content. Therefore, we establish the following diagram (see Figure 7) as the first proposal for an IMS-LD self-assessment meta-model.

Table 4. Correspondence between the terminology of the IMS-LD and that of the IMS-LD meta-model of sharing space

IMS-LD Meta-Model of the Sharing Space	IMS-LD Model
Activity	Activity
Task, and subtask of project	Activity structure
Prerequisite	Prerequisite
Project phase	Play
Members, and team	Person
Coordinator, teacher, and tutor	Staff
Learner	Learner
Notification	Notification
Project objective	Learning Objective
Course	Learning Object
Tools	Services
Sharing space	Environment

The majority of the classes designed in our IMS-LD meta-model of the evaluation space correspond perfectly to the IMS-LD model, which makes their transformations possible. In Table 5, we have tried to collect all the classes of the IMS-LD meta-model of the evaluation space and their equivalent to the IMS-LD model.

6. IMS-LD Meta-Model of the Production Space

We offer an IMS-LD meta-model for the production space designed to meet the needs of learners requiring online assistance, and the needs of teachers in terms of production when responding to the content of assessment, activity, and QUIZ. Consequently, we establish the following diagram (see Figure 8) as the first proposition of an IMS-LD production meta-model.

The majority of the classes designed in our IMS-LD meta-model of the production space correspond perfectly to the IMS-LD model, which makes their transformations possible. In Table 6, we have tried to collect all the classes of the IMS-LD meta-model of the production space and their equivalent to the IMS-LD model.

Figure 7. IMS-LD conceptual meta-model of the evaluation space

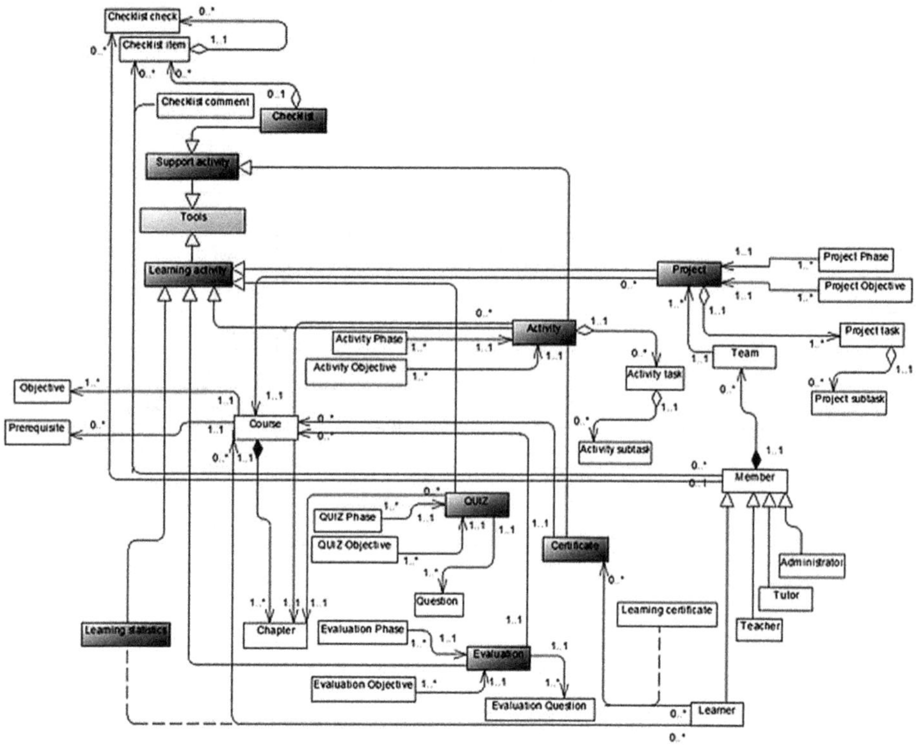

Table 5. Correspondence between the terminology of the IMS-LD and that of the IMS-LD meta-model of evaluation space

IMS-LD Meta-Model of the Evaluation Space	IMS-LD Model
Activity, project; QUIZ and evaluation	Activity
Task, and subtask of project or activity	Activity structure
Prerequisite	Prerequisite
The phase of activity, project, QUIZ, or evaluation	Play
Members, and team	Person
Coordinator, teacher, and tutor	Staff
Learner	Learner
Activity, project, QUIZ, or evaluation Objective	Learning objective
Course and Chapter	Learning Object
Tools	Services
Evaluation space	Environment

Figure 8. IMS-LD conceptual meta-model of the production space

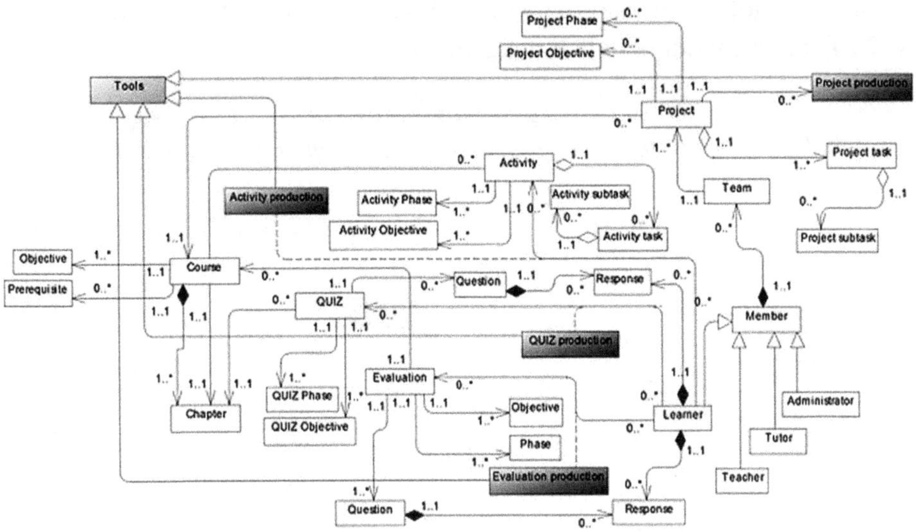

Table 6. Correspondence between the terminology of the IMS-LD and that of the IMS-LD meta-model of production space

IMS-LD Meta-Model of the Production Space	IMS-LD Model
Activity, project, QUIZ, and evaluation	Activity
Task and subtask of project or activity	Activity structure
Prerequisite	Prerequisite
Activity, project, QUIZ, or evaluation phase	Play
Members, and team	Person
Coordinator, teacher, and tutor	Staff
Learner	Learner
Activity, project, QUIZ, and evaluation production	Outcome
The objective of activity, project, QUIZ, or evaluation	Learning objective
Course and Chapter	Learning object
Tools	Services
Production space	Environment

7. IMS-LD Meta-Model of the Self-Management Space

We offer an IMS-LD meta-model for the self-management space designed to meet the needs of learners requiring online self-management, and the needs of teachers in terms of educational content management. Consequently, we establish the following diagram (see Figure 9) as the first proposition of an IMS-LD meta-model of self-management.

Figure 9. IMS-LD conceptual meta-model of the self-management space

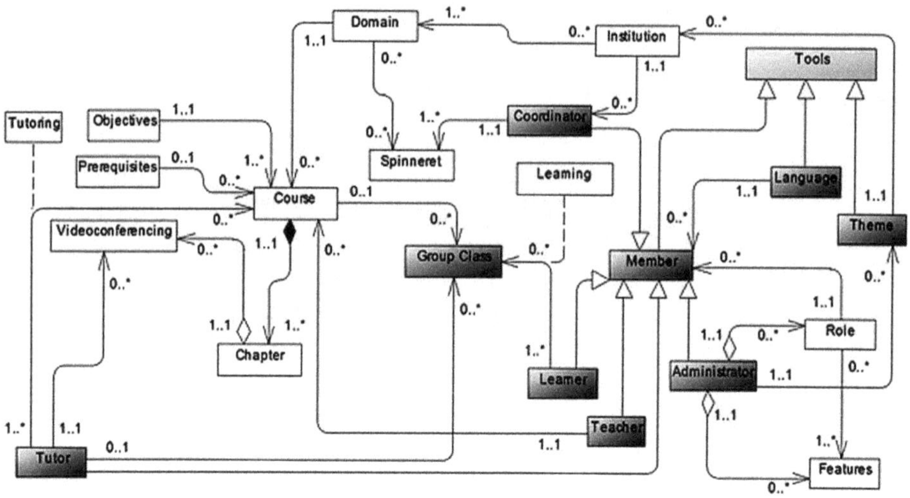

The majority of the classes designed in our IMS-LD meta-model of the self-management space correspond perfectly to the IMS-LD model, which makes their transformations possible. In Table 7, we have tried to collect all the classes of the IMS-LD meta-model of the self-management space and their equivalent to the IMS-LD model.

8. IMS-LD Meta-Model of the Assistance Space

We offer an IMS-LD meta-model for the support space designed to meet the needs of learners requiring online assistance, and the needs of teachers in terms of assistance when creating educational content. Consequently, we establish the following diagram (see Figure 10) as the first proposal for an IMS-LD meta-model of assistance.

The majority of the classes designed in our IMS-LD meta-model of the assistance space correspond perfectly to the IMS-LD model, which makes their transformations possible. In Table 8, we have tried to collect all the classes of the IMS-LD meta-model of the assistance space and their equivalent to the IMS-LD model.

Table 7. Correspondence between the terminology of the IMS-LD and that of the IMS-LD meta-model of self-management space

IMS-LD Meta-Model of the Self-Management Space	IMS-LD Model
Prerequisite	Prerequisite
The role, and features	Role
Member	Person
Coordinator, teacher, and tutor	Staff
Learner	Learner
Objective	Learning Objective
Course and chapter	Learning Object
Tools	Services
Self-management space	Environment

Figure 10. IMS-LD conceptual meta-model of the assistance space

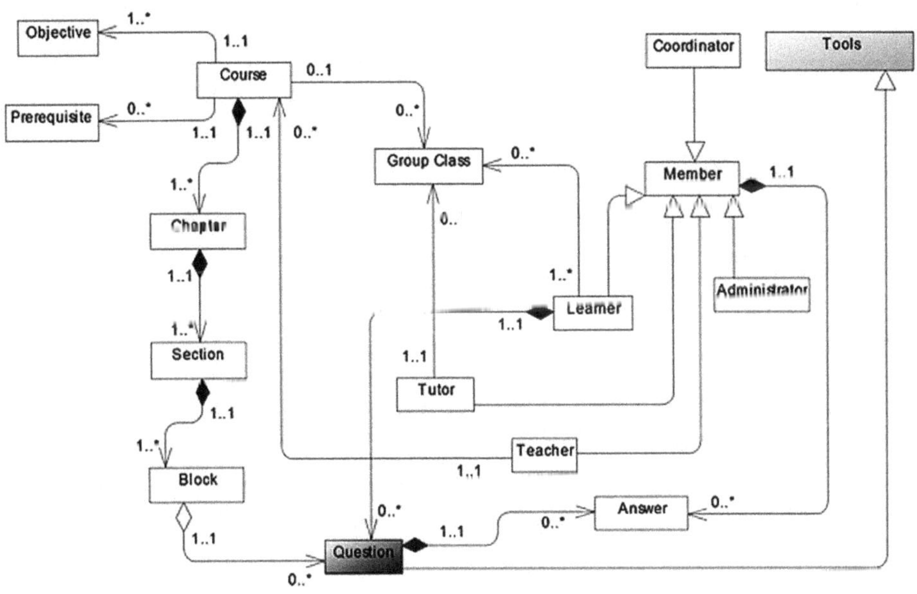

CONCLUSION

In our work, we are on the way to the design and modeling of meta-model content for a new smart Learning Management System compatible with IMS-LD. This design is based on active teaching learner-centered, and as an example of the pedagogy, we opted for four learning theories as a basis for teaching this LMS, namely the social constructivism, behaviorism, traditional pedagogy, and cognitivism. The latter allows us to reach a teaching object through the implementation of the courses divided into tasks performed by students collaboratively or individually. To achieve a goal, we need to reach the model validation step, which is one of the tasks to be performed in our future work; also, we seek a framework that will guide us better to start the development part of the smart LMS.

Table 8. Correspondence between the terminology of the IMS-LD and that of the IMS-LD meta-model of assistance space

IMS-LD Meta-Model of the Assistance Space	IMS-LD Model
Prerequisite	Prerequisite
Member	Person
Coordinator, teacher, and tutor	Staff
Learner	Learner
Answer	Outcome
Objective	Learning Objective
Course, chapter, section, and block	Learning Object
Tools	Services
Assistance space	Environment

REFERENCES

Alfanet Project. (2008). *CopperCore V 3.3*. Author.

ATLAS Group, LINA, & INRIA Nantes. (2006). *Atlas transformation language. ATL user manual - version 0.7*. Technical report, INRIA University of Nantes.

Bézivin, J., Dupé, G., Jouault, F., Pitette, G., & Eddine Rougui, J. (2003). *First experiments with the ATL model transformation language: Transforming xslt into xquery*. In OOPSLA 2003 Workshop, Anaheim, CA.

Bolton. (2005). *RELOAD Project: Editor*. The University of Bolton, The University of Strathclyde and JISC.

Boulet, P., Dekeyser, J. L., Dumoulin, C., & Marquet, P. (2003). Mda for soc embedded systems design, intensive signal processing experiment. In SIVOESMDA workshop at UML 2003, San Francisco, CA.

Brunel, S., Girard, P., & Lamago, M. (2015). Des plateformes pour enseigner à distance : vers une modélisation générale de leurs fonctions. In AIP Primeca 2015, La Plagne, France.

Burgos, Arnaud, Neuhauser, & Koper. (2005). *IMS Learning Design*. Association EPI.

Canals, Le Camus, Feau, Jolly, Bonnafous, & Bazavan. (2005). Une utilisation opérationnelle d'ATL : L'intégration de la transformation de modèles dans le projet TOPCASED. *Génie logiciel*, 21–26.

Caron, P. A., Hoogstoel, F., Le Pallec, X., & Warin, B. (2007). Construire des dispositifs sur la plateforme moodle - application de l'ingénierie bricoles. In MoodleMoot-2007, Castres, France.

Chouchane, K. (2012). *"Modélisation et réalisation d'une approche pour le m-learning," Magister en Informatique Option Système d'Informatique et de Communication (SIC)*. Université Hadj Lakhdar – Batna – Algérienne.

Clave. (2004). *D'UML à MDA en passant par les métas modèles*. Technical report, La Lettre d'ADELI.

Combemale & Rougemaille. (2005). *ATL - Atlas Transformation Language*. Master 2 Recherche SLCP, module rtm edition.

Dyke & Lund. (2006). *Implications d'un modèle de coopération pour la conception d'outils collaboratifs*. Academic Press.

El-Moudden, Aammou, & Khaldi. (2014). A Tool to Generate a Collaborative Content Compatible with IMS-LD. *International Journal of Software and Web Sciences, 11*(1), 1-8.

El-Moudden, F., Khaldi, M., & Aammou, S. (2015). Designing an IMS-LD Model for Collaborative Learning. *IJACSA*, *1*(6), 42–48.

Ferraris, Lejeune, Vignollet, & David. (2005). *Modélisation de scénarios pédagogiques collaboratifs*. Academic Press.

Henri, F., Rabardel, P., & Pastré, P. (Eds.). (2005). Modèles du sujet pour la conception. International Journal of ELearning & Distance Education, 22(1), 101–106.

Koper. (2001). *Modeling Units of Study from a Pedagogical Perspective, the pedagogical meta-model behind EML.* Academic Press.

Lejeune, A. (2004). *IMS Learning Design: Étude d'un langage de modélisation pédagogique* (Vol. 2). Revue Distances et Savoirs.

OMG/RFP/QVT MOF 2.0 Query/Views/Transformations RFP. (2002). OMG, Object Management Group.

Ouadoud, M., Chkouri, M. Y., & Nejjari, A. (2018a, March). Learning Management System and the Underlying Learning Theories: Towards a new Modeling of an LMS. *International Journal of Information Science and Technology*, *2*(1), 25–33.

Ouadoud, M., Chkouri, M. Y., & Nejjari, A. (2018b, January). LeaderTICE: A Platforms Recommendation System Based on a Comparative and Evaluative Study of Free E-learning Platforms. *International Journal of Online Engineering*, *14*(01), 132–161. https://doi.org/10.3991/ijoe.v14i01.7865

Ouadoud, M., Chkouri, M. Y., Nejjari, A., & El Kadiri, K. E. (2017, February). Exploring a Recommendation System of Free eLearning Platforms: Functional Architecture of the System. *International Journal of Emerging Technologies in Learning*, *12*(02), 219–226. https://dx.doi.org/10.3991/ijet.v12i02.6381

Ouadoud, M., Nejjari, A., Chkouri, M. Y., & El-Kadiri, K. E. (2017b). Learning Management System and the Underlying Learning Theories. *Innovations in Smart Cities and Applications*, 732–744. doi:10.1007/978-3-319-74500-8_67

Ouadoud, M., Nejjari, A., Chkouri, M. Y., & Kadiri, K. E. E. (2017a). Educational modeling of a learning management system. *2017 International Conference on Electrical and Information Technologies (ICEIT),* 1–6. doi:10.1109/EITech.2017.8255247

Sadiq & Talbi. (2010). *Modélisation des unités d'apprentissage sur des plates-formes de formation à distance*. Association EPI.

Survey of Educational Modelling Languages (EMLs). Version 1. (2002). *CEN/ISS WS/LT, Learning Technologies Workshop.*

Thi-Lan-anh, D., Olivier, G., & Houari, S. (2005). Gestion de modèles: définitions, besoins et revue de littérature. *Premières Journées sur l'Ingénierie Dirigée par les Modèles*, 1–15.

Wake, J. D. (2001). *Evaluating the Organising of a Collaborative Telelearning Scenario from an Instructor Perspective œ an Activity Theoretical Approach* (Ph.D. dissertation). Dept. of Information Science, University of Bergen.

ADDITIONAL READING

Ouadoud, M., Chafiq, T., Rida, N., & Chkouri, M. Y. (2019). Generate a Meta-Model Content for Collaboration Space of Learning Management System Compatible with IMS-LD. *International Journal of Interactive Mobile Technologies, 13*(01), 37–52. doi:10.3991/ijim.v13i01.9440

Ouadoud, M., & Chkouri, M. Y. (2019). Generate a Meta-Model Content for Communication Space of Learning Management System Compatible with IMS-LD. In M. Ezziyyani (Ed.), *Advanced Intelligent Systems for Sustainable Development (AI2SD'2018), Advances in Intelligent Systems and Computing* (pp. 24–39). Springer International Publishing. doi:10.1007/978-3-030-11928-7_3

Ouadoud, M., & Chkouri, M. Y. (2019). Designing an IMS-LD Model for Communication Space of Learning Management System. In M. Ezziyyani (Ed.), *Advanced Intelligent Systems for Sustainable Development (AI2SD'2018), Advances in Intelligent Systems and Computing* (pp. 40–54). Springer International Publishing. doi:10.1007/978-3-030-11928-7_4

KEY TERMS AND DEFINITIONS

IMS: Instructional management systems.

LMS: Learning management system.

Methods: The word "method" used by IMS-LD means the unfolding of the scenario.

SCORM: The SCORM® (Sharable Content Object Reference Model) was created to address these interoperability, reusability, and durability challenges. As a reference model, it was intentionally designed to leverage standard web technologies as well as existing learning technology specifications that already existed. SCORM® is comprised of a collection of interrelated technical specifications and guidelines designed to meet the DoD's high-level requirements for creating interoperable, plug-n-play, browser-based e-learning content. It consists of three different technical specifications "books" that collectively address challenges associated with interoperability, portability, reusability, and the instructional sequencing of self-paced e-learning content (Available at https://www.adlnet.gov/adl-research/scorm).

Social Constructivism: Is centered on the learner. The learner learns through its representations. The construction of knowledge although personal is carried out in a social setting. The context and come from both what we think and what others bring as interactions.

Chapter 7
Modeling a New Smart Learning Management System Based on the EML

ABSTRACT

The context of this work is that of designing an IMS-LD model for a new smart LMS. The work is specifically in the field or seeking to promote using information technology from a distance. The approach is to first think about the conditions for creating a real new smart LMS between learners and designing the IT environment that supports this LMS. In this chapter, the authors try to adapt the IMS-LD model with a new smart LMS based on traditional pedagogy, behaviorism, cognitivism, and social constructivism. This adaptation will go through three stages: first, the development of an LMS model; second, the study of the correspondence between the developed model and the IMS-LD model; finally, their transformation to the IMS-LD model.

INTRODUCTION

In the 20th century, there was an international movement in favor of e-learning integration in higher education. This movement has been operationalized due to the variety of the educational offer by universities, which most have opted to diversify knowledge dissemination platforms to meet the needs of their target public.

DOI: 10.4018/978-1-7998-4021-3.ch007

E-learning is promoted through e-learning platforms: integrated systems offer a wide range of activities in the learning process. Teachers use the platforms to monitor or evaluate the work of students. They use LMSs to create courses, tests, etc. However, the LMS e-learning platforms do not offer personalized services and therefore do not take into account the aspects of personalization such as the level of knowledge, interest, motivation, and goals of learners. They access the same resource sets in the same way.

We present an easy model of the new smart LMS to create and administer the educational content online. This tool allows the generation and editing structures of websites through a database rather than pedagogical models, with a variety of choices that ensures better adaptation to the teaching of the course and learning style. Therefore, it is necessary to find a method to model all LMS types. To model the new smart LMS we have based ourselves upon the IMS-LD specification focusing on learning theory that was judged the most important and relevant to our modeling, namely social constructivism. Then, this learning theory which has inspired for a long time the design of computer applications is combined and put into perspective with several emergent pedagogical functionalities to build original modeling for our LMS. This reveals that this proposed modeling that is presented to readers here looks for ways to leverage technology for learning by considering users as being human actors and not human factors (Henri and al., 2005).

The IMS-LD specification or instructional design engineering uses pedagogical concepts, allowing to model learning units. IMS-LD takes into account a wide variety of teaching models it is there its flexibility. A course plan extract of a general or specific database can be modeled with IMS-LD, through the description of the different roles, activities, environments, methods, properties, conditions, and notifications. It is used to transform the course plans into formal learning units (UOL) that can be performed with an IMS-LD editor based on an engine such as Copper core (Alfanet project, 2008). These executable units can be designed from the beginning using an editor such as Reload (Bolton, 2005).

Based on these various research works, which seemed to us incomplete, we proposed a modeling portrait of designing an IMS-LD model for a new smart LMS platform. The latter is anthropocentric and relies on a learning conception that is located at the intersection of the most used learning theory. Indeed, the idea is to orient the design work research towards great and optimal compatibility between the services offered by e-learning platforms and the needs of all users, particularly learners, for better optimization of online learning.

To make our modeling work concrete, we present in the second section the different activity spaces for teaching and learning activities. We also present in the third section, the IMS-LD e-learning specification. Then in the last section, we present the design of our new smart LMS, of which we create the LMS use case diagrams. Thus, we try to adapt the LMS class diagram models to the IMS-LD model.

LMS AND ACTIVITY SPACES

The LMS consists of different activity spaces for activities of teaching and learning (Ouadoud and al., 2018; Ouadoud and al., 2017), in these spaces, both teachers and learners can have:

- Disciplinary information space.
- Communication space.
- Collaboration space.
- Sharing space.
- Evaluation space.
- Production space.
- Self-management space.
- Assistance space.

INSTRUCTIONAL MANAGEMENT SYSTEMS - LEARNING DESIGN

IMS-LD was published in 2003 by the IMS/GLC. (Instructional Management Systems Global Learning Consortium: Consortium for global learning management systems with training, the original name when IMS was started in 1997 Instructional Management Systems project) (Lejeune, 2004; Burgos and al., 2005). Reminds us of its origins: the source (EML1) of the proposed language was assessed by the European Committee for Standardization (CEN) in a comparative study of different SRMS (CEN/ISS WS/LT, 2002), (Burgos and al., 2005), as best suited to satisfy the criteria definition of an EML. EML is defined by CEN / ISS as *"an information aggregation and semantic model describing the content and processes involved in a unit of learning from an educational perspective and to ensure the reusability and interoperability."*

(Burgos and al., 2005; El-Moudden and al., 2015). In this context, the North American IMS consortium undertook a study and provided a specification of such a language, giving birth in February 2003, the Learning Design specification V1.0 (IMS-LD). She adds that the proposal, largely inspired by EML developed by (Koper, 2001), (Burgos and al., 2005) (OUNL) provides a conceptual framework for modeling a Learning Unit and claims to offer a good compromise between on the one hand to the generic implement a variety of instructional approaches and secondly, the power of expression that allows an accurate description of each learning unit.

This specification allows us to represent and encode learning structures for learners both alone and in groups, compiled by roles, such as *"learners"* and *"Team"* (see Figure 1) (Burgos and al., 2005). We can model a lesson plan in IMS-LD, defining roles, learning activities, services, and many other elements and building learning units. The syllabus is modeled and built with resources assembled in a compressed Zip file, then started by an executable *("player")*. It coordinates the teachers, students, and activities as long as the respective learning process progresses. A user takes a "role" to play and execute the activities related to achieve a satisfactory learning unit. In all, the unit structure, roles, and activities to build the learning scenario to be executed in a system compatible with IMS-LD.

Figure 1. The conceptual model of Instructional Management Systems - Learning Design (Burgos and al., 2005)

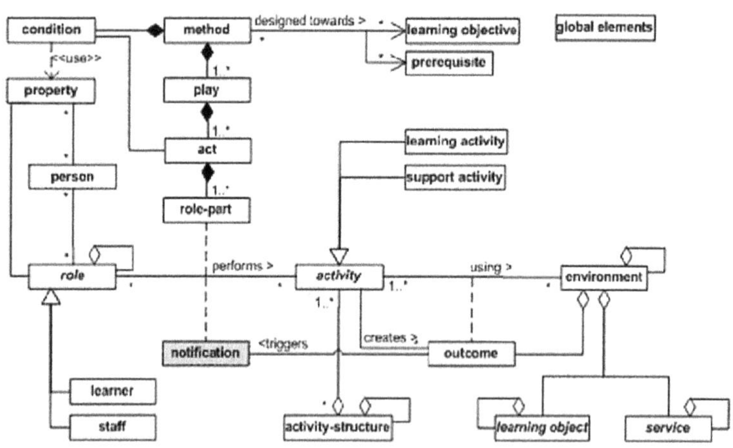

IMS-LD does not impose a particular pedagogical model but can be used with a large number of scenarios and pedagogic models, demonstrating its flexibility. Therefore, IMS-LD is often called a meta-pedagogic model. Previous eLearning initiatives claim to be pedagogically neutral; IMS-LS is not intended for pedagogical neutrality but seeks to raise awareness of eLearning on the need for a flexible approach.

IMS-LD has been developed for eLearning and virtual classes, but a course face to face can be done and integrated into a structure created by this specification, as an activity of learning or support activity. If the ultimate goal to create rich learning units, with support to achieve the learning objectives by providing the best possible experience, face-to-face meetings, and any other learning resource are permitted such as video conferencing, collaborative table, or any field action research.

IMS-LD uses the theatrical metaphor, which implies the existence of roles, resources, and learning scenarios itself: one room is divided into one or more acts and conducted by several actors who can take on different roles at different times. Each role is to carry out some activities to complete the learning process. Besides, all roles must be synchronized at the end of each act before processing the next act.

DESIGN OF AN IMS-LD MODEL OF A NEW SMART LMS

In our work we will try to design e-learning models, so we have to create a use case diagram model and class diagrams based on the theoretical study of our current work and will simultaneously ensure its projections to the models, also that we will try to recognize our models with the IMS-LD model. This compatibility will not be a direct means, i.e. we will use the same IMS-LD terminology for all the classes of our proposed LMS models, there is an equivalent class in the IMS-LD meta-models of the activity spaces, proposed in the previous chapter, which will greatly help us in the design level.

1. Use Case Diagrams

The use case diagrams identify the functionality provided by the model (use case); users interact with the system (actors), and the interactions between them. The main objectives of the use case diagrams are:

- Provide a high-level view of the model.
- Identify users ("actors") of the model.
- Define the roles of the actors in the model.

Each diagram represents an activity space, in these spaces teachers and learners can:

- Present structured information (disciplinary information space);
- Interact and collaborate with other actors (collaboration space);
- Communicate with one or more actors (communication space);
- Share resources with one or more actors (sharing space);
- Evaluate themselves and other resources (evaluation space);
- Produce information (production space);
- Select and use different tools according to their needs (self-management space);
- Offer and/or receive personalized assistance (assistance space).

1.1 Disciplinary Information Space

Table 1 describes the service functions for each actor in the disciplinary information space. Figure 2, presents the disciplinary information space use case diagram, representing the external actors who will interact with the system, and how they will use it.

1.2 Collaboration Space

Table 2 describes the service functions for each actor in the collaboration space. Figure 3, presents the collaboration space use case diagram, representing the external actors who will interact with the system, and how they will use it.

1.3 Communication Space

Table 3 describes the service functions for each actor in the communication space. Figure 4, presents the communication space use case diagram, representing the external actors who will interact with the system, and how they will use it.

Table 1. Functions' description of the disciplinary information space

Actor	Function	Description
Learners	Consult the course	The learner can view the course, prerequisites, and its objectives at any time
	Browse calendar	The learner can browse the defined task calendar.
	View documents	Learners read the downloaded documents.
	Download documents	The learner can download the documents
	Upload documents	The learner can upload documents
	Download documents	The learner can download the documents
Tutor	Supervise the learners	The tutor adds, modifies or deletes his learners
	Manage groups	The tutor adds, modifies or deletes groups
	Assign students to groups	The tutor can assign learners to groups
	Set calendar	The teacher can set schedules for the tasks and phases
	Consult the intervention schedules	Tutor can consult the intervention schedules of the learners
Teacher	Create courses	The teacher can create courses
	Set prerequisites	The teacher can set prerequisites for course
	Set objectives	The teacher can set objectives for course, projects, activities, QUIZs, and assessments
	Upload documents	The teacher can upload documents
	Download documents	Teachers can download the documents
	Planning of teaching resources	The teacher must plan of teaching resources
Administrator	Set in place groups	The administrator can set in place the classes' groups
	Assignment of courses to tutors	The administrator can assignment of courses to tutors according to the specialty of each one
	Management of the courses	The administrator can management of the courses
	Manage access rights	The administrator can manage the access rights of teachers and learners.
Coordinator	Manage teachers	The coordinator adds, modifies, or deletes a teacher
	Set in place groups	The coordinator can set in place the classes' groups
	Assignment of courses to tutors	The coordinator can assignment of courses to tutors according to the specialty of each one
	Management of the courses	The coordinator can management of the courses

Figure 2. Use case diagram of disciplinary information space

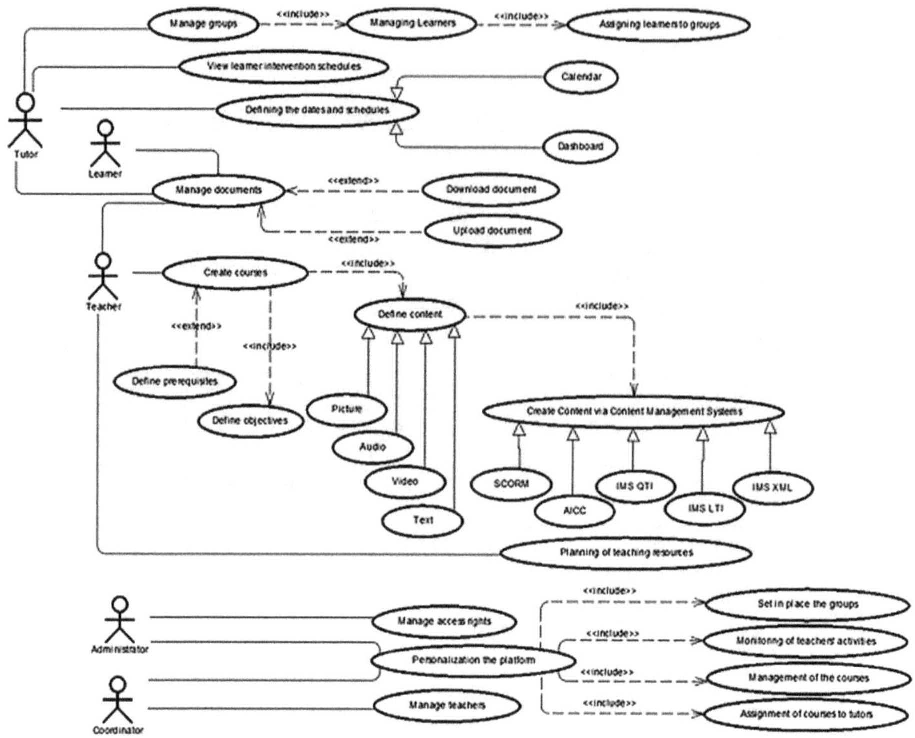

1.4 Sharing Space

Table 4 describes the service functions for each actor in the sharing space. Figure 5, presents the sharing space use case diagram, representing the external actors who will interact with the system, and how they will use it.

1.5 Evaluation Space

Table 5 describes the service functions for each actor in the evaluation space. Figure 6, presents the evaluation space use case diagram, representing the external actors who will interact with the system, and how they will use it.

Table 2. Functions' description of the collaboration space

Actor	Function	Description
Learners	Consult the project	The learner can view the project and its objectives at any time
	View documents	Learners read the downloaded documents.
	Download documents	The learner can download the documents
	Upload documents	The learner can upload documents
	Download documents	The learner can download the documents
Tutor	Manage groups	The tutor adds, modifies or deletes groups
	Assign students to groups	The tutor can assign learners to groups
	Initiate collaboration	The tutor can start collaboration
	Set phases	The tutor can set phases of project
	Set tasks	The tutor can set tasks
	Assign tasks	The tutors can assign tasks to learners
	Support the learners	Tutor can keep tracking of learners
Teacher	Create courses	The teacher can create courses
	Create projects	The teacher can create projects
	Set objectives	The teacher can set objectives for projects
	Upload documents	The teacher can upload documents
	Download documents	Teachers can download the documents
	Planning of teaching re sources	The teacher must plan of teaching resources
Administrator	Set in place groups	The administrator can set in place the classes' groups
	Management of the courses	The administrator can management of the courses
	Manage access rights	The administrator can manage the access rights of teachers and learners.
Coordinator	Manage teachers	The coordinator adds, modifies, or deletes a teacher
	Monitoring of teachers' activities	The coordinator can monitor of teachers' activities
	Assignment of courses to tutors	The coordinator can assignment of courses to tutors according to the specialty of each one

1.6 Production Space

Table 6 describes the service functions for each actor in the production space. Figure 7, presents the production space use case diagram, representing the external actors who will interact with the system, and how they will use it.

Figure 3. Use case diagram of collaboration space.

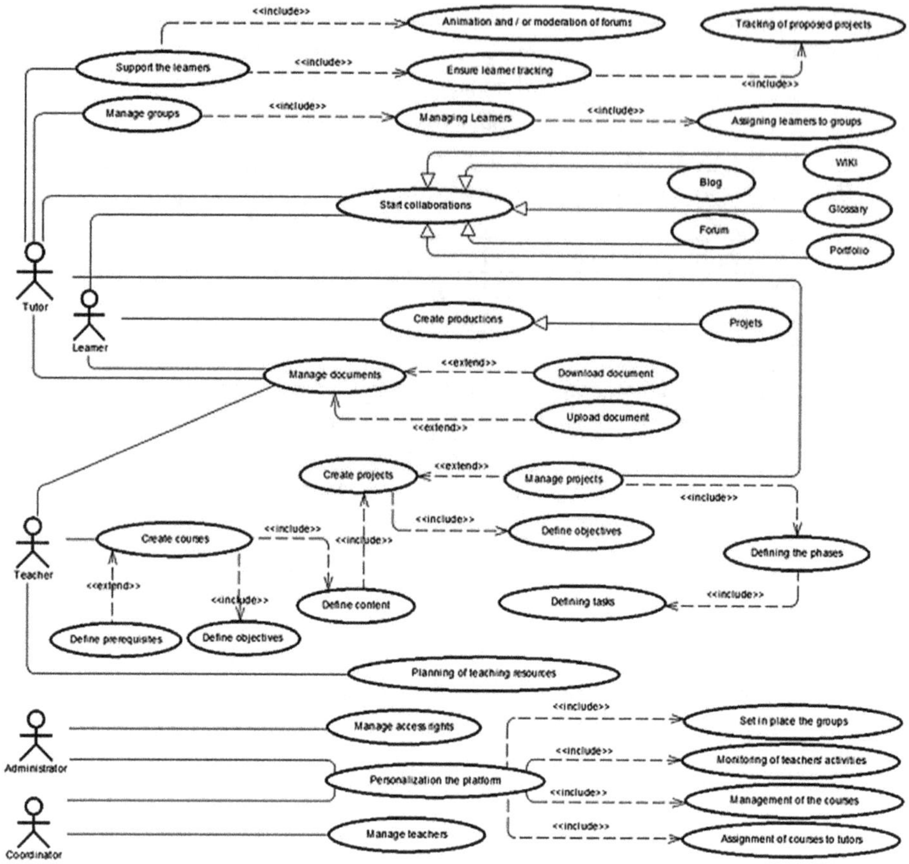

1.7 Self-management Space

Table 7 describes the service functions for each actor in the self-management space. Figure 8, presents the self-management space use case diagram, representing the external actors who will interact with the system, and how they will use it.

1.8 Assistance Space

Table 8 describes the service functions for each actor in the assistance space. figure 9, presents the assistance space use case diagram, representing the external actors who will interact with the system, and how they will use it.

Table 3. Functions' description of the communication space

Actor	Function	Description
Learner	Consult the course	The learner can view the course, prerequisites, and its objectives at any time
	View documents	Learners read the downloaded documents.
	Initiate discussions	The learner can start discussions
	Upload documents	The learner can upload documents
	Download documents	The learner can download the documents
Tutor	Manage groups	The tutor adds, modifies or deletes groups
	Assign students to groups	The tutor can assign learners to groups
	Initiate discussions	The tutor can start discussions
	Set tasks	The tutor can set tasks
	Assign tasks	The tutors can assign tasks to learners
	Support the learners	Tutor can keep tracking of learners
Teacher	Create courses	The teacher can create courses
	Set prerequisites	The teacher can set prerequisites for course
	Set objectives	The teacher can set objectives for course
	Upload documents	The teacher can upload documents
	Download documents	Teachers can download the documents
	Planning of teaching resources	The teacher must plan of teaching resources
Administrator	Set in place groups	The administrator can set in place the classes' groups
	Management of the courses	The administrator can management of the courses
	Manage access rights	The administrator can manage the access rights of teachers and learners.
Coordinator	Manage teachers	The coordinator adds, modifies, or deletes a teacher
	Monitoring of teachers' activities	The coordinator can monitor of teachers' activities
	Assignment of courses to tutors	The coordinator can assignment of courses to tutors according to the specialty of each one

2. Correspondence Between the Terminology of IMS-LD and That of the LMS Model

In this research, we try to adapt the model IMS-LD with our LMS model. This adaptation will go through three stages, first the development of an LMS model; secondly, the study of the correspondence between the developed model and IMS-LD model, and their transformation to the IMS-LD model that reduced the MDA approach in a transformation that based on the rules implemented in the ATL language. However, we will talk about the IT design of our LMS model without using the transformation that is based on the rules implemented in the ATL language, because we have detected the same problems as in El-Moudden's works (El-Moudden and al., 2015). In IMS-LD, we do not have the opportunity to build a course, which consists of several chapters, because, there is at this level a semantic loss.

This led us to develop our proposal for an IMS-LD model of a new smart LMS through the main lines of the diagrams in which we will finally identify the characteristics of the constituent entities of our activity spaces of our new smart LMS.

Figure 4. Use case diagram of communication space.

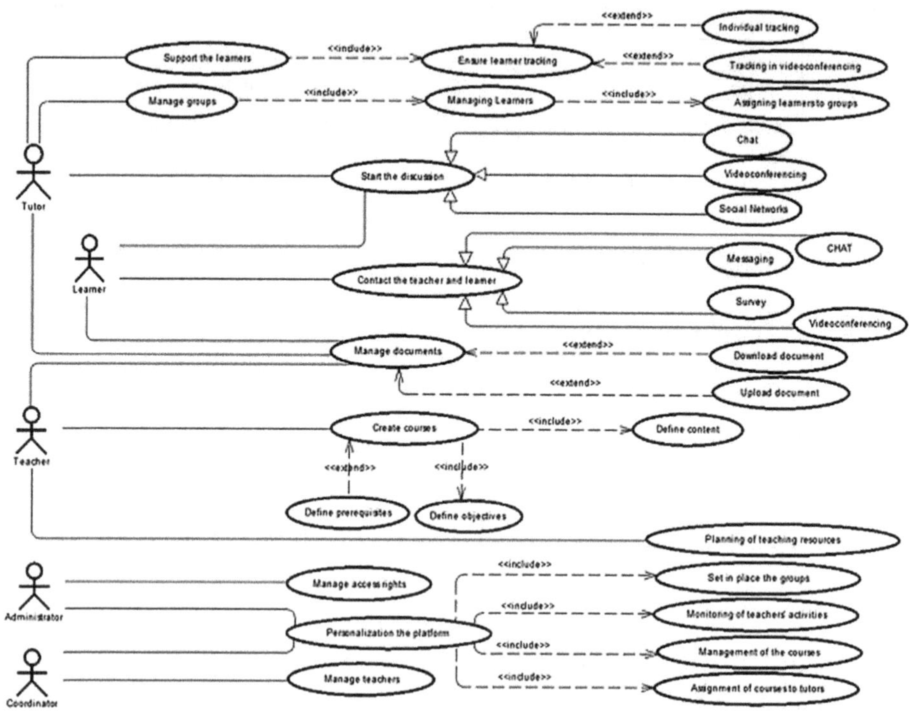

3. Class Diagrams of the LMS's IMS-LD Model

In this section, the LMS consists of class diagrams of different spaces of teaching and learning activities (Ouadoud and al, 2017; Ouadoud and al, Jan. 2018; Ouadoud and al, Mar. 2018), namely:

Table 4. Functions' description of the sharing space

Actor	Function	Description
Learner	Consult the course	The learner can view the course, its prerequisites, and its objectives at any time
	Consult the project	The learner can view the project and its objectives at any time
	Check notifications	The learner can always check notifications.
	View documents	Learners can view documents.
	Upload documents	The learner can upload documents
	Download documents	The learner can download documents
Tutor	Supervise the learners	The tutor can add, modify or delete his learners
	Manage groups	The tutor can add, modify or delete groups
	Assign learners to groups	The tutor can assign learners to groups
	Create notifications	The tutor can create notifications
	Set phases	The tutor can set phases of project
	Set tasks	The tutor can set tasks of project
Teacher	Create courses	The teacher can create courses
	Create projects	The teacher can create projects
	Set prerequisites	The teacher can set prerequisites for course
	Set objectives	The teacher can set objectives for course and projects
	Upload documents	The teacher can upload documents
	Download documents	Teachers can download documents
Administrator	Set in place groups	The administrator can set in place the classes' groups
	Assignment of courses to tutors	The administrator can assign courses to tutors according to the specialty of each one
	Management of the courses	The administrator can manage the courses
	Manage access rights	The administrator can manage the access rights of teachers and learners
Coordinator	Manage teachers	The coordinator can add, modify, or delete teachers
	Set in place groups	The coordinator can set in place the classes' groups
	Assignment of courses to tutors	The coordinator can assign courses to tutors according to the specialty of each one
	Management of the courses	The coordinator can manage the courses

- IMS-LD model of the disciplinary information space class diagram
- IMS-LD model of the collaboration space class diagram
- IMS-LD model of the communication space class diagram
- IMS-LD model of the sharing space class diagram
- IMS-LD model of the evaluation space class diagram
- IMS-LD model of the production space class diagram
- IMS-LD model of the self-management space class diagram
- IMS-LD model of the assistance space class diagram

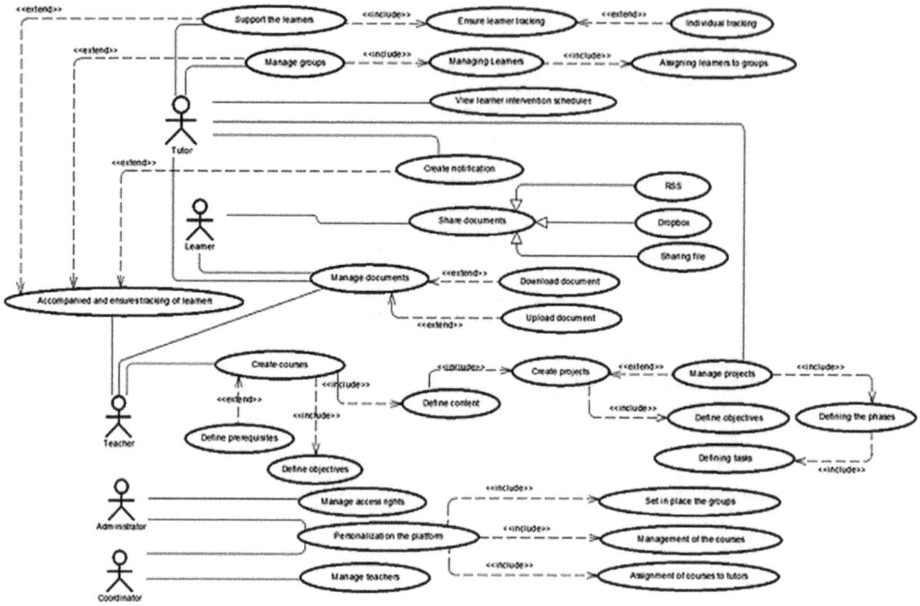

Figure 5. Use case diagram of sharing space.

3.1 IMS-LD Model of the Disciplinary Information Space Class Diagram

In our LMS, we propose a class diagram model for the disciplinary information space (cf. Figure 10) from our meta-model proposed in chapter 6.

In the latter, we have defined the properties of each class and the relationships between them. The majority of the classes designed in our class diagram model correspond perfectly to the meta-model proposed in Figure 4 of Chapter 6, which makes their transformations possible. The transformation of models is a technique aiming to put links between models to avoid unnecessary reproductions.

3.2 IMS-LD Model of the Collaboration Space Class Diagram

In our LMS, we propose a class diagram model for the collaboration space (see Figure 11) from our meta-model proposed in chapter 6. In this last one, we have defined the properties of each class and the relations between them. The majority of the classes designed in our class diagram model correspond perfectly to the meta-model proposed in Figure 5 of Chapter 6, which makes their transformations possible. The transformation of models is a technique aiming to put links between models to avoid unnecessary reproductions.

Table 5. Functions' description of the evaluation space

Actor	Function	Description
Learners	Consult the course	The learner can view the course, its prerequisites, and its objectives at any time
	Consult the QUIZs	The learner can view the QUIZs and its objectives at any time
	Consult the activities	The learner can view the activities and its objectives at any time
	Consult the project	The learner can view the project and its objectives at any time
	Consult the assessment	The learner can view the assessment and its objectives at any time
	Browse calendar	The learner can browse the defined task calendar.
	Upload documents	The learner can upload documents
	Download documents	The learner can download documents
Tutor	Supervise the learners	The tutor can add, modify or delete his learners
	Manage groups	The tutor can add, modify or delete groups
	Assign learners to groups	The tutor can assign learners to groups
	Set calendar	The teacher can set schedules for the tasks and phases
	Set phases	The tutor can set phases of project, activities, QUIZs, and assessments
	Set tasks	The tutor can set tasks
	Assign tasks	The tutors can assign tasks to learners
	Support the learners	Tutor can keep tracking of learners
	Consult the intervention schedules	Tutor can consult the intervention schedules of the learners
Teacher	Create courses	The teacher can create courses
	Create QUIZs	The teacher can create QUIZs
	Create activities	The teacher can create activities
	Create projects	The teacher can create projects
	Create assessments	The teacher can create assessments
	Set prerequisites	The teacher can set prerequisites for course
	Set objectives	The teacher can set objectives for course, projects, activities, QUIZs, and assessments
	Upload documents	The teacher can upload documents
	Download documents	Teachers can download documents
	Plan teaching resources	The teacher can plan teaching resources
Administrator	Set in place groups	The administrator can set in place the classes' groups
	Assignment of courses to tutors	The administrator can assign courses to tutors according to the specialty of each one
	Management of the courses	The administrator can manage the courses
	Manage access rights	The administrator can manage the access rights of teachers and learners.
Coordinator	Manage teachers	The coordinator can add, modify, or delete teachers
	Monitoring of teachers' activities	The coordinator can monitor teachers' activities
	Set in place groups	The coordinator can set in place the classes' groups
	Assignment of courses to tutors	The coordinator can assign courses to tutors according to the specialty of each one
	Management of the courses	The coordinator can manage the courses

Figure 6. Use case diagram of evaluation space.

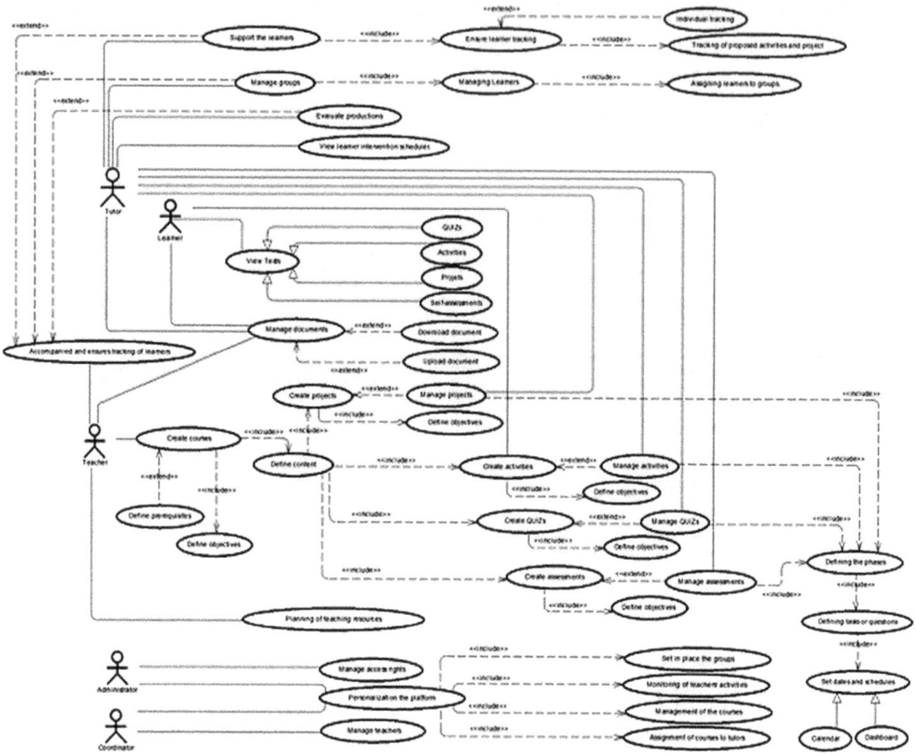

3.3 IMS-LD Model of the Communication Space Class Diagram

In our LMS, we propose a class diagram model for the communication space (see Figure 12) from our meta-model proposed in the chapter. In the latter, we have defined the properties of each class and the relationships between them. The majority of classes designed in our class diagram model correspond perfectly to the meta-model proposed in Figure 6 of Chapter 6, which makes their transformations possible. The transformation of models is a technique aiming to put links between models to avoid unnecessary reproductions.

3.4 IMS-LD Model of the Sharing Space Class Diagram

In our LMS, we propose a class diagram model for the sharing space (see Figure 13) from our meta-model proposed in chapter 6. In the latter, we have defined the properties of each class and the relations between them. The majority of the classes designed in our class diagram model correspond perfectly to the meta-model proposed in Figure 7 of Chapter 6, which makes their transformations possible. The transformation of models is a technique aiming to put links between models to avoid unnecessary reproductions.

Table 6. Functions' description of the production space

Actor	Function	Description
Learner	Consult the course	The learner can view the course, its prerequisites and its objectives at any time
	Consult the quizzes	The learner can view the QUIZZES and their objectives at any time
	Consult the activities	The learner can visualize the activity and its objectives at any time
	Consult the projects	The learner can visualize the project and its objectives at any time
	View evaluations	The learner can view the evaluation and its objectives at any time
	Consult the calendar	The learner can go through the defined task schedule
	Produce the quizzes	The learner can answer the quizzes at any time
	Produce activities	The learner can respond to the 'activities at any time
	Produce projects	The learner can respond to projects at any time
	Produce the evaluations	Learner can respond to evaluations at any time
	Import documents	The learner can import documents
	Export documents	The learner can export documents
Tutor	Supervise learners	The tutor can add, modify or delete his learners
	Manage groups	The tutor can add, modify or delete groups
	Assign students to groups	Tutor can assign learners to groups
	Set the schedule	Tutor can set schedules for tasks and phases
	Define the phases	The tutor can define the phases of the project, activities, QUIZZES and evaluations
	Define tasks	The tutor can define tasks
	Assign tasks	Tutor can assign tasks to learners
	Consult the intervention schedules	The tutor can consult the intervention schedules of the learners
Teacher	Create courses	The teacher can create the courses
	Create quizzes with correction	The teacher can create the quizzes with their corrections
	Create activities with correction	The teacher can create the activities with their corrections
	Create the projects with correction	The teacher can create the projects with their corrections
	Create evaluations with correction	The teacher can create the evaluations with their corrections
	Define the prerequisites	The teacher can define the prerequisites for a course
	Define the objectives	Teacher can set objectives for courses, projects, activities, QUIZ and evaluations
	Import documents	The teacher can import documents
	Export documents	The teacher can export documents
	Planning of educational resources	The teacher must plan the teaching resources
Administrator	Set up groups Course	The administrator can set up class groups
	Assignment to tutors	The administrator can assign courses to tutors according to each person's specialty
	Course management	The administrator can manage the courses
	Manage access rights	The administrator can manage the access rights of teachers and learners
Coordinator	Manage teachers	The coordinator can add, modify or delete a teacher
	Monitor teachers' activities	The coordinator can monitor teachers' activities
	Set up groups	The coordinator can set up class groups
	Assignment of courses to tutors	The coordinator can assign courses to tutors according to the specialty of each
	Course management	The coordinator can manage the courses

Figure 7. Use case diagram of production space.

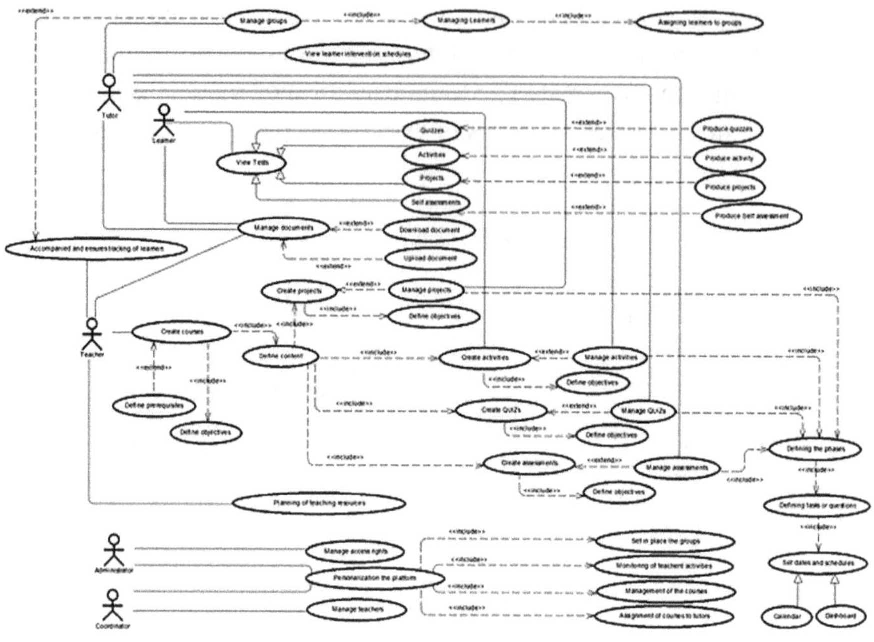

3.5 IMS-LD Model of the Evaluation Space Class Diagram

In our LMS, we propose a class diagram model for the evaluation space (cf. Figure 14) from our meta-model proposed in chapter 6. In the latter, we have defined the properties of each class and the relationships between them. The majority of the classes designed in our class diagram model correspond perfectly to the meta-model proposed in Figure 8 of Chapter 6, which makes their transformations possible. Model transformation is a technique aiming to put links between models to avoid unnecessary reproductions.

3.6 IMS-LD Model of the Production Space Class Diagram

In our LMS, we propose a class diagram model for the production space (see Figure 15) from our meta-model proposed in chapter 6. In the latter, we have defined the properties of each class and the relations between them. The majority of the classes designed in our class diagram model correspond perfectly to the meta-model proposed in Figure 9 of Chapter 6, which makes their transformations possible. The transformation of models is a technique aiming to put links between models to avoid unnecessary reproductions.

Table 7. Functions' description of the self-management space

Actor	Function	Description
Learner	Set language	The learner can define the language of these studies
	Set theme	The learner can define the theme of his personal office
	View documents	Learners can view documents.
	Upload documents	The learner can upload documents
Tutor	Manage courses	The tutor can add, modify or delete courses
	Manage groups	The tutor can add, modify or delete groups
	Assign learners to groups	The tutor can assign learners to groups
	Set language	The tutor can define the language of study for their learners
	Set theme	The tutor can define the theme of the personal offices of these learners
Teacher	Create Quizzes	The teacher can create Quizzes
	Create activities	The teacher can create activities
	Create projects	The teacher can create projects
	Create assessments	The teacher can create assessments
	Set prerequisites	The teacher can set prerequisites for course
	Set objectives	The teacher can set objectives for course, projects, activities, quizzes, and assessments
	Set language	The teacher can define the language of study for their learners
	Set theme	The tutor can define the theme of the personal offices of these learners
	Upload documents	The teacher can upload documents
	Plan teaching resources	The teacher can plan teaching resources
Administrator	Set in place groups	The administrator can set in place the classes' groups
	Assignment of courses to tutors	The administrator can assign courses to tutors according to the specialty of each one
	Management of the courses	The administrator can manage the courses
	Manage access rights	The administrator can manage the access rights of teachers and learners.
Coordinator	Manage teachers	The coordinator can add, modify, or delete teachers
	Monitoring of teachers' activities	The coordinator can monitor teachers' activities
	Set in place groups	The coordinator can set in place the classes' groups
	Assignment of courses to tutors	The coordinator can assign courses to tutors according to the specialty of each one
	Management of the courses	The coordinator can manage the courses

Figure 8. Use case diagram of self-management space.

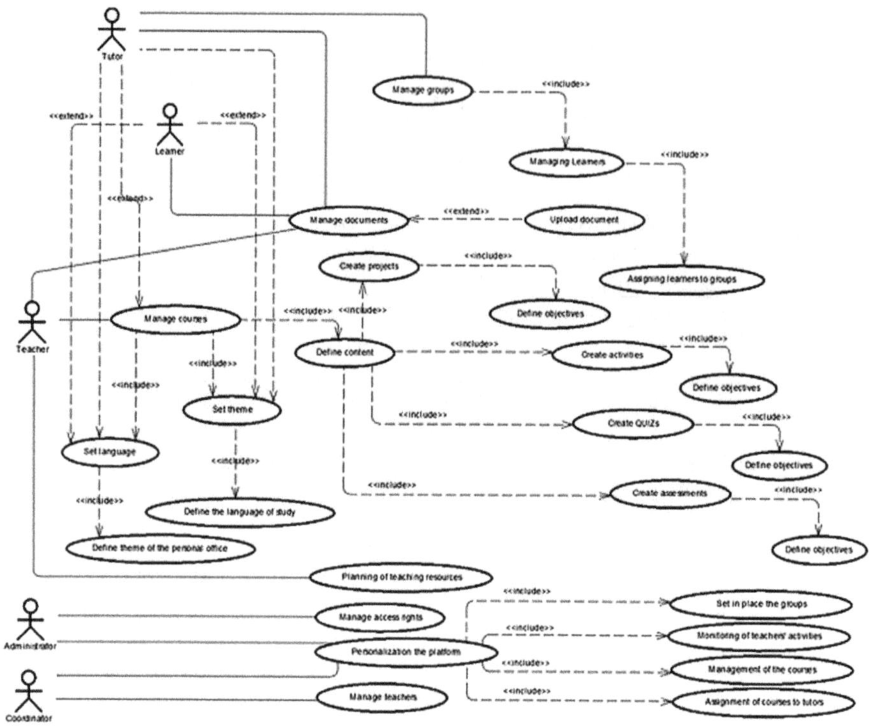

3.7 IMS-LD Model of the Self-Management Space Class Diagram

In our LMS, we propose a class diagram model for the self-management space (see Figure 16) from our meta-model proposed in chapter 6. In the latter, we have defined the properties of each class and the relationships between them. The majority of the classes designed in our class diagram model correspond perfectly to the meta-model proposed in Figure 10 of Chapter 6, which makes their transformations possible. The transformation of models is a technique aiming to put links between models to avoid unnecessary reproductions.

3.8 IMS-LD Model of the Assistance Space Class Diagram

In our LMS, we propose a class diagram model for the assistance space (cf. Figure 17) from our meta-model proposed in Chapter 6. In this last one, we have defined the properties of each class and the relationships between them.

The majority of the classes designed in our class diagram model correspond perfectly to the meta-model proposed in Figure 11 of Chapter 6, which makes their transformations possible. Model transformation is a technique aiming to put links between models to avoid unnecessary reproductions.

Table 8. Functions' description of the assistance space

Actor	Function	Description
Learner	Consult the course	The learner can view the course, its prerequisites and its objectives at any time
	View documents	Learners can read the downloaded documents
	Contact the teacher	The learner can contact the teacher
	Ask for help	The learner can ask for help by asking questions
Tutor	Give some help	The teacher can help by answering learners' questions
	Support learners	The tutor can keep the follow-up of the learners
	Consult the intervention schedules	The tutor can consult the intervention schedules of the learners
Teacher	Create courses	The teacher can create the courses
	Give some help	The teacher can help by answering learners' questions
	Export documents	The teacher can export documents
	Planning of teaching resources	The teacher must plan the teaching resources
Administrator	Course assignment to tutors	The administrator can assign courses to tutors according to the specialty of each
	Course management	The administrator can manage the courses
	Manage access rights	The administrator can manage the access rights of teachers and learners
Coordinator	Monitor teachers' activities	The coordinator can monitor teachers' activities
	Assignment of courses to tutors	The coordinator can assign courses to tutors according to the specialty of each
	Course management	The coordinator can manage the courses

CONCLUSION

In our work, we are on the way to the design and modeling of model content for a new smart Learning Management System compatible with IMS-LD. This design is based on active teaching learner-centered, and as an example of the pedagogy, we opted for four learning theories as a basis for teaching this LMS, namely the social constructivism, behaviorism, traditional pedagogy, and cognitivism. The latter allows us to reach a teaching object through the implementation of the courses divided into tasks performed by students collaboratively or individually. To achieve a goal, we need to reach the model validation step, which is one of the tasks to be performed in our future work; also, we seek a framework that will guide us better to start the development part of our new smart LMS.

Figure 9. Use case diagram of assistance space.

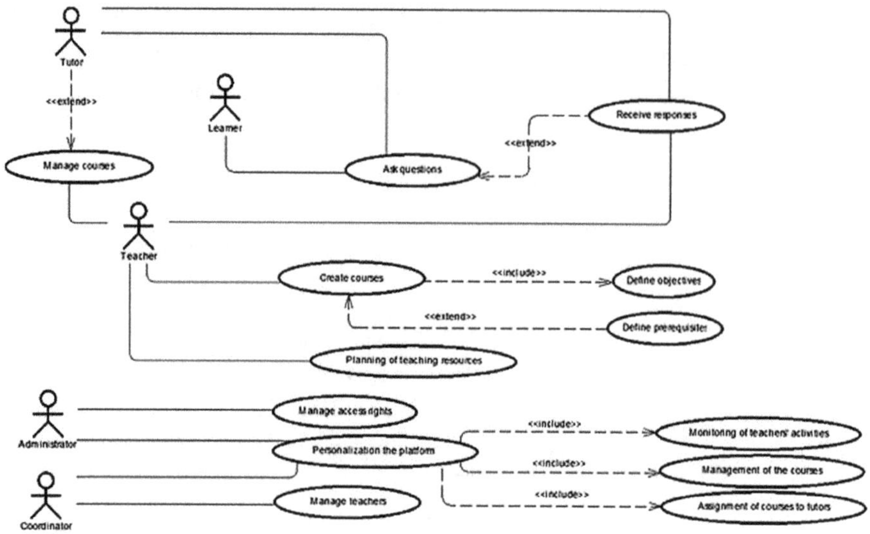

Figure 10. IMS-LD model of the disciplinary information space class diagram.

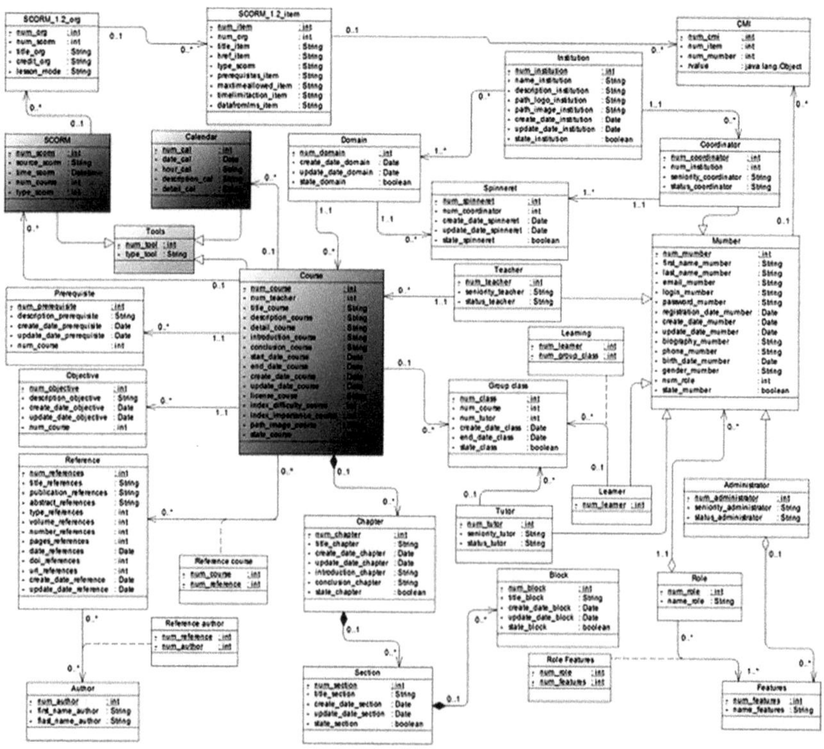

Figure 11. IMS-LD model of the collaboration space class diagram.

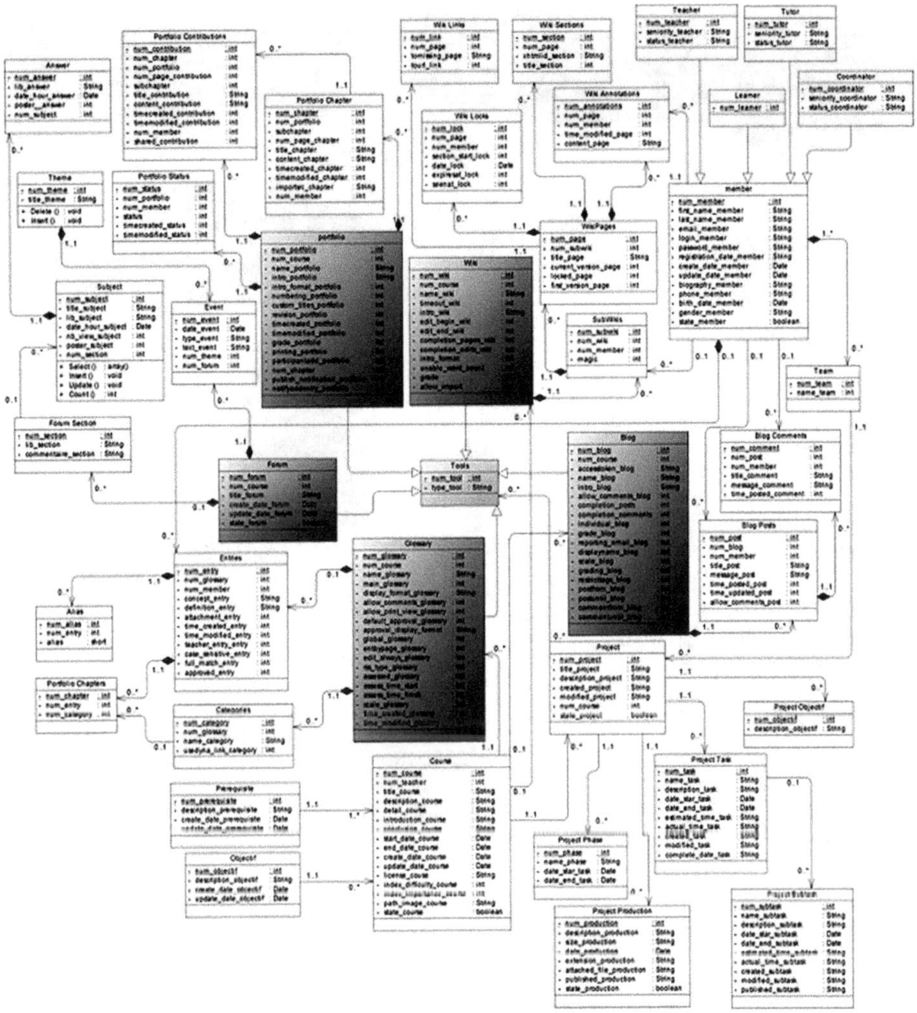

Figure 12. IMS-LD model of the communication space class diagram.

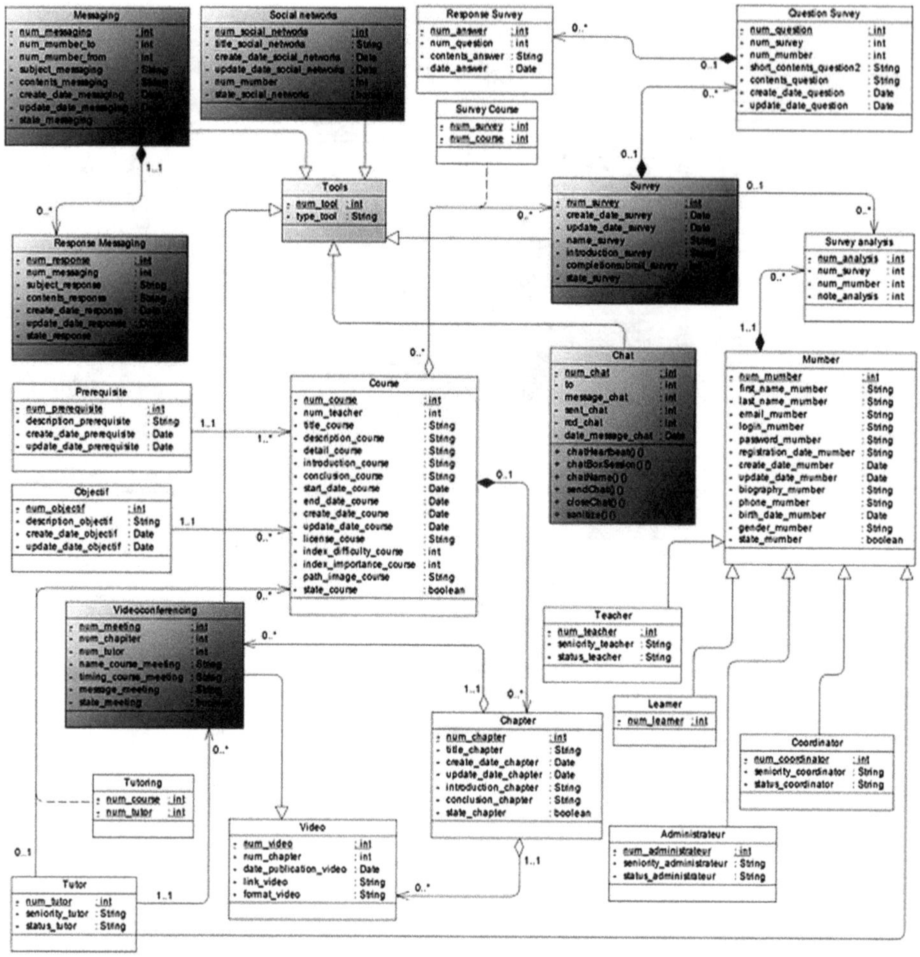

Figure 13. IMS-LD model of the sharing space class diagram.

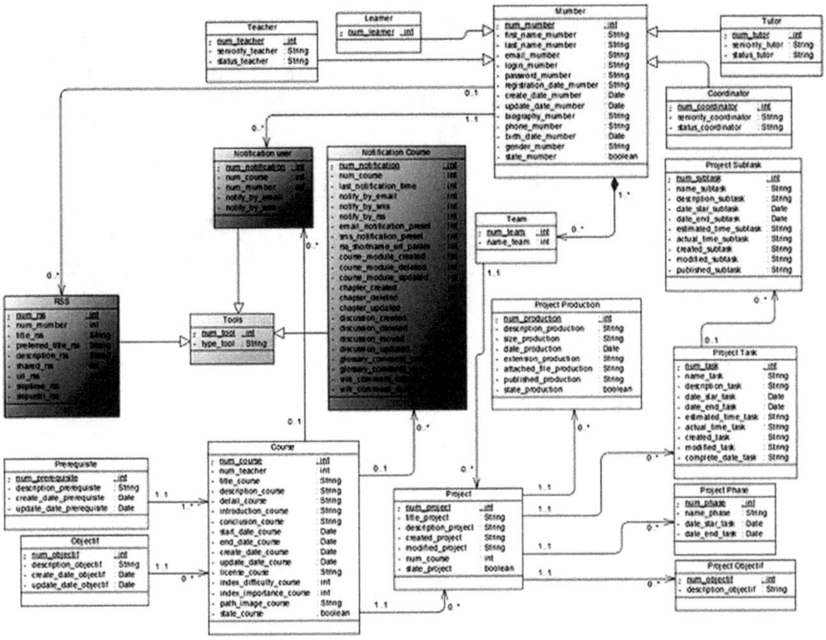

Figure 14. IMS-LD model of the evaluation space class diagram.

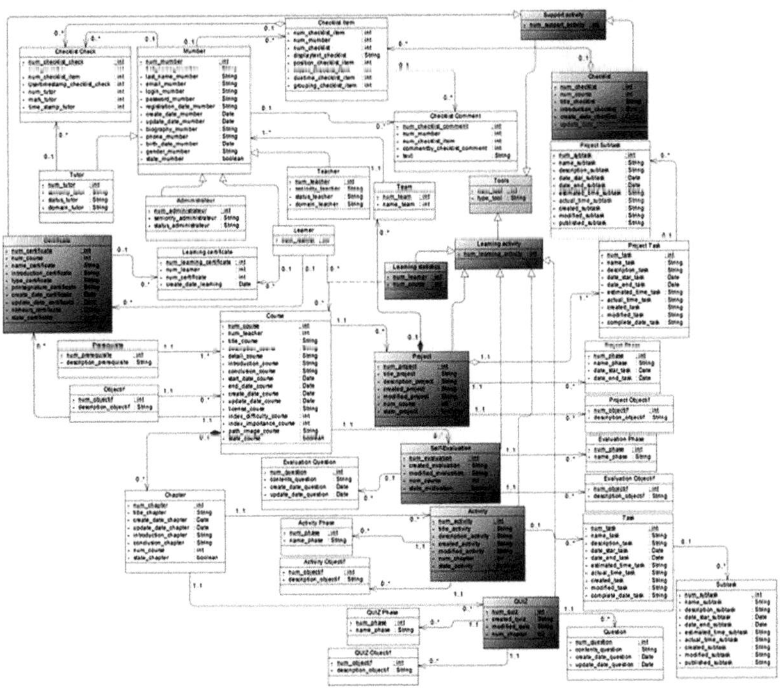

Figure 15. IMS-LD model of the production space class diagram.

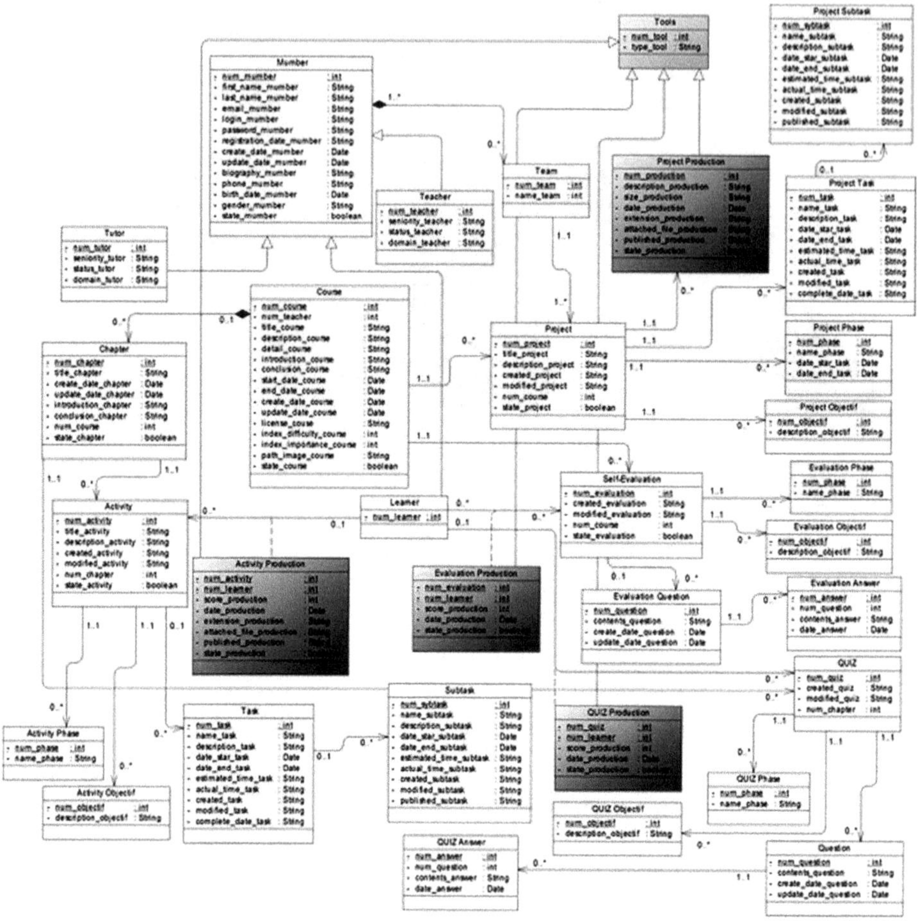

Figure 16. IMS-LD model of the self-management space class diagram.

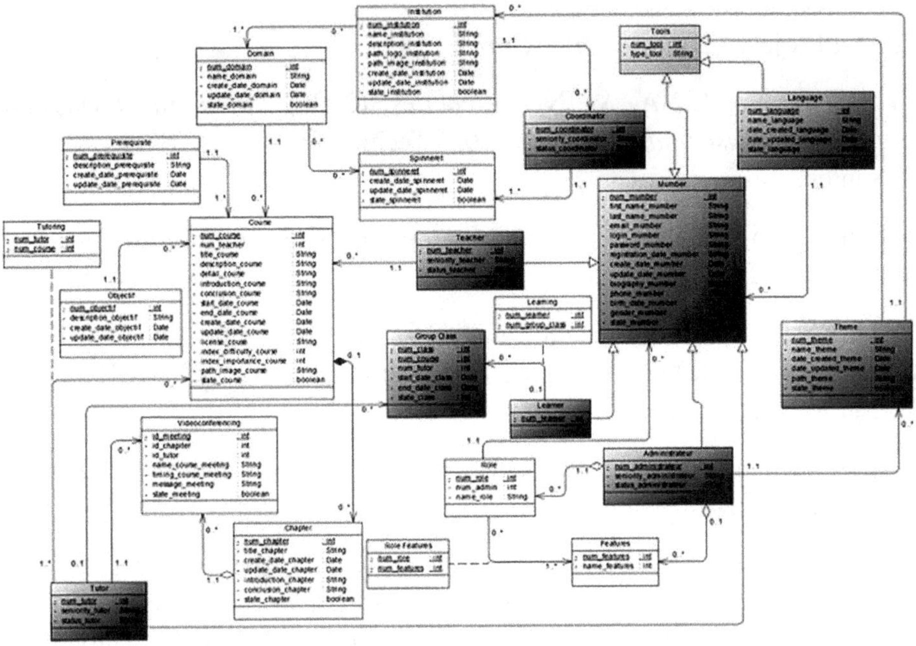

Figure 17. IMS-LD model of the assistance space class diagram.

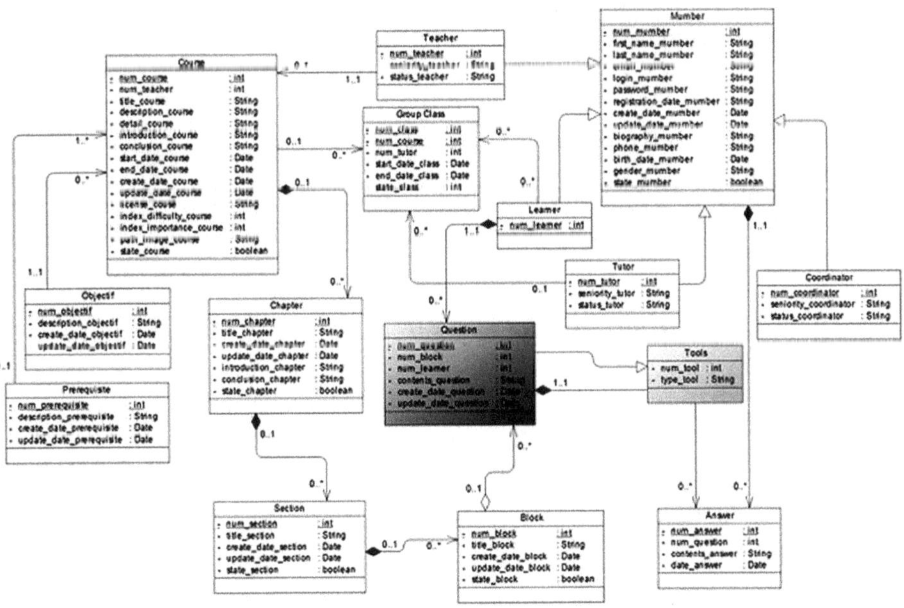

REFERENCES

Alfanet Project. (2008). *CopperCore V 3.3*. Author.

ATLAS Group, LINA, & INRIA Nantes. (2006). *Atlas transformation language. ATL user manual - version 0.7*. Technical report, INRIA University of Nantes.

Bolton. (2005). *RELOAD Project: Editor*. The University of Bolton, The University of Strathclyde, and JISC.

Brunel, S., Girard, P., & Lamago, M. (2015). Des plateformes pour enseigner à distance : vers une modélisation générale de leurs fonctions. In AIP Primeca 2015, La Plagne, France.

Burgos, Arnaud, Neuhauser, & Koper. (2005). *IMS Learning Design*. Association EPI.

Dahmani. (2010). *Modélisation basée ontologies pour l'apprentissage interactif - Application à l'évaluation des connaissances de l'apprenant* (PhD dissertation). Computer Science Department, Mouloud Mammeri University of Tizi-Ouzou, Algeria.

El-Moudden, Aammou, & Khaldi. (2014). A Tool to Generate a Collaborative Content Compatible with IMS-LD. *International Journal of Software and Web Sciences, 11*(1), 1-8.

El-Moudden, F., Khaldi, M., & Aammou, S. (2015). Designing an IMS-LD Model for Collaborative Learning. *IJACSA*, *1*(6), 42–48.

Henri, F., Rabardel, P., & Pastré, P. (Eds.). (2005). Modèles du sujet pour la conception. International Journal of ELearning & Distance Education, Octares Éditions, 22(1).

Koper. (2001). *Modeling Units of Study from a Pedagogical Perspective, the pedagogical meta-model behind EML*. Academic Press.

Lejeune, A. (2004). *IMS Learning Design: Étude d'un langage de modélisation pédagogique* (Vol. 2). Revue Distances et Savoirs.

Ouadoud, M., Chkouri, M. Y., & Nejjari, A. (2018a, March). Learning Management System and the Underlying Learning Theories: Towards a new Modeling of an LMS. *International Journal of Information Science and Technology*, *2*(1), 25–33.

Ouadoud, M., Chkouri, M. Y., & Nejjari, A. (2018b, January). LeaderTICE: A Platforms Recommendation System Based on a Comparative and Evaluative Study of Free E-learning Platforms. *International Journal of Online Engineering*, *14*(01), 132–161. https://doi.org/10.3991/ijoe.v14i01.7865

Ouadoud, M., Chkouri, M. Y., Nejjari, A., & El Kadiri, K. E. (2017, February). Exploring a Recommendation System of Free ELearning Platforms: Functional Architecture of the System. *International Journal of Emerging Technologies in Learning*, *12*(02), 219–226. doi:10.3991/ijet.v12i02.6381

Ouadoud, M., Nejjari, A., Chkouri, M. Y., & El-Kadiri, K. E. (2017b). Learning Management System and the Underlying Learning Theories. *Innovations in Smart Cities and Applications*, 732–744. doi:10.1007/978-3-319-74500-8_67

Ouadoud, M., Nejjari, A., Chkouri, M. Y., & Kadiri, K. E. E. (2017a). Educational modeling of a learning management system. *2017 International Conference on Electrical and Information Technologies (ICEIT),* 1–6. doi:10.1109/EITech.2017.8255247

Survey of Educational Modelling Languages (EMLs). Version 1. (2002). *CEN/ISS WS/LT, Learning Technologies Workshop.*

ADDITIONAL READING

Ouadoud, M., Chafiq, T., Rida, N., & Chkouri, M. Y. (2019). Generate a Meta-Model Content for Collaboration Space of Learning Management System Compatible with IMS-LD. *International Journal of Interactive Mobile Technologies*, *13*(01), 37–52. doi:10.3991/ijim.v13i01.9440

Ouadoud, M., & Chkouri, M. Y. (2019). Generate a Meta-Model Content for Communication Space of Learning Management System Compatible with IMS-LD. In M. Ezziyyani (Ed.), *Advanced Intelligent Systems for Sustainable Development (AI2SD'2018), Advances in Intelligent Systems and Computing* (pp. 24–39). Springer International Publishing. doi:10.1007/978-3-030-11928-7_3

Ouadoud, M., & Chkouri, M. Y. (2019). Designing an IMS-LD Model for Communication Space of Learning Management System. In M. Ezziyyani (Ed.), *Advanced Intelligent Systems for Sustainable Development (AI2SD'2018), Advances in Intelligent Systems and Computing* (pp. 40–54). Springer International Publishing. doi:10.1007/978-3-030-11928-7_4

KEY TERMS AND DEFINITIONS

IMS: Instructional management systems.

IMS-LD: Instructional management systems - learning design.

LMS: Learning management system.

Methods: The word "method" used by IMS-LD means the unfolding of the scenario.

Social Constructivism: Is centered on the learner. The learner learns through its representations. The construction of knowledge although personal is carried out in a social setting. The context and come from both what we think and what others bring as interactions.

UML: The unified modeling language (UML) is a general-purpose, developmental, modeling language in the field of software engineering that is intended to provide a standard way to visualize the design of a system.

ENDNOTE

1 **EML**: Educational Modelling Language.

Chapter 8
Prototyping a New Smart Learning Management System Based on the NoSQL

ABSTRACT

The context of this work is that of prototyping a disciplinary information space for a new LMS. The work is specifically in the field or seeking to promote, using information technology from a distance, a collective knowledge construction. The approach is to first think about the conditions for creating a real LMS between learners and designing the IT environment that supports this LMS. The authors chose to base on the hybridization between four learning theories as a basis for teaching this LMS, namely the traditional pedagogy, behaviorism, cognitivism, and social constructivism. These pedagogies have already proven themselves, mostly in learning situations in the classroom. The LMS consists of different activity spaces for teaching and learning activities. The authors limit themselves in this work to the prototyping of disciplinary information space for a new smart LMS based on IMS-LD, the NoSQL, MongoDB database, and the Symfony framework.

INTRODUCTION

eLearning is a fast and efficient way of providing and sharing knowledge with learners in different parts of the world.

DOI: 10.4018/978-1-7998-4021-3.ch008

According to (Liu, 2010; Faten, 2013), it is defined as the following: "eLearning uses the Internet or other digital content for learning and education activities, that takes full advantage of modern educational technology to provide a new mechanism for communication and learning environment rich in resources to achieve a new way of learning."

eLearning is promoted through educational platforms: integrated systems offer a wide range of activities in the learning process. Teachers use the platforms to monitor or evaluate the work of students. They use LMSs to create courses, tests, etc. However, the LMS does not offer personalized services and therefore does not take into account the aspects of personalization such as the level of knowledge, interest, motivation, and goals of learners. They access the same resource sets in the same way.

We present an easy disciplinary information model of the new smart LMS to create and administer the educational content online. This tool allows the generation and editing structures of websites through a database rather than pedagogical models, with a variety of choices that ensures better adaptation to the teaching of the course and learning style. Therefore, it is necessary to find a method to model all LMSs types. To model the disciplinary information space of our new LMS we have based ourselves upon the IMS-LD specification focusing on four learning theories that were judged the most important and relevant to our modeling, namely the traditional pedagogy, behaviorism, cognitivism, and social constructivism. Then, these learning theories which have inspired for a long time the design of computer applications are combined and put into perspective with several emergent pedagogical functionalities to build original modeling of disciplinary information space for our new smart LMS. This reveals that this proposed modeling that is presented to readers here looks for ways to leverage technology for learning by considering users as being human actors and not human factors (Henri and al., 2007).

The IMS-LD specification or instructional design engineering uses pedagogical concepts, allowing to model learning units. IMS-LD takes into account a wide variety of teaching models it is there its flexibility. A course plan extract of a general or specific database can be modeled with IMS-LD, through the description of the different roles, activities, environments, methods, properties, conditions, and notifications. It is used to transform the course plans into formal learning units (UOL) that can be performed with an IMS-LD editor based on an engine such as Copper core (Alfanet project, 2008). These executable units can be designed from the beginning using an editor such as Reload (Bolton, 2005).

Based on these various research works, which seemed to us incomplete, we proposed a modeling portrait of designing an IMS-LD model of the disciplinary information space for our new smart LMS. The latter is anthropocentric and relies on a learning conception that is located at the intersection of the most used learning theories. Indeed, the idea is to orient the design work research towards great and optimal compatibility between the services offered by eLearning platforms and the needs of all users, particularly learners, for better optimization of online learning.

LMS AND THE ACTIVITY SPACES

1. Definition

An LMS or eLearning platform is software including a range of services that assist teachers with the management of their courses. It offers many services allowing the management of content, particularly by creating, importing, and exporting learning objects. The set of available tools in the LMS represents all these services that help in managing the teaching process and the interaction between users such as the access control services, synchronous and asynchronous tools of communication, and user administration services. More precisely these services are linked to the following variety of functionalities:

- The management of pedagogical content (creating, importing, and exporting learning objects),
- The creation of an individual's paths in the training modules,
- The availability of sharing tools,
- The distribution of communication tools,
- The student registration and the management of their files (training tracking and results),
- The distribution of online courses and many other pedagogical resources.

Figure 1 illustrates the general principle of the operation of an LMS by presenting the key features associated with the main actors: learners, teachers, tutors, coordinators, and administrators. The learner can consult and/or download the resources made at his/her disposal by the teacher, he/she can create his/her learning activities while following his/her progress in training. The teacher, who is responsible for one or more modules, can create and manage the educational content he/she wishes to broadcast via the platform. He/she can also build tools for monitoring learners' activities. The tutor accompanies and monitors each learner by providing the tools of communication and collaboration. Concerning the coordinator, he/she ensures the management of the overall system. Finally, the administrator is responsible for the customization of the platform having the rights of the administration deriving from it (system installation, maintenance, access management...).

2. Activity Spaces

The LMS consists of different activity spaces for activities of teaching and learning (Ouadoud and al., 2018; Ouadoud and al., 2017; Ouadoud and al., 2017). Each model represents a space, in these spaces, both teachers and learners can have a disciplinary information space, a collaboration space, a communication space, a sharing space, an evaluation space, a production space, a self-management space, and an assistance space.

2.1 Disciplinary Information Space

In the disciplinary information space, teachers or tutors can export content from the LMS as IMS/SCORM conformant Content Packages that can be viewed offline, or imported into the LMS. Entire courses or individual course units can be packaged for viewing or redistribution.

2.2 Communication Space

Communication is the act of conveying intended meanings from one entity or group to another using mutually understood signs and semiotic rules. Learners can communicate with others through their Inbox using LMS's private mail, through the discussion forums, or the chat rooms.

2.3 Collaboration Space

Collaboration is the process of two or more people or organizations working together to realize or achieve something successfully (Martinez-Moyano, 2006). Collaboration requires leadership, although the form of leadership can be social within a decentralized and egalitarian group (Spence, 2005). Teams that work collaboratively can obtain greater resources, recognition, and reward when facing competition for finite resources.

Figure 1. The general architecture of the LMS. Please reduce the image size

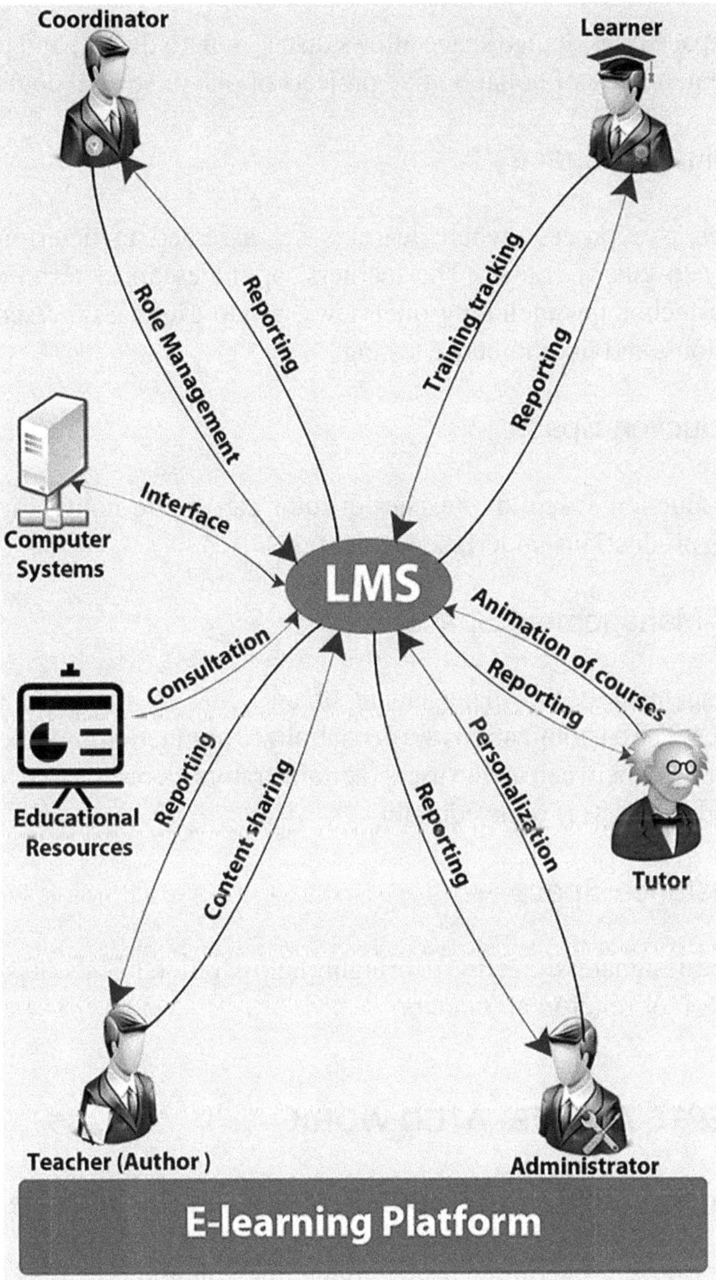

2.4 Sharing Space

Sharing space or exchange space allows discussion, to define, and to follow the implementation of collaborative projects of one or several courses.

2.5 Evaluation Space

Evaluation is a process where learners are assessed to determine their suitability to take a course. The learners' aptitudes are determined by a variety of techniques including interviews, group exercises, presentations, examinations, and psychometric testing.

2.6 Production Space

In the production space, the teacher or tutor can create notifications, and assess the productions undertaken by learners.

2.7 Self-Management Space

Self-management is the management of an LMS by the administrators themselves. The customizations are decentralized as much as possible and the sharing of tasks between all the users (administrators, coordinators, teachers, tutors, and learners) is done equitably.

2.8 Assistance Space

Assistance designates the action of bringing help or relief. It is about providing aid, support, or relief in all matters.

CONCEPTS AND RELATED WORK

1. Instructional Management Systems – Learning Design

There are several eLearning specifications, for example, SCORM, DCMI, IMS-SS, or IMS-CP. Among these, IMS-LD, one of the last publications, seeks to incorporate pedagogical flexibility and complements certain aspects treated by others.

IMS-LD was published in 2003 by the IMS/GLC. (Instructional Management Systems Global Learning Consortium: Consortium for global LMSs with training, the original name when IMS was started in 1997 Instructional Management Systems project) (Lejeune, 2006; Burgos and al., 2005). Reminds us of its origins: the source (EML) of the proposed language was assessed by the European Committee for Standardization (CEN) in a comparative study of different SRMS (CEN/ISS WS/LT, 2002; Burgos and al., 2005), as best suited to satisfy the criteria definition of an EML. EML is defined by CEN / ISS as "an information aggregation and semantic model describing the content and processes involved in a unit of learning from an educational perspective and to ensure the reusability and interoperability." (El-Moudden and al., 2015) In this context, the North American IMS consortium undertook a study and provided a specification of such a language, giving birth in February 2003, the Learning Design specification V1.0 (IMS-LD). She adds that the proposal, largely inspired by EML developed by (Koper, 2001; Burgos and al., 2005) (OUNL) provides a conceptual framework for modeling a Learning Unit and claims to offer a good compromise between on the one hand to the generic implement a variety of instructional approaches and secondly, the power of expression that allows an accurate description of each learning unit.

This specification allows us to represent and encode learning structures for learners both alone and in groups, compiled by roles, such as "learners" and "Team". (Burgos and al., 2005) We can model a lesson plan in IMS-LD, defining roles, learning activities, services, and many other elements and building learning units. The syllabus is modeled and built with resources assembled in a compressed Zip file then started by an executable ("player"). It coordinates the teachers, students, and activities as long as the respective learning process progresses. A user takes a "role" to play and execute the activities related to achieve a satisfactory learning unit. In all, the unit structure, roles, and activities build the learning scenario to be executed in a system compatible with IMS-LD (see Figure 2).

IMS-LD does not impose a particular pedagogical model but can be used with a large number of scenarios and pedagogic models, demonstrating its flexibility. Therefore, IMS-LD is often called a meta-pedagogic model. Previous eLearning initiatives claim to be pedagogically neutral, IMS-LS is not intended for pedagogical neutrality but seeks to raise awareness of eLearning on the need for a flexible approach.

Figure 2. The conceptual model of Instructional Management Systems - Learning Design (Burgos and al., 2005).

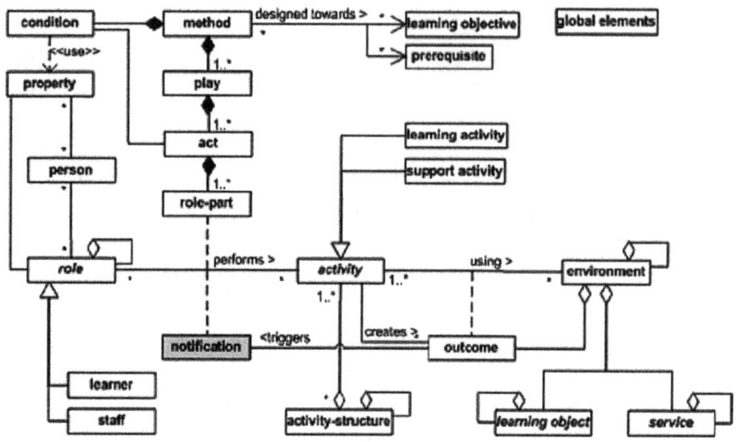

IMS-LD has been developed for eLearning and virtual classes, but a course face to face can be done and integrated into a structure created with this specification, as an activity of learning or support activity. If the ultimate goal to create rich learning units, with support to achieve the learning objectives by providing the best possible experience, face-to-face meetings, and any other learning resource are permitted such as video conferencing, collaborative table, or any field action research.

IMS-LD uses the theatrical metaphor, which implies the existence of roles, resources, and learning scenario itself: one room is divided into one or more acts and conducted by several actors who can take on different roles at different times. Each role is to carry out several activities to complete the learning process. Besides, all roles must be synchronized at the end of each act before processing the next act.

2. NoSQL Databases

A NoSQL (originally referring to "No SQL" or "non-relational") database provides a mechanism for storage and retrieval of data that is modeled in means other than the tabular relations used in relational databases. Such databases have existed since the late 1960s but did not obtain the "NoSQL" moniker until a surge of popularity in the early twenty-first century (Leavitt, 2010), triggered by the needs of Web 2.0 companies such as Facebook, Google, and Amazon (Mohan, 2013). NoSQL databases are increasingly used in big data and real-time web applications (Andlinger, 2013). NoSQL systems are also sometimes called "Not Only SQL" to emphasize that they may support SQL-like query languages (Rouse and al., 2017; Fowler, 2012).

Motivations for this approach include simplicity of design, simpler "horizontal" scaling to clusters of machines (which is a problem for relational databases) (Leavitt, 2010), and finer control over availability. The data structures used by NoSQL databases (e.g. key-value, wide column, graph, or document) are different from those used by default in relational databases, making some operations faster in NoSQL. The particular suitability of a given NoSQL database depends on the problem it must solve. Sometimes the data structures used by NoSQL databases are also viewed as "more flexible" than relational database tables (Vogels, 2012).

Many NoSQL stores compromise consistency (in the sense of the CAP theorem) in favor of availability, partition tolerance, and speed. Barriers to the greater adoption of NoSQL stores include the use of low-level query languages (instead of SQL, for instance, the lack of ability to perform ad-hoc joins across tables), lack of standardized interfaces, and huge previous investments in existing relational databases (Grolinger and al., 2013). Most NoSQL stores lack true ACID transactions, although a few databases, such as MarkLogic, Aerospike, FairCom, c-treeACE, Google Spanner (though technically a NewSQL database), Symas LMDB, and OrientDB have made them central to their designs.

Most NoSQL databases offer a concept of "eventual consistency" in which database changes are propagated to all nodes "eventually" (typically within milliseconds) so queries for data might not return updated data immediately or might result in reading data that is not accurate, a problem known as stale reads. Additionally, some NoSQL systems may exhibit lost writes and other forms of data loss. Fortunately, some NoSQL systems provide concepts such as write-ahead logging to avoid data loss. For distributed transaction processing across multiple databases, data consistency is an even bigger challenge that is difficult for both NoSQL and relational databases. Even current relational databases "do not allow referential integrity constraints to span databases". Few systems maintain both ACID transactions and X/Open XA standards for distributed transaction processing.

3. Related Works

A great deal of research is focusing in one way or another on the platforms engineering for distance education, including LMSs. For example, Chekour (Chekour and al., 2015), presented a synthesis of the main learning theories in the digital era, namely: behaviorism, cognitivism, constructivism, and social constructivism. El-Mhouti (El Mhouti and al., 2013) highlighted the ICT use in the service of active pedagogies, based on the social constructivist approach, the principles that structure the instructional design approaches, and the assessment of the social constructivist activities.

These works, among many others, emphasized the contribution of learning theories in the design and development of learning systems. The direct application of each of these theories allows particularly providing supporting methods for the design and development of LMSs. The hybridization of the learning theories that we presented in this chapter as an original conceptual model has allowed us to design a new smart LMS whose benefit resides essentially in the richness of the proposed functionalities in a way that fits the needs of all its final users: teachers and learners.

Furthermore, several kinds of research (Benslimane and al., 2016; Zoubaidi and al., 2014; Chemsi and al., 2011) had a goal to implement and present the functionalities of LMSs (such as Moodle) and their possibilities to effectively manage users' assessment approach (teachers and/or learners) within training institutions. Paquette (Paquette, 2000) elaborated eLearning portals editor that opens the way to more diverse and evolved pedagogical models on the pedagogical plan, focusing more on the quality of interactions. Moreover, in the framework of the European project Mediasite (Bechina and al., 2001), a reference model for the process of distance learning has been developed. This theoretical framework has led to the integration of several applications (video-conferencing, document manager, portal...) to define an electronic training platform for online communication and/or collaboration.

Besides, much work has been done in the field of collaborative learning and IMS-LD specification. For example, Dyke (Dyke and Lund, 2006) explains how models' socio-cognitive interaction is related to the properties of collaborative tools. Ferraris (Ferraris and al., 2005) expresses collaborative learning scenarios by teachers animating virtual classrooms to promote re-use and share teaching practices. He proposes an approach led by the models per the recommendations of the Model Driven Architecture OMG. He presents a meta-model based on IMS-LD enhanced by the concepts of the participation model to capture the richness of the interactions inherent in collaborative activities. Moreover, El-Moudden (El-Moudden and al., 2015; El-Moudden and al., 2015) proposes designing an IMS-LD model for collaborative learning. He works is specifically in the field or seeking to promote, using information technology from a distance, a collective knowledge construction. His approach is to first think about the conditions for creating a real collective activity between learners and designing the IT environment that supports these activities.

On the other hand, other research aimed at proposing the modeling of new units, approaches, architecture, or adaptive, flexible, and interactive eLearning systems. For example, Sadiq proposed the modeling of learning units on eLearning platforms, which relies on the application of the standard IMS-LD in the production of adaptive learning units (Sadiq and Talbi, 2010). Tonye proposed a distance education model adapted to the African context (Tonye, 2010). Chouchane proposed the modeling of an adaptive agent-based approach to mLearning for efficient and flexible mobile learning systems (Chouchane, 2012). Moreover, Brunel proposed a modeling work based on the following five fundamental functions: organize learning, inform, collaborate, accompany, and produce. His modeling work shows that mastering the overall logic of functioning of these digital learning environments helps to avoid the focus on the tools and providing active pedagogy adapted to the context and needs of all users (Brunel and al., 2015).

Aammou proposed implementing traditional features of adaptive hypermedia in an open environment, for describing learning objects and architectural models based on the use of ontologies (Aammou and al., 2010). Dahmani also presented ontology-based modeling for interactive learning. His work deals with interactive learning and focuses particularly on the possibility of using the results of ontological engineering in the modeling of educational domains as well as in the knowledge assessment of learners in the case of computer-assisted learning exercises (Née Dahmani, 2010).

Based on these various research works, which seemed to us incomplete, we proposed a modeling portrait of designing an IMS-LD Model for the LMS. For us, this is not the same case and the same vision as our modelization is more general, it aims at one hand to create a new smart LMS from which teachers can animate virtual groups for the re-use and sharing of teaching practices and on the other hand, the re-use of the content created in other frameworks. The latter is anthropocentric and relies on a learning conception that is located at the intersection of the most used learning theories. Indeed, the idea is to orient the design work research towards great and optimal compatibility between the services offered by LMSs and the needs of all users, particularly learners, for better optimization of online learning.

TRANSFORMATION RULES

1. Atlas Language Transformation (ATL)

In their operational ATL, Canals use. (Canals and al., 2005; El-Moudden and al., 2015) State that to deal with the transformation of models; it is difficult and cumbersome to use object languages since we spend so much effort on the development of transformation definitions of Framework for the set work. The use of XSLT as a language if is more direct and adapted by rest against difficulty to maintain (Canals and al., 2005; El-Moudden and al., 2015). We follow their choice by focusing on the implementation of approaches centered on the MDA (Model Driven Architecture), MDE (Model Driven Engineering), and QVT (Queries View Transformation) tools. Query / View / Transformation (QVT) (OMG/RFP/QVT, 2002; El-Moudden and al., 2015) is a standard defined by the OMG. This is a standardized language to express model transformations. QVT is not advanced sufficiently now in its definition for Queries and View aspects. Against transformation by the appearance expressed by the MDA, the approach has resulted in various experiments (eg Triskell, ATL ...) on both academic and commercial levels. To determine the transformation, it is necessary to have tools of transformation. These are based on language transformations that must respect the QVT standard (OMG/RFP/QVT, 2002; El-Moudden and al., 2015) proposed by the OMG (Bézivin and al., 2003; El-Moudden and al., 2015). There is an offer of free tools (ATL, MTF, MTL, QVTP, etc.) and commercial (eg MIA). We chose ATL (Atlas Transformation Language) from the provision of free tools to the extent that only ATL has a spirit consistent with OMG / MDA / MOF / QVT (Canals and al., 2005; El-Moudden and al., 2015).

2. ATL Description

Atlas Transformation Language (ATL) has been designed to perform transformations within the MDA Framework proposed by the OMG (ATLAS group, 2006; Combemale and Rougemaille, 2005), and (El-Moudden and al., 2015). The ATL language is mainly because the models are first-class entities.

Indeed, the transformations are considered models of Transformation. Since transformations are considered themselves as models, we can apply their transformations. This possibility of ATL is considered an important point. Indeed, it provides the means to achieve higher-order transformations (HOT Higher-Order Processing) (Combemale and Rougemaille, 2005; El-Moudden and al., 2015). A higher-order transformation is a transformation including source and target models that are themselves transformations. As ATL is among the languages model transformation respecting the QVT (OMG/RFP/QVT, 2002) standard proposed by OMG (Bézivin and al., 2003; El-Moudden and al., 2015), we describe its structure about this standard (QVT).

The study of the abstract syntax of the ATL language is to study two features provided by this language more than rules changes. The first feature, navigation, allows studying the possibility of navigation between meta-models sources and targets. The second feature, Operations, is used to describe the ability to define operations on model elements. Finally, the study of the transformation rules is used to describe these types of rules, how they are called and the type of results they return.

- Navigation (ATLAS group, 2006; Bézivin and al., 2003; El-Moudden and al., 2015) this feature is offered by ATL language (Object Constraint Language). Navigation is allowed only if the model elements are fully initialized. The elements of the target model cannot be definitively initialized at the end of the execution of the transformation. Therefore, the navigation in ATL can only be made between elements of the model (or meta-model) source and model (or meta-model) target.
- Operations: (ATLAS group, 2006; El-Moudden and al., 2015) this feature ATL is also provided by the OCL (Object Constraint Language). In OCL, operations can be defined on the elements of the model. ATL takes this opportunity to OCL to allow defining operations on elements of the source model and the transformation model (Bézivin and al., 2003; El-Moudden and al., 2015).

The transformation rules: there are several types of transformation rules based on how they are called and what kind of results they return (see figure 3).

CalledRule (ATLAS group, 2006) rule explicitly called by its name and by setting its parameters.

MatchedRule (ATLAS group, 2006) rule executed when a guy (InPattern) scheme is recognized in the source model.

Figure 3. ATL Transformation rules (El-Moudden and al., 2015)

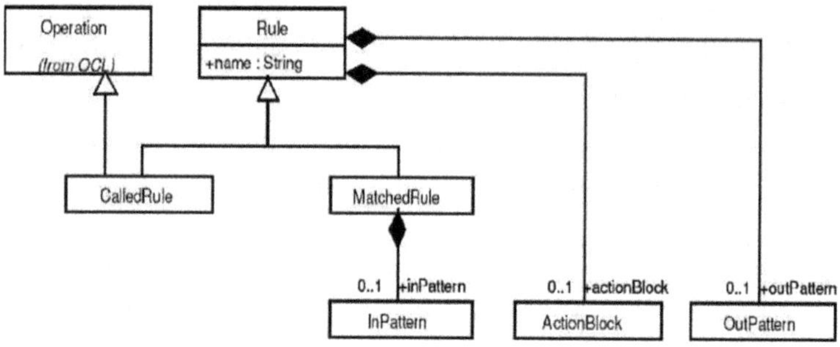

The result of a rule may be a set of predefined models (OutPattern) or a block of mandatory (ActionBlock). If the rule is MatchedRule type and if its result is a set of elements of the target model (OutPattern), it was named declarative. If it is CalledRule type whose result is a block of statements, it is then called procedure. Combinations of rules (declarative and imperative) are called hybrid rules (Bézivin and al., 2003).

3. Contribution

In this research, we try to adapt the model IMS-LD with a disciplinary information meta-model supporting LMS. This adaptation will go through three stages, first the development of a disciplinary information meta-model for the new smart LMS. Secondly, the study of the correspondence between the developed meta-model. Finally, the IMS-LD model and their transformation to the IMS-LD meta-model reduced the MDA approach in a transformation that is based on the rules implemented in the ATL language. However, we will talk about the IT design of our disciplinary information meta-model for new smart LMS without using the transformation that is based on the rules implemented in the ATL language, because we have detected the same problems as in several works (El-Moudden, 2015). In IMS-LD, we do not have the opportunity to build a course, which consists of several chapters. For this, there is at this level a semantic loss.

MODEL-DRIVEN ENGINEERING

1. Modeling Driven Architecture (MDA)

In November 2000, the OMG in the field of software engineering consortium of over 1,000 companies, has initiated the process MDA [OMG MDA], the concepts-oriented models rather than object-oriented. The Model Driven Architecture MDA [OMG MDA] offers the power of abstraction, refinement, and different views of the models. This standard has to add a new way to design applications by separating business logic from business, any technical platform to increase the reuse of previously developed code, reducing development time, and facilitating the integration of new technology (Boulet and al., 2003). It allows developing independent models platforms and implementation (Thi-Lan-Anh and al., 2005) environment. MDA is used to separate two extreme views of the same system (Clave, 2004):

- Its functional specifications on the one hand.
- Its physical implementation on the other hand.

Including several aspects of the life of the software, namely its tests, its quality requirements, the definition of successive iterations, etc. MDA architecture consists of four layers. In the center, there is a UML (Unified Modeling Language) standard MOF (Meta-Object Facility) and CWM (Common Warehouse Meta-model). The second layer contains the XMI (XML Metadata Interchange) standard for dialogue between the middleware (Java, CORBA, .NET, and Web services). The next layer refers to the services to manage events, transaction security, and directories. The last layer offers specific frameworks in scope (Telecommunications, medicine, electronic commerce, finance, etc.) A designer to create his application can use UML as it can use other languages. So according to this architecture-independent technical context, MDA proposes to structure the front needs to engage in a transformation of this functional modeling technical modeling while testing each product model (Clave, 2004). This application model is to be created independently of the target implementation (hardware or software). This allows greater reuse of patterns. MDA is considered an approach with the ambition to offer the widest possible view of the life cycle of the software, not content with only its production. Moreover, this is an intended overview described in a unified syntax. One of the assumptions underlying the MDA is that the operationalization of an abstract model is not a trivial problem. One of the benefits of MDA is to solve this problem (Caron and al., 2007). MDA proposes to design an application through a software chain that is divided into four phases with the aim of flexible implementation, integration, maintenance, and test:

- The development of a computer model without concern (CIM: Computer Independent Model).
- The manual transformation into a model in a particular technological context (PIM: Platform Independent Model).
- The automatic transformation into a pattern associated with the target implementation of the platform (PSM: Platform Specific Model) model to be refined,
- Its implementation in the target platform.

2. Generate a Disciplinary Information Meta-Model

In our research, we propose a meta-model for a system designed to achieve the needs of the LMS and the needs of teachers and learners. Therefore, we establish the disciplinary information space diagram as the first proposal of a meta-model for new smart LMS:

In the disciplinary information space, teachers or tutors can export content from the LMS as IMS/SCORM conformant Content Packages that can be viewed offline, or imported into the LMS. Content packages can be imported and exported with QTI Tests, and AccessForAll adapted content together in a single package. Teachers and tutors can create disciplinary information through the meta-model tools presented in figure 4 and these technological advances:

- My Courses. Teachers, tutors, or learners can manage the LMS courses they teach and/or are enrolled in. When learners register, they are automatically logged into My Courses.
- SCORM. Upload and configure SCORM packages, enabling interoperability and accessibility of web-based learning content.
- IMS QTI. Import and export interoperable QTI test packages or question banks.
- IMS LTI. Support for IMS Learning Tool Integration (LTI) for simple, standards-based integration with third-party tools running outside LMS.

- Course elements provide pre-shaped pedagogic bricks that can be used as resources in a course. The latter provide high semantic level objects that are commonly used on written learning content, such as Important, local goals, reminders, work description, tips, and tricks... Other course elements provide a pre-styled constant way of course headings, section, block, and sequence headings.
- Calendar. View a weekly or monthly summary of scheduled events, either for a course or work site or for an active individual in one or more LMS.

Figure 4. IMS-LD conceptual meta-model of the disciplinary information space

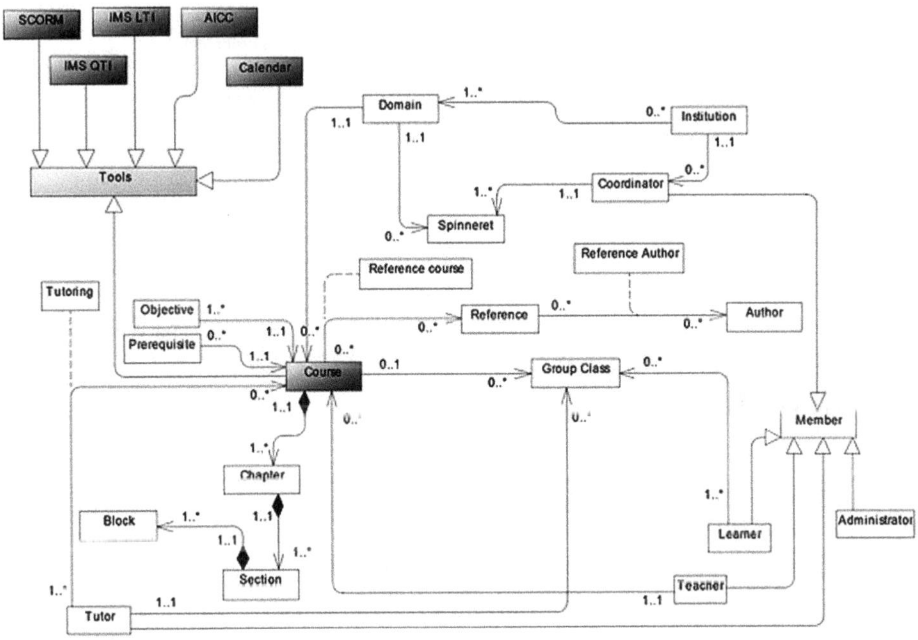

3. Correspondence Between the Terminology of IMS-LD and that of the Disciplinary Information Meta-Model

The majority of classes designed in our disciplinary information space meta-model for the new smart LMS correspond perfectly with the IMS-LD model, which makes possible their transformations to it. The transformation of models is a technique that aims to put links between models to avoid unnecessary reproductions.

In table I, we have tried to collect all the disciplinary information space meta-model classes for LMS and their equivalent at the IMS-LD:

Table 1. Correspondence between the terminology of the IMS-LD and that of the IMS-LD meta-model of disciplinary information

IMS-LD meta-model of the disciplinary information space	IMS-LD model
Prerequisite	Prerequisite
Phase	Play
The role, and features	Role
Members	Person
Coordinator, tutor, and teacher	Staff
Learner	Learner
Objective	Learning Objective
Disciplinary information space	Environment
Course, chapter, section, and block	Learning Object
Tools	Services

MODELING A DISCIPLINARY INFORMATION SPACE BASED ON IMS-LD

In our previous section, we tried to design an LMS meta-model of learning online, beginning with the study of the IDM approach (Model-based Engineering) based on the four stages of implementation.

In this section, we will talk about the IT design of our disciplinary information model for new smart LMS without using the same approach that El-Moudden has adopted in his previous works (El-Moudden and al., 2015; El-Moudden and al., 2015) because we have detected the same problems as him of semantic loss during the transformation of the model.

This led us to develop our model through the outline of the diagram in which we will eventually identify the features of the constituent entities of our use case model and the class diagram in which we will specify the different classes' constituents of our disciplinary information model for new smart LMS.

1. Use Case Diagram

The use case diagrams identify the functionality provided by the model (use case); users interact with the system (actors), and the interactions between them. The main objectives of the use case diagrams are:

- Provide a high-level view of the model.
- Identify users ("actors") of the model.
- Define the roles of the actors in the model.

Table 2 describes the service function for each actor.

Table 2. Table function description

Actor	Function	Description
Learners	Consult the course	The learner can view the course, prerequisites, and its objectives at any time
	Browse calendar	The learner can browse the defined task calendar.
	View documents	Learners read the downloaded documents.
	Download documents	The learner can download the documents
	Upload documents	The learner can upload documents
	Download documents	The learner can download the documents
Tutor	Supervise the learners	The tutor adds, modifies or deletes his learners
	Manage groups	The tutor adds, modifies or deletes groups
	Assign students to groups	The tutor can assign learners to groups
	Set calendar	The teacher can set schedules for the tasks and phases
	Consult the intervention schedules	The tutor can consult the intervention schedules of the learners
Teacher	Create courses	The teacher can create courses
	Set prerequisites	The teacher can set prerequisites for course
	Set objectives	The teacher can set objectives for course, projects, activities, quizzes, and assessments
	Upload documents	The teacher can upload documents
	Download documents	Teachers can download the documents
	Planning of teaching resources	The teacher must be planning of teaching resources

Figure 5 describes the use case diagram of the disciplinary information space model representing the external actors who will interact with the system and how they will use it.

2. IMS-LD Class Diagram

In this part, we will try to create models based on the theoretical study of our current work and allows simultaneously ensure its projections to the model, on top of that we will try to recognize our model with the IMS-LD model, this compatibility will not be a direct way c to d, one will use the same terminology but IMS-LD for all classes of our proposed model of disciplinary information space, there is an equivalent class in the IMS-LD, which will greatly help us in the implementation level, we present in table 2 the different classes of our model and the IMS-LD model.

Figure 5. Use Case Diagram of disciplinary information space.

In figure 6, we propose a model of disciplinary information space for a system designed to achieve the needs of the LMS and the needs of teachers and learners. Therefore, we establish the following class diagram as a proposal for a disciplinary information model for the new smart LMS.

DESIGNING A DISCIPLINARY INFORMATION SPACE BASED ON MONGODB

1. Why Choosing NOSQL Databases?

Before drawing a comparison between SQL and NoSQL, we must evaluate our preferences. This means that we need to be clear about the type of database we need. Here are some comparisons to help us choose better.

Figure 6. Class Diagram of disciplinary information space for LMS

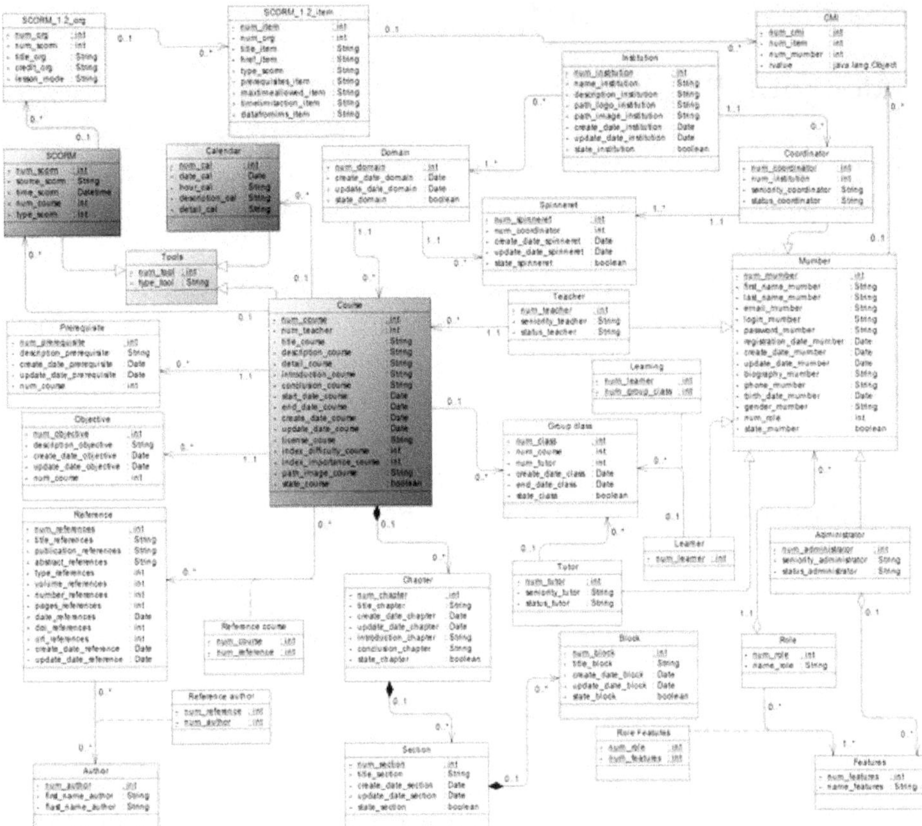

- Type of organization. In an organization with real-time applications requiring a huge amount of data traffic and Big Data, NoSQL is the obvious choice.
- Flexibility. The ability to store different types of data is thus an attribute owned by the NoSQL database. As the NoSQL database is document-based, it can combine all types of data in its document.
- Speed. With easy access and flexible structure, NoSQL succeeds in the SQL database in the speed department. It simply means that NoSQL takes less time to access data than SQL.
- Cloud Storage. Storing data in the cloud requires that data be stored on multiple servers. For it to take place, the database we choose must be highly scalable. NoSQL databases are templates to be scalable on multiple servers.

After this comparison, we opted for NoSQL databases to develop our LMS for easy quick access and flexible structure of data.

2. MongoDB Database

MongoDB is a free and open-source cross-platform document-oriented database program. Classified as a NoSQL database program, MongoDB uses JSON-like documents with schemas.

MongoDB supports field, range queries, regular expression searches. Queries can return specific fields of documents and include user-defined JavaScript functions. Queries can also be configured to return a random sample of results of a given size.

3. Designing a Disciplinary Information Space Based on the MongoDB Database

We chose to develop our disciplinary information space of LMS via the MongoDB database, for the following main features:

- Deploy, operate, and scale a MongoDB database in the cloud with just a few clicks. Fully elastic and highly available by default.
- Secure from the start. Authentication, network isolation, encryption, and role-based access controls keep your data protected. MongoDB has been independently audited and confirmed to meet privacy and compliance standards.
- Continuous backups. MongoDB includes a continuous backup solution with point-in-time restores and queryable snapshots, which allow you to perform queries against your backup snapshots and restore data at the document level in minutes.
- Comprehensive monitoring and customizable alerts. Optimized dashboards highlight key historical metrics. View performance in real-time, customize alerts, or dig into the details with ease. Easily integrate with DataDog, New Relic, Sumo Logic, and other monitoring tools.
- Live migration. Live to migrate your data into MongoDB with minimal impact on your application.

To build our database we used MongoDB Compass, which facilitated the construction of the database of the disciplinary information space of our LMS.

MongoDB Compass allows us to quickly visualize the structure of the data in our database and perform ad hoc queries, without any knowledge of the MongoDB query language. Figure 7 shows an example of a JSON document from the course collection via MongoDB Compass.

Figure 7. JSON document from the course collection interpreted via MongoDB Compass

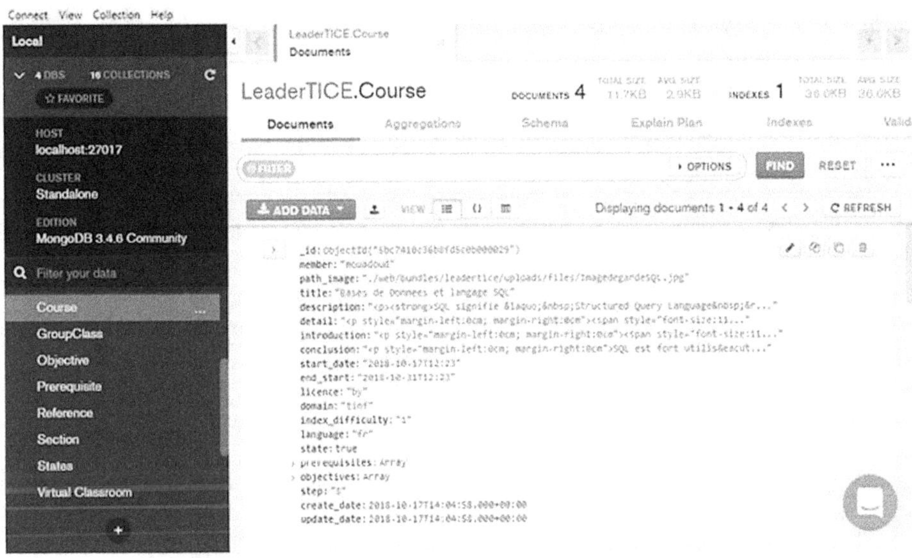

3.1 Course Collections

Teachers, tutors, or learners can manage the LMS courses they teach and/or are enrolled in. When learners register, they are automatically logged into My Courses.

Table 3 describes the schema of the course, chapters, sections, blocs, prerequisites, objectives, and references collections of the NoSQL MongoDB database, of the disciplinary information space of our new LMS.

3.2 Virtual Classroom Collection

The virtual classroom is a teaching and learning environment in which participants can interact, communicate, view and discuss presentations, and use learning resources while working in groups, all online. Support will use the BigBlueButton video conferencing application, which allows multiple users to be connected at the same time via the Internet, allowing users from virtually anywhere to participate.

In this way, the virtual classroom recreates the conditions for traditional classroom training at a distance. Thanks to its interactive and educational tools, it makes it possible to organize distance training as effectively as that carried out in the field.

Table 3. Course collections of the disciplinary information space based on NoSQL MongoDB database

<table>
<tr><th>Course Collection</th><th>Reference Collection</th></tr>
<tr><td rowspan="3">{
"_id":"ID of the course",
"title_course":"title of the course",
"description_course":"description of the course",
"detail_course":"detail of the course",
"introduction_course":"introduction of the course",
"conclusion_course":"conclusion of the course",
"start_date_course":"start date of the course",
"end_date_course":"end date of the course",
"create_date_course":"create date of the course",
"update_date_course":"update date of the course",
"licence_course":"licence of the course",
"index_difficulty_course":"difficulty index of the course",
"index_importance_course":"importance index of the course",
"path_picture_course":"path picture of the course",
"state_course":"state of the course",
"chapter_ids_cascade":[chp_number1...chp_numberN],
"reference_ids":[ref_number1...ref_numberN],
"objective_ids":[obj_number1...obj_numberN],
"prerequisite_ids":[pre_number1...pre_numberN],
"calendar_ids":[cal_number1...cal_numberN],
"groupClass_ids":[grpC_number1...grpC_numberN],
"scorm_ids":[sc_number1...sc_numberN],
"tools_id":"tools ID of the course"
}</td><td>{
"_id":"ID of the reference",
"title_reference":"title of the reference",
"publication_reference":"publication of the reference",
"abstract_reference":"abstract of the reference",
"type_reference":"type of the reference",
"volume_reference":"volume of the reference",
"number_reference":"number of the reference",
"pages_reference":"pages of the reference",
"date_reference":"date of the reference",
"doi_reference":"doi of the reference",
"url_reference":"url of the reference",
"create_date_reference":"create date of the reference",
"update_date_reference":"update date of the reference",
"course_ids":[course_number1...course_numberN],
"author_ids"[author_number1...author_numberN]
}</td></tr>
<tr><th>Author Collection</th></tr>
<tr><td>{
"_id":"ID of the author"
"first_name_author":"first name of the author",
"last_name_author":"last name of the author",
"reference_ids"[reference_number1...reference numberN]
}</td></tr>
<tr><th>Chapter Collection</th><th>Section Collection</th></tr>
<tr><td>{
"_id":"ID of the chapter",
"title_chapter":"title of the chapter",
"create_date_chapter":"create date of the chapter",
"update_date_chapter":"update date of the chapter",
"introduction_chapter":"introduction of the chapter",
"conclusion_chapter":"conclusion of the chapter",
"state_chapter":"state of the chapter",
"course_id":"course ID of the chapter",
"section_ids_cascade":[sec_number 1...sec_number N]
}</td><td>{
"_id":"ID of the section",
"title_section":"title of the section",
"create_date_section":"create date of the section",
"update_date_section":"update date of the section",
"state_section":"state of the section",
"chapter_id":"chapter ID of the section",
"block_ids_cascade":[blc_number 1...block number N]
}</td></tr>
<tr><th colspan="2">Block Collection</th></tr>
<tr><td colspan="2">{
"_id":"ID of the block",
"title_block":"title of the block",
"create_date_block":"create date of the block",
"update_date_block":"update date of the block",
"section_id":"section ID of the block"
}</td></tr>
<tr><th>Prerequisite Collection</th><th>Objective Collection</th></tr>
<tr><td>{
"_id":"ID of the prerequisite",
"description_prerequisite":"description of the prerequisite",
"create_date_prerequisite":"create date of the prerequisite",
"update_date_prerequisite":"update date of the prerequisite",
"course_id":"course ID of the prerequisite"
}</td><td>{
"_id":"ID of the objective",
"description_objective":"description of the objective",
"create_date_objective":"create date of the objective",
"update_date_objective":"update date of the objective",
"course_id":"course ID of the objective"
}</td></tr>
</table>

Table 4. Virtual Classroom collection of the disciplinary information space based on NoSQL MongoDB database

Virtual classroom collection
{
"_id":"ID of the virtual classroom",
"member_id":"tutor ID of the virtual classroom",
"course_id":"course ID of the virtual classroom",
"start_date_class":"start date of the virtual classroom",
"end_date_class":"end date of the virtual classroom",
"state_class":"state of the virtual classroom"
}

Figure 8 shows an example of a JSON document from the virtual classroom collection via MongoDB Compass.

Table 4 describes the virtual classroom schema representing the collection that interacts with the NoSQL MongoDB database of the disciplinary information space.

Figure 8. JSON document from the virtual classroom collection interpreted via MongoDB Compass

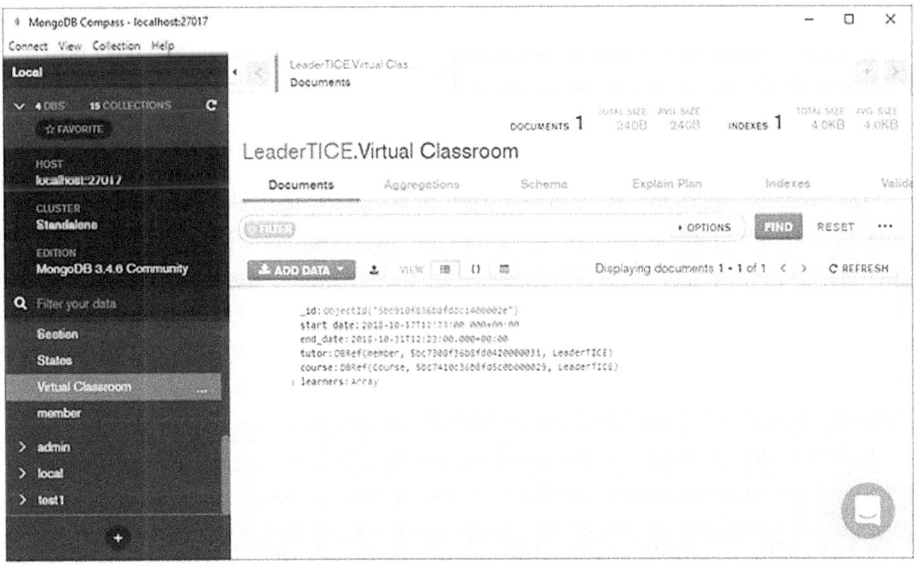

3.3 Institution Collections

A virtual institution is a set of online tools that allow remote access to digital resources. We also talk about the digital work environment, virtual office, online binder, and collaborative work platform. LMS for distance education and can offer services similar to a digital workspace.

Table 5 describes the institution schema representing the collections that interact with the NoSQL MongoDB database of the disciplinary information space.

Table 5. Institution collection of the disciplinary information space based on NoSQL MongoDB database

<table>
<tr><th>institution Collection</th><th>Domain Collection</th></tr>
<tr><td rowspan="3">{
"_id":"ID of the institution",
"name_institution":"name of the institution",
"description_institution":"description of the institution",
"path_logo_institution":"path logo of the institution",
"path_picture_institution":"path picture of the institution",
"create_date_institution":"create date of the institution",
"update_date_institution":"update date of the institution",
"state_institution":"state of the institution",
"theme_id":"theme of the institution ",
"member_ids":[memberNumber1...memberNumberN],
"domain_ids":[domainNumber1...domainNumberN]
}</td><td>{
"_id":"ID of the domain",
"create_date_domain":"create date of the domain",
"update_date_domain":"update date of the domain",
"state_domain":"state of the domain",
"institution_ids":[institutionNumber1...institutionNumberN],
"spinneret_ids":[spinneretNumber1...spinneretNumberN]
}</td></tr>
<tr><th>Spinneret Collection</th></tr>
<tr><td>{
"_id":"ID of the spinneret",
"create_date_spinneret":"create date of the spinneret",
"update_date_spinneret":"update date of the spinneret",
"domain_id":"domain ID of the spinneret",
"member_id":"member ID of the spinneret"
}</td></tr>
</table>

3.4 Member Collections

The member collections illustrate the general principle of the functioning of an LMS by presenting the main characteristics associated with the main actors: learners, teachers, tutors, coordinators, administrators, and anonymous users.

- The learner is a user within the activity space. All users who are registered in an activity space have the role of “learner”.
- The author or teacher can create, open, copy, download, and edit resources, but does not have administration rights for the activity spaces.
- The tutor manages the activity spaces: the creation of resources, registration of users ...

- Concerning the coordinator, he/she ensures the management of the overall system.
- The administrator is responsible for the customization of the platform having the rights of the administration deriving from it (system installation, maintenance, access management...)
- And the anonymous user can access without identification the activity spaces and resources of the LMS which are configured in this way. These activity spaces and resources can, therefore, be public, open to everyone with free access.

Figure 9 shows an example of a JSON document from the member collection via MongoDB Compass.

Table 6 describes the member schema representing the collections that interact with the NoSQL MongoDB database of the disciplinary information space.

Table 6. Member collections of the disciplinary information space based on NoSQL MongoDB database

<table>
<tr><th>Member collection</th><th>Role collection</th></tr>
<tr><td rowspan="3">{
"_id":"ID of the member",
"first_name_member":"first name of the member",
"last_name_member":"last name of the member",
"email_member":"email of the member",
"login_member":"login of the member",
"password_member":"password of the member",
"create_date_member":"create date of the member",
"update_date_member":"update date of the member",
"biography_member":"biography of the member",
"phone_member":"phone of the member",
"birth_date_member":"birth date of the member",
"gender_member":"gender of the member",
"seniority_member"."seniority of the member",
"status_member":"status of the member",
"state_member":"state of the member",
"url_picture_member":"url picture of the member",
"url_facebook_member":"url facebook of the member",
"url_twitter_member":"url twitter of the member",
"url_google_plus_member":"url google plus of the member",
"virtualClassroom_ids":[virtualClassroom number1...virtualClassroom numberN],
"feature_ids":[feature_number 1...feature numberN],
"cmi_ids":[cmi_number 1, cmi_number 2...cmi numberN],
"spinneret_ids":[spinneret_number 1...spinneret_numberN],
"role_id":"role ID of the member",
"institution_id":"institution ID of the member",
"language_id":"language date of the member",
"theme_ids":[theme_number 1...theme_numberN],
}</td><td>{
"_id":"ID of the role"
"name_role":"name of the role",
"member_ids":[member number1... member numberN],
"feature_ids":[feature number 1... feature number N]
}</td></tr>
<tr><th>Features collection</th></tr>
<tr><td>{
"_id":"ID of the features"
"name_features":"name of the features",
"member_id":"member ID",
"role_ids":[role number 1...role number N]
}</td></tr>
</table>

Figure 9. JSON document from the member collection interpreted via MongoDB Compass

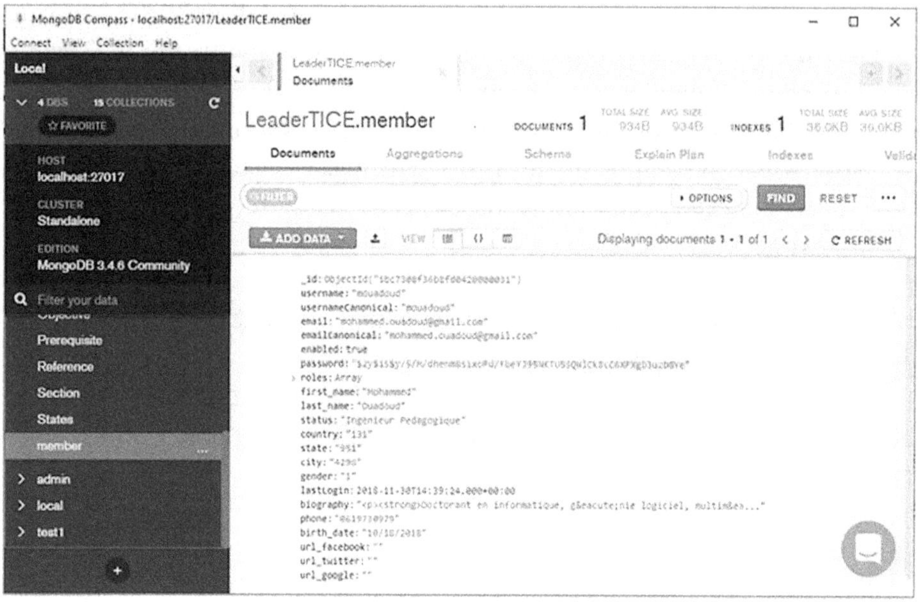

3.5 SCORM Collections

SCORM, for the Sharable Content Object Reference Model, is a set of standards and specifications used for learning management systems. It standardizes communications and data exchange formats and precisely defines packets for file transfer. The XML format is used internally.

Table 7 describes the SCORM schema representing the collections that interact with the NoSQL MongoDB database of the disciplinary information space.

3.6 Calendar Collection

An agenda is a system for locating dates as a function of time. This system has the role of dividing and organizing time over long periods. The latter displays a weekly or monthly summary of planned events, either for a course or a site or for a person active in one or more LMS.

Table 8 describes the calendar schema representing the collection that interacts with the NoSQL MongoDB database of the disciplinary information space.

Table 7. SCORM collections of the disciplinary information space based on NoSQL MongoDB database

SCORM Collection	scorm_1.2_item collection

{
"**_id**":"ID of the scorm",
"**source_scorm**":"source of the scorm",
"**time_scorm**":"time of the scorm",
"**type_scorm**":"type of the scorm",
"**scorm_1.2_org**":[scorm_org number 1...scorm_org number N],
"**course_id**":"course ID of the scorm",
"**tools_id**":"tools ID of the scorm"
}
	{
	"**_id**":"ID of the scorm_1.2_item",
	"**title_item**":"title of the scorm_1.2_item",
	"**href_item**":"href of the scorm_1.2_item",
	"**type_scorm**":"type of scorm_1.2_item",
	"**prerequisites_item**":"prerequisites of the scorm_1.2_item",
	"**maxtimeallowed_item**":"max time allowed for the scorm_1.2_item",
	"**datafromlms_item**":"data from LMS of the scorm_1.2_item",
	"**scorm_1.2_org_id**":"scorm_1.2_org ID of the scorm_1.2_item",
	"**cmi_ids**":[cmi number 1, cmi number 2...cmi number N]
	}

scorm_1.2_org collection	**CMI collection**

{
"**_id**":"ID of the scorm_1.2_org",
"**title_org**":"title of the scorm_1.2_org",
"**credit_org**":"credit of the scorm_1.2_org",
"**lesson_mode**":"lesson mode of the scorm_1.2_org",
"**scorm_id**":"scorm ID of the scorm_1.2_org",
"**scorm_1.2_item_ids**":[scorm_item number 1 ... scorm_item number N]
}
	{
	"**_id**":"ID of the cmi",
	"**rvalue**":"rvalue of the cmi",
	"**scorm_1.2_item_id**":"scorm_1.2_item ID of the cmi",
	"**member_id**":"member ID of the cmi"
	}

Table 8. Calendar collection of the disciplinary information space based on NoSQL MongoDB database

Calendar Collection

{
"**_id**":"ID of the calendar",
"**date_cal**":"date of the calendar",
"**hour_cal**":"hour of the calendar",
"**description_cal**":"description of the calendar",
"**detail_cal**":"detail of the calendar",
"**course_id**":"course ID of the calendar",
"**tools_id**":"tools ID of the calendar"
}

Table 9. Theme, tool, and language collections of the disciplinary information space based on NoSQL MongoDB database

Collection Theme	Collection tool

{
"**_id**":"ID of the theme",
"**name_theme**":"name of the theme",
"**date_created_theme**":"create date of the theme",
"**date_updated_theme**":"update date of the theme",
"**state_theme**":"state of the theme",
"**path_theme**":"path of the theme",
"**member_id**":"member ID",
"**institution_ids**":[institution number1... institution numberN]
}
	{
	"**_id**":"ID of the tool",
	"**type_tool**":"type of the tool",
	"**calendar_ids**":[calendar number1...calendar numberN],
	"**course_ids**":[course number1... course numberN],
	"**scorm_ids**":[scorm number1... scorm numberN]
	}

	Collection Language

	{
	"**_id**":"ID of the language",
	"**name_language**":"name of the language",
	"**date_created_language**":"create date of the language",
	"**date_updated_language**":"update date of the language",
	"**state_language**":"state of the language",
	"**member_ids**":[member number1... member numberN]
	}

3.7 Theme, Tool, and Language Collections

Table 9 describes the theme, tool, and language schema representing the collections that interact with the NoSQL MongoDB database of the disciplinary information space.

PROTOTYPING A DISCIPLINARY INFORMATION SPACE BASED ON SYMFONY FRAMEWORK

1. Symfony Framework

The Symfony framework is a PHP web application framework and a set of reusable PHP components/libraries.

We chose to develop our LMS via this framework, for the following majors' objectives:

- Symfony aims to speed up the creation and maintenance of web applications and to replace repetitive coding tasks.
- Symfony has a low-performance overhead used with a bytecode cache.
- Symfony is aimed at building robust applications, and aims to give developers full control over the configuration: from the directory structure to the foreign libraries, almost everything can be customized. To match development guidelines, Symfony is bundled with additional tools to help developers test, debug, and document projects.

2. Prototyping a Disciplinary Information Space

In this subsection, we limit ourselves to presenting the general information interface of the course in the disciplinary information space.

2.1 General Information Interface

In the latter (see Figure 10), the author/teacher has several privileges, which he needs for the creation of a course, which respects academic standards. For this, we have given the author/teacher the right to:

- Add a general title, an image, and a short description of a course, which are displayed when the course appears for the first time.
- Add a short introduction, the details, and the conclusion of a course, which are displayed if the learner wants to see more details about the course.
- Select the start and end date of a course, which indicates the duration of a course session, thus, they allow you to close the session if the course duration has elapsed.
- Determine the license of a course, to respect copyright.
- Add the difficulty index of a course, to recommend the courses adapted to the level of each learner.
- Choose the language of a course, to recommend the course adapted to each learner.
- Choose the course area, to simplify the search for a course by area.
- Make the general course information active, by clicking on the "active" checkbox, if the general course information is well written, or leave it inactive, by clicking on the "inactive" checkbox, if the general information of the course requires certain modifications.

2.2 The Prerequisite Course Interface

In the course prerequisite interface (see Figure 11); the author/teacher has several privileges, which he needs to create the objectives of a course that meet academic standards. For this, we have given the author/teacher the right to quote the necessary prerequisites so that the learner can start the session of the course.

2.3 The Course Objectives Interface

In the course objectives interface (see Figure 12), the author/teacher has several privileges, which he needs to create the objectives of a course that meet academic standards. For this, we have given the author/teacher the right to cite all the objectives of the course so that the learner can determine if the course meets his needs.

Figure 10. General information interface developed by the NoSQL MongoDB database and the Symfony framework.

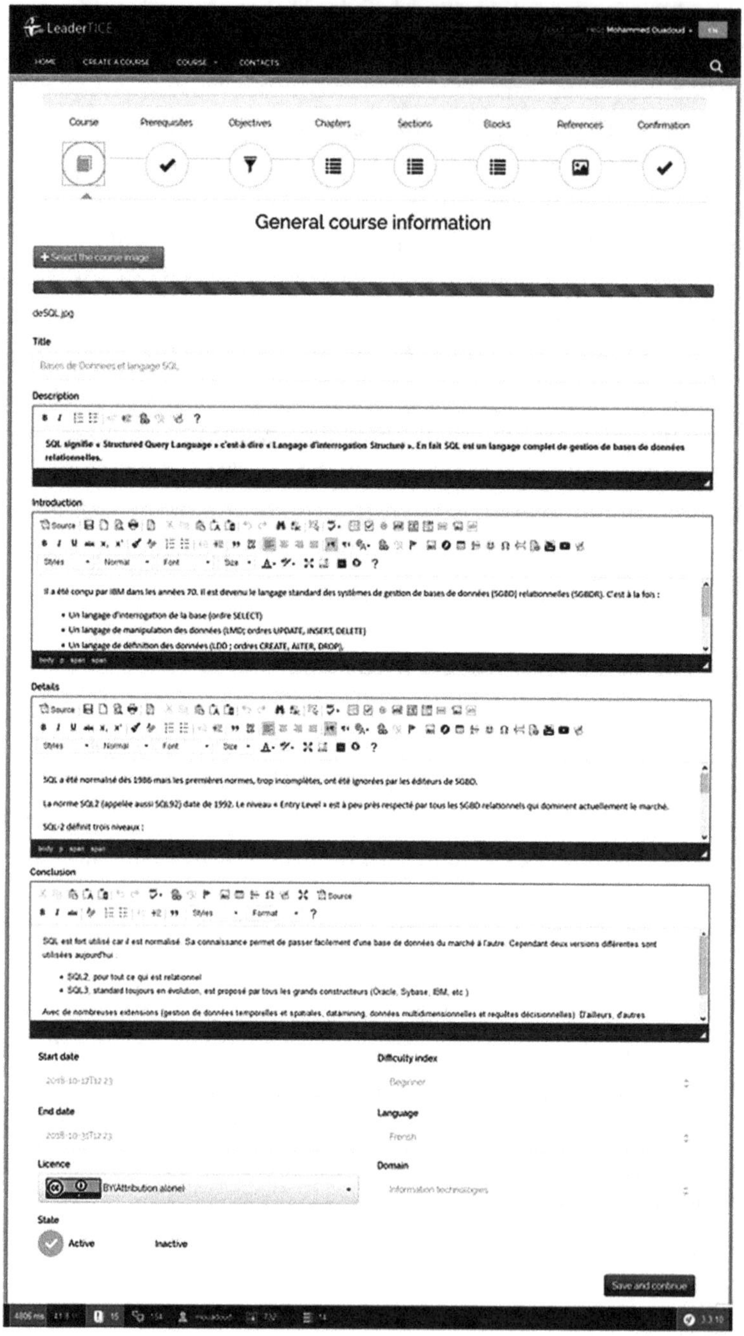

Figure 11. Course prerequisite interface developed by the NoSQL MongoDB database and the Symfony framework

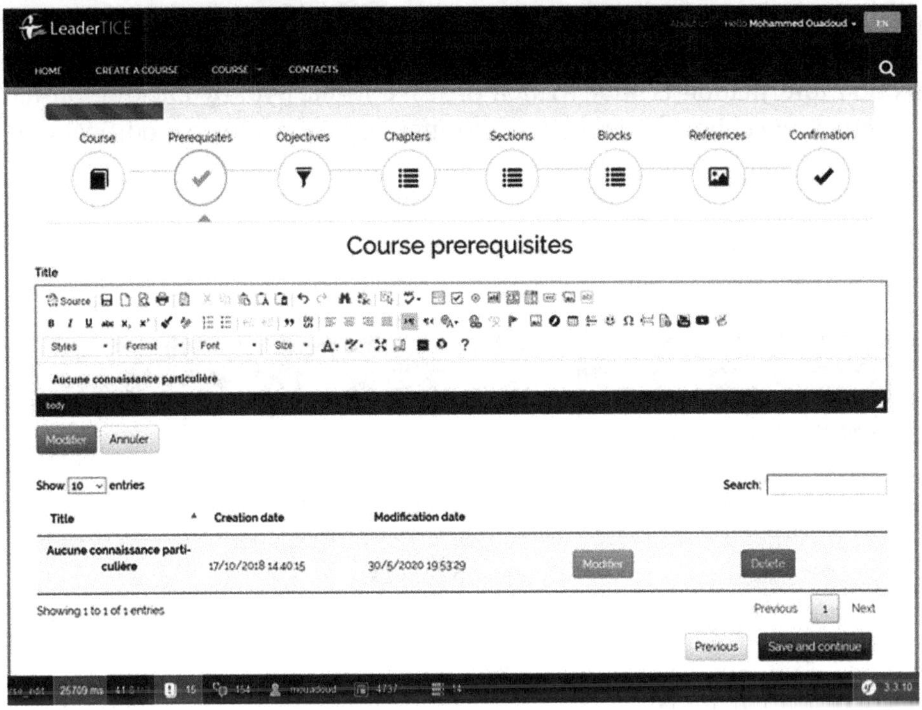

2.4 The Course Chapters Interface

In the chapter interface of the course (see Figure 13), the author/teacher has several privileges, which he needs for the creation of the chapters of a course that respects the academic standards. For this, we have given the author/teacher the right to insert the title, introduction, and conclusion of all chapters of a course that the learner can determine if the course meets his needs.

To make the chapters of the course active, by clicking on the checkbox “active”, if the chapters are well written, or leave it inactive, by clicking on the checkbox “inactive”, if the chapters require certain modifications.

2.5 The Sections Interface of a Chapter

In the section interface of a course chapter (see Figure 14), the author/teacher has several privileges, which he needs for the creation of chapter sections that comply with academic standards. For this, we have given the author/teacher the right to choose the chapter in which he wants to add sections. For each section of a selected chapter, the author/teacher can insert the title of the section and the type of media to use (text, audio, video, etc.).

To make the section active, by clicking on the "active" checkbox, if the section information is well written or leave it inactive, by clicking on the "inactive" checkbox, if the section information requires some modifications.

Figure 12. Course objective interface developed by the NoSQL MongoDB database and the Symfony framework

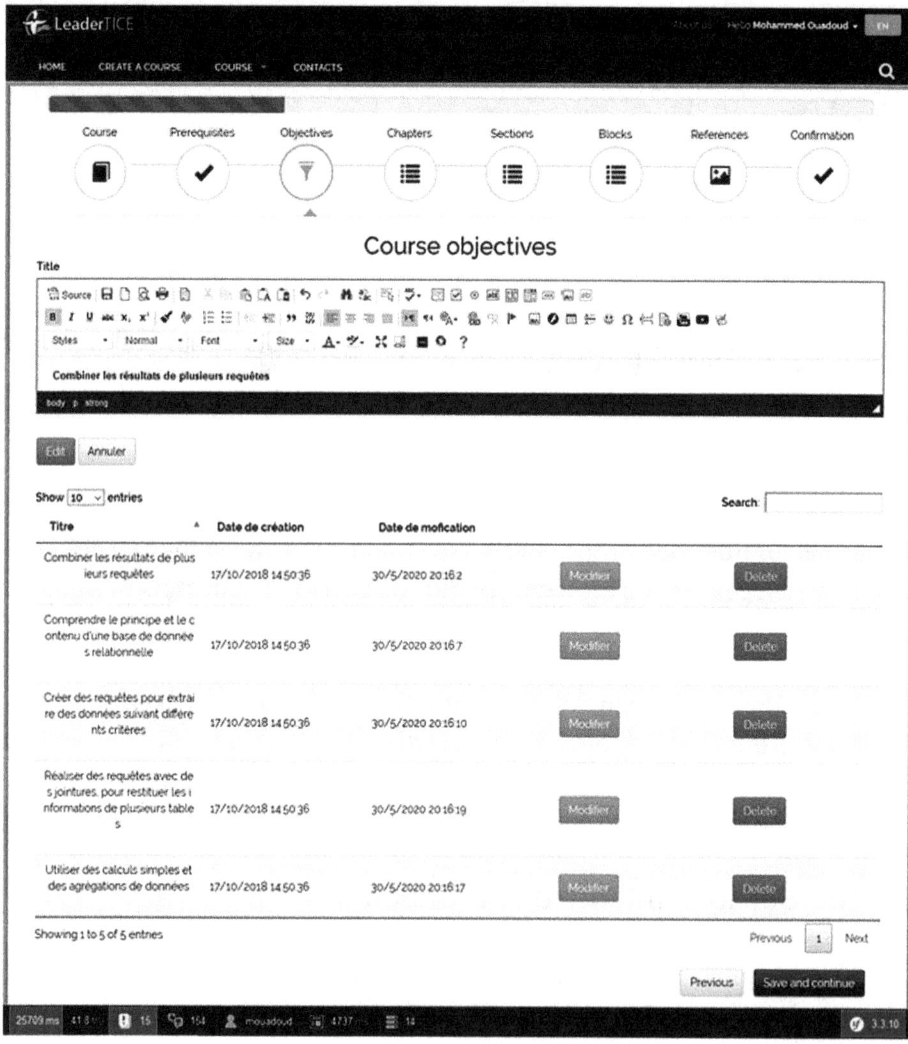

Figure 13. Course chapters interface developed by the NoSQL MongoDB database and the Symfony framework

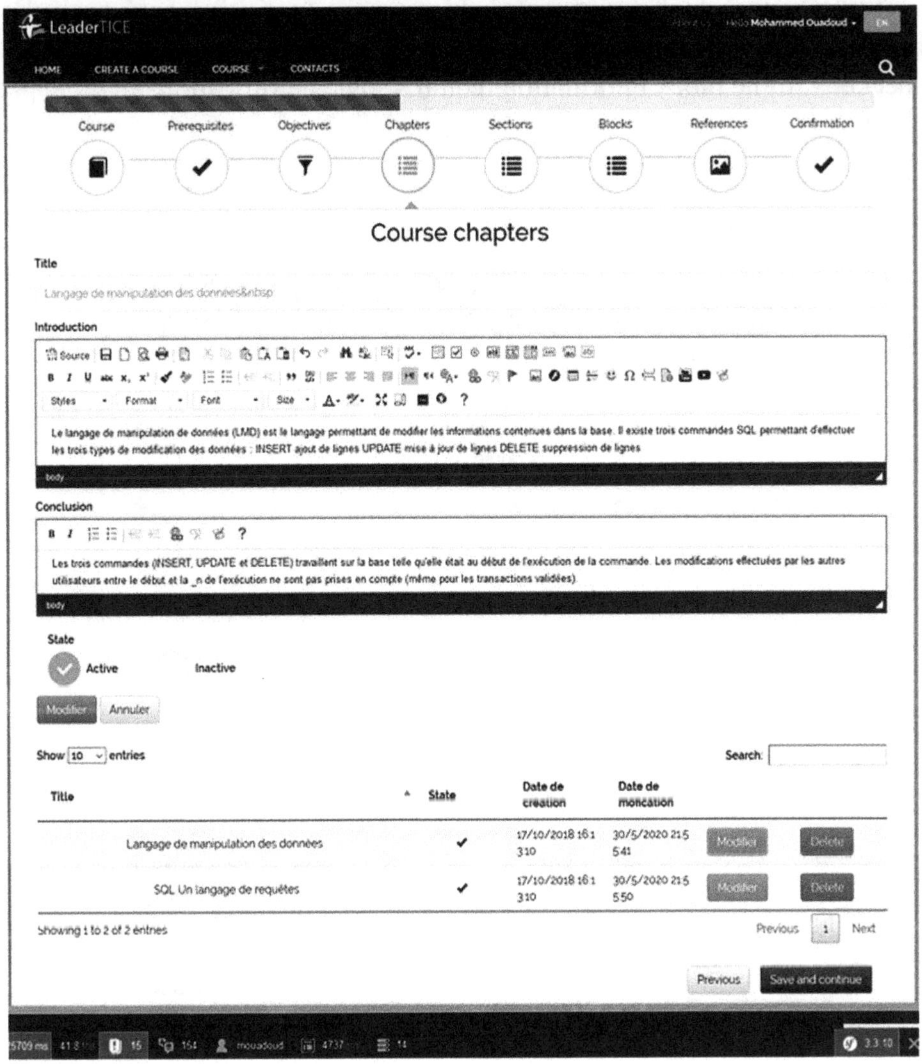

2.6 The Block Interface of a Section

In the block interface of a chapter section (see Figure 15), the author/teacher has several privileges, which he needs to create the blocks of a section that meet academic standards. For this, we have given the author/professor the right to choose the chapter and section in which he wishes to add blocks. For each section block of a selected chapter, the author/teacher can insert the title and the content of the block.

To make the block active, by clicking on the "active" checkbox, if the block information is well written, or to leave it inactive, click on the "inactive" checkbox, if the block information requires some modifications.

Figure 14. Course sections interface developed by the NoSQL MongoDB database and the Symfony framework.

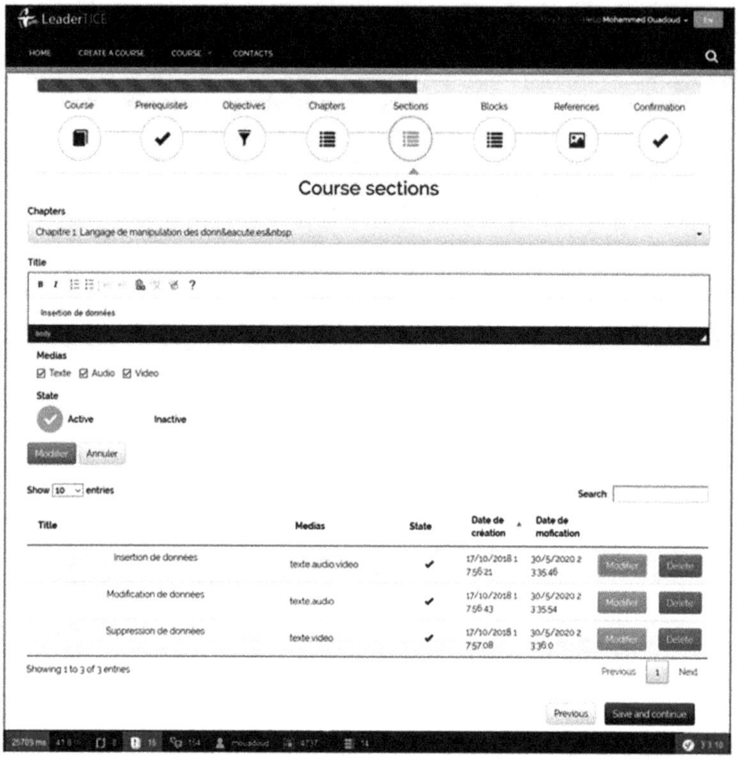

2.7 The Course References Interface

In the course references interface (see Figure 16), the author/teacher has several privileges, which he needs for creating course references that meet academic standards. For this, we have given the author/teacher the right to:

- Select the type of reference (article, chapter, book, thesis, manuscript, report, web page, etc.

Figure 15. Course blocs interface developed by the NoSQL MongoDB database and the Symfony framework.

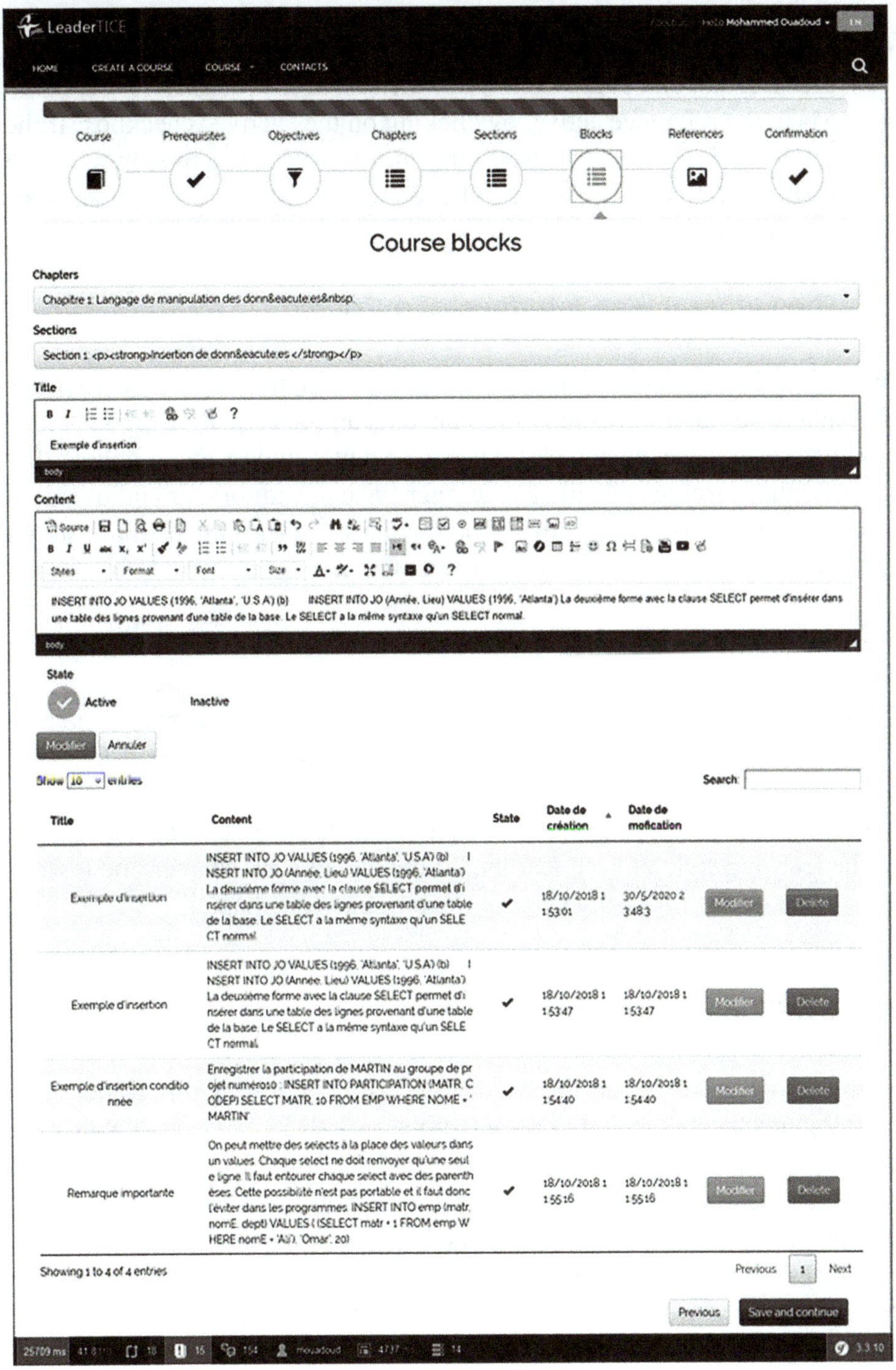

- Add a title, publication date, and a summary of the reference,
- Add the list of authors, to indicate the first, second ... until the last author for each reference,
- Indicate the volume, issue, DOI, publication journal, and numbers of the start and end page, to simplify the search for each reference,
- Make the reference active, by clicking on the "active" checkbox, if the reference information is well written, or leave it inactive, by clicking on the "inactive" checkbox, if the reference information requires some modifications.

2.8 The General Plan Interface of a Course

In the interface "general plan of a course" (see Figure 17), the learner has the right to see all the chapters, sub-chapters, and references of a course. He also has several means, which he needs to better understand a course that respects the learning style of each learner (visual, auditory, or audiovisual). For this, we gave the learner the right to choose the learning medium suited to his learning style, audio, video, image, text...

2.9 The Course Details Interface

In the "course details interface" (see Figure 18), the learner has several means, which he needs to better understand a course that respects each learner's learning style (visual, auditory, or audio-visual). The system after several choices of means of learning, a few recommend the means of learning adapted to the learning style of each learner. At the end of each chapter, the learner must click on the following symbol to go to the next chapter.

CONCLUSION

In this chapter, we are on the way to modeling and designing a model of learning management system compatible with IMS-LD and NoSQL, to develop a prototype of the disciplinary information space of the LMS via the Symfony Framework. This conception is based on active teachings centered on the learner, and as an example of pedagogies; we opted for four learning theories as a basis for teaching this LMS, namely traditional pedagogy, behaviorism, cognitivism, and social constructivism. This allows us to achieve a teaching object through the implementation of projects, activities, and QUIZ which are divided into tasks performed by the students in collaboration or individually. To reach an objective, we must reach the validation stage of the model, which is one of the tasks to be accomplished in our future work; besides, we are developing the rest of our LMS via the Symfony Framework, which will facilitate the implementation phase.

Figure 16. Course references interface developed by the NoSQL MongoDB database and the Symfony framework.

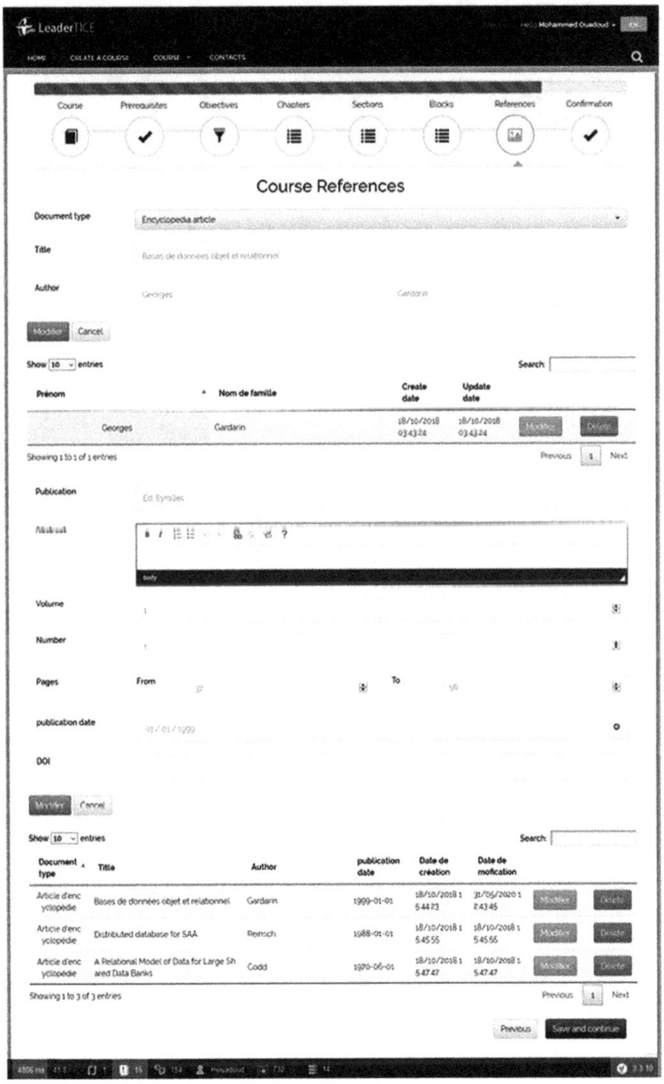

Figure 17. The general plan of a course developed via Symfony Framework.

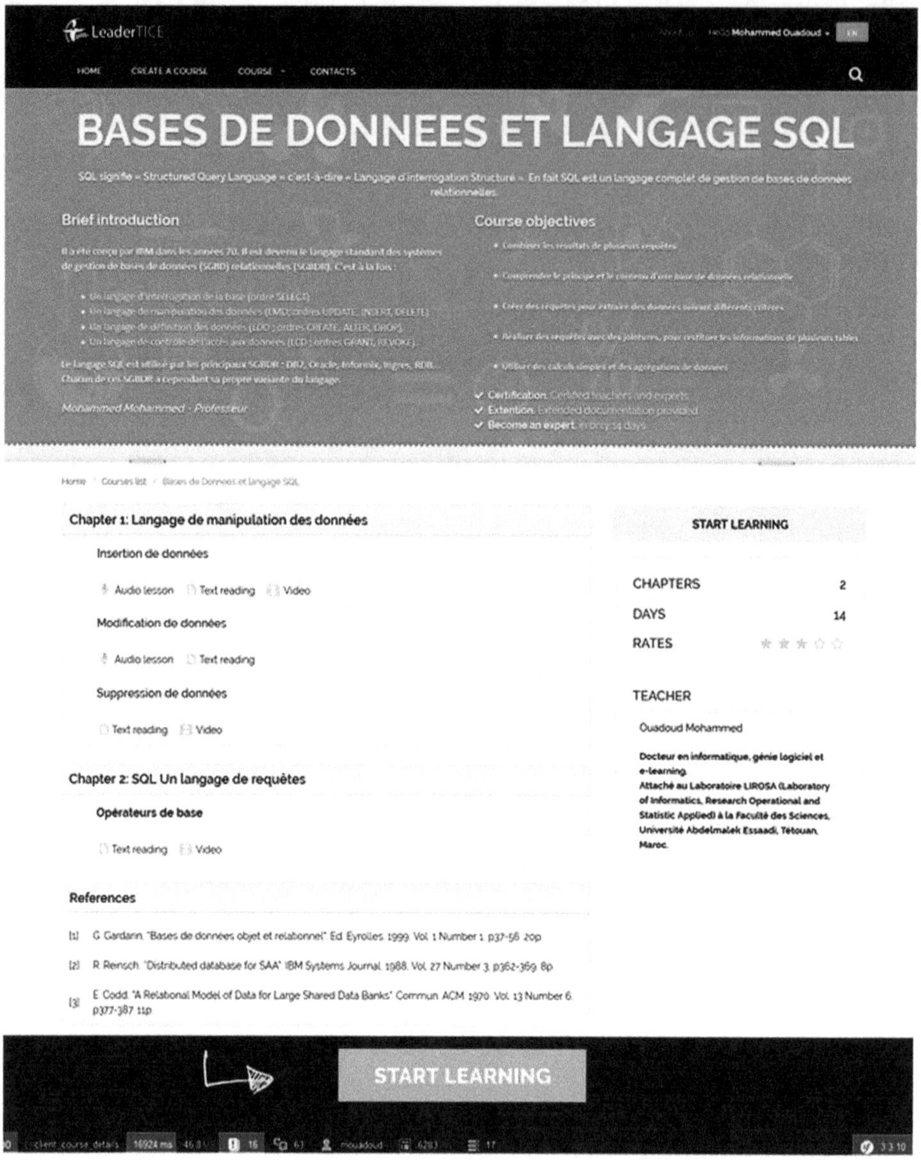

Figure 18. Details of a course developed via Symfony Framework.

REFERENCES

Ouadoud, M., Chkouri, M. Y., Nejjari, A., & El Kadiri, K. E. (2017, February). Exploring a Recommendation System of Free eLearning Platforms: Functional Architecture of the System. *International Journal of Emerging Technologies in Learning*, *12*(02), 219–226. doi:10.3991/ijet.v12i02.6381

Lejeune, A. (2006). *IMS Learning Design: Étude d'un langage de modélisation pédagogique* (Vol. 2). Revue Distances et Savoirs.

Survey of Educational Modelling Languages (EMLs). Version 1. (2002). *CEN/ISS WS/LT, Learning Technologies Workshop*.

Koper, R. (2001). *Modeling Units of Study from a Pedagogical Perspective, the pedagogical meta-model behind EML*. http://eml.ou.nl/introduction/docs/pedmetamodel.pdf

Burgos, D., Arnaud, M., Neuhauser, P., & Koper, R. (2005). *IMS Learning Design*. Association EPI. Available: http://www.epi.asso.fr/revue/articles/a0512c.htm

Leavitt, N. (2010, February). Will NoSQL Databases Live Up to Their Promise? *Computer*, *43*(2), 12–14.

Mohan, C. (2013). History Repeats Itself: Sensible and NonsenSQL Aspects of the NoSQL Hoopla. *Proc. 16th Int'l Conf. on Extending Database Technology*, 11–16.

Liu, C.-H. (2010). The comparison of learning effectiveness between traditional face-to-face learning and eLearning among goal-oriented users. In *Digital Content, Multimedia Technology and its Applications (IDC), 2010 6th International Conference on*. IEEE.

Faten, K., & Goodwin, R. (2013, October-December). Using Cloud Computing in ELearning Systems. *International Journal of Advanced Research in Computer Science & Technology*, *1*(1), 66–67.

Henri, F., Rabardel, P., & Pastré, P. (Eds.). (2005). Modèles du sujet pour la conception. International Journal of ELearning & Distance Education, Octares Éditions, 22(1), 101–106.

Sadiq, M., & Talbi, M. (2010). *Modélisation des unités d'apprentissage sur des plates-formes de formation à distance*. Association EPI. Available: https://www.epi.asso.fr/revue/articles/a1003e.htm

Tonye, E. (2010). *Modeling a framework for open and distance learning in sub-Saharan African countries*. Available: http://www.frantice.net/docannexe.php?id=339

Chouchane, K. (2012). *Modélisation et réalisation d'une approche pour le m-learning*. Magister en Informatique Option Système d'Informatique et de Communication (SIC), Université Hadj Lakhdar – Batna – Algérienne. Available: http://theses.univ-batna.dz/index.php?option=com_docman&task=doc_details&gid=3074&Itemid=4

Brunel, S., Girard, P., & Lamago, M. (2015). *Des plateformes pour enseigner à distance : vers une modélisation générale de leurs fonctions.* In AIP Primeca 2015, La Plagne, France. Available: https://hal.archives-ouvertes.fr/hal-01128532

Née Dahmani, B. F. (2010). *Modélisation basée ontologies pour l'apprentissage interactif - Application à l'évaluation des connaissances de l'apprenant* (PhD dissertation). Computer Science Department, Mouloud Mammeri University of Tizi-Ouzou, Algeria. Available: http://docplayer.fr/4482022-These-de-doctorat-modelisation-basee-ontologies-pour-l-apprentissage-interactif-application-a-l-evaluation-des-connaissances-de-l-apprenant.html

Alfanet project. (2008). *CopperCore V 3.3*. Available: http://coppercore.sourceforge.net

Bolton. (2005). *RELOAD Project: Editor*. The University of Bolton, The University of Strathclyde and JISC. Available: http://www.reload.ac.uk/editor.html

El-Moudden, F., Aammou, S., & Khaldi, M. (2014). A Tool to Generate a Collaborative Content Compatible with IMS-LD. *International Journal of Software and Web Sciences, 11*(1), 1-8.

Dyke, G., & Lund, K. (2006). *Implications d'un modèle de coopération pour la conception d'outils collaboratifs*. Academic Press.

Ferraris, C., Lejeune, A., Vignollet, L., & David. J. P. (2005). *Modélisation de scénarios pédagogiques collaboratifs*. Academic Press.

El-Moudden, F. (2015, December). Designing an IMS-LD Model for Collaborative Learning. *IJACSA, 1*(6), 42–48.

Chekour, M., Laafou, M., & Janati-Idrissi, R. (2015). *L'évolution des théories de l'apprentissage à l'ère du numérique*. Association EPI. Available: http://www.epi.asso.fr/revue/articles/a1502b.htm

El Mhouti, A., Nasseh, A., & Erradi, M. (2013). *Les TIC au service d'un enseignement-apprentissage socioconstructiviste*. Association EPI. Available: http://www.epi.asso.fr/revue/articles/a1301g.htm

Benslimane, M., Zine, O., Derouich, A., & Talbi, A. (2016). Proposition et implémentation sur Moodle d'une approche de conception d'un cours en ligne : cas d'un cours d'algorithmique. *Workshop International sur les Approches Pédagogiques & ELearning*. Available: http://docplayer.fr/12209814-Proposition-et-implementation-sur-moodle-d-une-approche-de-conception-d-un-cours-en-ligne-cas-d-un-cours-d-algorithmique.html

Zoubaidi, X., Ait Daoud, M., Namir, A., Talbi, M., & Nachit, B. (2014). *La formation de formateurs d'éducateurs du préscolaire: mise en place d'un dispositif de formation à distance*. Association EPI. Available: http://www.epi.asso.fr/revue/articles/a1401d.htm

Chemsi, G., Radid, M., Sadiq, M., & Talbi, M. (2011). *Une plate-forme d'évaluation des enseignements et des formations à distance : EVAL-EFD*. Association EPI. Available: http://www.epi.asso.fr/revue/articles/a1109b.htm

Bechina, A., Keith, B., & Brinkschulte, U. (2001). *Mediasite: Une nouvelle plate-forme dédiée à l'enseignement à distance*. IRES.

Paquette, G. (2000). Construction de portails de téléapprentissage Explor@ - Une diversité de modèles pédagogiques. *Science et Techniques Educatives, 7*(1), 207-226. Available: http://tecfa.unige.ch/tecfa/teaching/FFL/Textes/Textes_secondaires/paquette_2000.pdf

Boulet, P., Dekeyser, J. L., Dumoulin, C., & Marquet, P. (2003). Mda for soc embedded systems design, intensive signal processing experiment. In SIVOESMDA workshop at UML 2003, San Francisco, CA.

Thi-Lan-anh, D., Olivier, G., & Houari, S. (2005). Gestion de modèles: définitions, besoins et revue de littérature. *Premières Journées sur l'Ingénierie Dirigée par les Modèles*, 1–15.

Clave, A. (2004). *D'UML à MDA en passant par les métas modèles*. Technical report, La Lettre d'ADELI.

Caron, P. A., Hoogstoel, F., Le Pallec, X., & Warin, B. (2007). Construire des dispositifs sur la plateforme moodle - application de l'ingénierie bricoles. In MoodleMoot-2007, Castres, France.

Canals, A., Le Camus, C., Feau, M., Jolly, G., Bonnafous, V., & Bazavan, P. (2005). Une utilisation opérationnelle d'ATL : L'intégration de la transformation de modèles dans le projet TOPCASED. *Génie logiciel*, 21–26.

Bézivin, J., Dupé, G., Jouault, F., Pitette, G., & Eddine Rougui, J. (2003). *First experiments with the ATL model transformation language: Transforming XSLT into XQuery*. In OOPSLA 2003 Workshop, Anaheim, CA.

OMG/RFP/QVT MOF 2.0 Query/Views/Transformations RFP. (2002). OMG, Object Management Group.

ATLAS Group, LINA, & INRIA Nantes. (2006). *Atlas transformation language. ATL user manual - version 0.7*. Technical report, INRIA University of Nantes.

Combemale, B., & Rougemaille, S. (2005). *ATL - Atlas Transformation Language*. Master 2 Recherche SLCP, module rtm edition.

Martinez-Moyano, I. J. (2006). Exploring the dynamics of collaboration in interorganizational settings. *Creating a culture of collaboration: the International Association of Facilitators handbook*.

Spence, M. U. (2005). Graphic Design: Collaborative Processes. A course on collaboration, theory and practice. In *Art 325: Collaborative Processes. Fairbanks Hall*. Oregon State University.

Andlinger, P. (2013). *RDBMS dominate the database market, but NoSQL systems are catching up*. Available: https://db-engines.com/en/blog_post/23

Fowler, M. (2012). *NoSQL Definition*. Available: https://martinfowler.com/bliki/NosqlDefinition.html

Rouse, M., Vaughan, J., & Beal, B. (2017). *NoSQL (Not Only SQL database)*. Search-Data Management. Available: https://searchdatamanagement.techtarget.com/definition/NoSQL-Not-Only-SQL

Vogels, W. (2012). *Amazon DynamoDB – a Fast and Scalable NoSQL Database Service Designed for Internet-Scale Applications*. Available: https://www.allthingsdistributed.com/2012/01/amazon-dynamodb.html

Grolinger, K., Higashino, W. A., Tiwari, A., & Capretz, M. A. (2013, December). Data management in cloud environments: NoSQL and NewSQL data stores. *Journal of Cloud Computing: Advances, Systems and Applications*, *2*, 22. https://doi.org/10.1186/2192-113X-2-22

Ouadoud, M., Chkouri, M. Y., & Nejjari, A. (2018a). Generate a Meta-Models Content for Learning Management System Compatible with IMS-LD. International Journal of Emerging Technologies in Learning, 11(1), 11-20.

Ouadoud, M., Chkouri, M. Y., & Nejjari, A. (2018b, January). LeaderTICE: A Platforms Recommendation System Based on a Comparative and Evaluative Study of Free eLearning Platforms. *International Journal of Online Engineering*, *14*(01), 132–161. https://doi.org/10.3991/ijoe.v14i01.7865

Ouadoud, M., Chkouri, M. Y., & Nejjari, A. (2018c, March). Learning Management System and the Underlying Learning Theories: Towards a new Modeling of an LMS. *International Journal of Information Science and Technology*, *2*(1), 25–33.

Ouadoud, M., Nejjari, A., Chkouri, M. Y., & Kadiri, E. L. K. E. (2017a). Learning Management System and the Underlying Learning Theories. *Innovations in Smart Cities and Applications*, 732–744. doi:10.1007/978-3-319-74500-8_67

Ouadoud, M., Nejjari, A., Chkouri, M. Y., & Kadiri, E. L. K. E. (2017b). Educational modeling of a learning management system. *2017 International Conference on Electrical and Information Technologies (ICEIT)*, 1–6. doi:10.1109/EITech.2017.8255247

Aammou, S., Mohamed, K., Ahmed, I., & El-Kadiri, K. E. (2010). Adaptive hypermedia systems for eLearning. *IEEE EDUCON 2010 Conference*, 1799–1804. doi:10.1109/EDUCON.2010.5492421

ADDITIONAL READING

Ouadoud, M., Chafiq, T., Rida, N., & Chkouri, M. Y. (2019). Generate a Meta-Model Content for Collaboration Space of Learning Management System Compatible with IMS-LD. *International Journal of Interactive Mobile Technologies*, *13*(01), 37–52. doi:10.3991/ijim.v13i01.9440

Ouadoud, M., & Chkouri, M. Y. (2019). Generate a Meta-Model Content for Communication Space of Learning Management System Compatible with IMS-LD. In M. Ezziyyani (Ed.), *Advanced Intelligent Systems for Sustainable Development (AI2SD'2018), Advances in Intelligent Systems and Computing* (pp. 24–39). Springer International Publishing. doi:10.1007/978-3-030-11928-7_3

Ouadoud, M., & Chkouri, M. Y. (2019). Designing an IMS-LD Model for Communication Space of Learning Management System. In M. Ezziyyani (Ed.), *Advanced Intelligent Systems for Sustainable Development (AI2SD'2018), Advances in Intelligent Systems and Computing* (pp. 40–54). Springer International Publishing. doi:10.1007/978-3-030-11928-7_4

KEY TERMS AND DEFINITIONS

DCMI: Dublin core metadata initiative.

EML: Educational modelling language.

IMS: Instructional management systems.

IMS-CP: Instructional management systems-content packaging.

IMS-LD: Instructional management systems-learning design.

IMS-SS: Instructional management systems-simple sequencing.

LMS: Learning management system.

Methods: The word "method" used by IMS-LD means the unfolding of the scenario.

SCORM: The SCORM® (Sharable Content Object Reference Model) was created to address these interoperability, reusability, and durability challenges. As a reference model, it was intentionally designed to leverage standard web technologies as well as existing learning technology specifications that already existed. SCORM® is comprised of a collection of interrelated technical specifications and guidelines designed to meet the DoD's high-level requirements for creating interoperable, plug-n-play, browser-based e-learning content. It consists of three different technical specifications "books" that collectively address challenges associated with interoperability, portability, reusability, and the instructional sequencing of self-paced e-learning content.

About the Authors

Mohammed Ouadoud is a Ph.D. in Computer sciences, at the Laboratory of the Information System and Software Engineering (SIGL) at National School of Applied Sciences, Abdelmalek Essaâdi University. In 2018, He completed his Ph.D. thesis in computer science at the faculty of science of Tetouan, Morocco. His dissertation research focuses on Modeling and Prototyping a Learning Management System Based on the IMD-LD, the NoSQL, and the Hybridization between Learning Theories. He has a Master's degree in Mul-timedia Engineering of Instructional Design from the École Normale Supérieure of Martil, Morocco in 2013. His current research focuses on IT, E-learning, Public Health, and Software Engineering. He is a reviewer in several international journals.

Mohamed Yassin CHKOURI defended his thesis at VERIMAG (Grenoble) in 2010 on the modeling of real-time embedded systems using AADL for the automatic generation of formally verified applications. Before joining the National School of Applied Sciences (ENSA) of Tetouan as a senior teaching assistant professor in 2012, he has held positions of engineer / doctor in industry: EVOSYS (Asynchronous Model transformation in Synchronous models for formal verification by model checking - in rail couplings) and ALSTOM (Project ATS - Automatic Train Supervision). He defended his habilitation in 2014. He is the Head of Department of Computer Engineering since 10/2016, an academic coordinator of the e-val project (Erasmus +) since 11/2016, and the Leader and founder of the accredited research laboratory "Information Systems and Software Engineering" SIGL since 04/2014.

Index

H

I

L

M

N

O

P

R

S

T

U

V

W

www.ingramcontent.com/pod-product-compliance
Lightning Source LLC
LaVergne TN
LVHW081327300926
849161LV00008B/1898